Interpreter-mediated Police Interviews

Also by Ikuko Nakane

SILENCE IN INTERCULTURAL COMMUNICATION

Interpreter-mediated Police Interviews

A Discourse-Pragmatic Approach

Ikuko Nakane
Asia Institute, University of Melbourne, Australia

First published 2014 by
PALGRAVE MACMILLAN

Palgrave Macmillan in the UK is an imprint of Macmillan Publishers Limited, registered in England, company number 785998, of Houndmills, Basingstoke, Hampshire RG21 6XS.

Palgrave Macmillan in the US is a division of St Martin's Press LLC, 175 Fifth Avenue, New York, NY 10010.

Palgrave Macmillan is the global academic imprint of the above companies and has companies and representatives throughout the world.

Palgrave® and Macmillan® are registered trademarks in the United States, the United Kingdom, Europe and other countries.

ISBN 978–0–230–35514–9

This book is printed on paper suitable for recycling and made from fully managed and sustained forest sources. Logging, pulping and manufacturing processes are expected to conform to the environmental regulations of the country of origin.

A catalogue record for this book is available from the British Library.

A catalog record for this book is available from the Library of Congress.

Typeset by MPS Limited, Chennai, India.

Contents

List of Tables

Acknowledgements

I could not have completed this book without the generous support of my colleagues, family and friends. First, I would like to thank my colleagues at the University of Melbourne for their encouragement and support. My special thanks go to Michelle Hall, for her support as a brilliant librarian and a friend. Many thanks to Constance Ellwood for her meticulous proofreading of the manuscript, valuable comments and generous support. I would like to thank Kazumi Namiki and Ben Morgan for their excellent work as research assistants. I am also grateful to Richard Powell for sharing interesting discussions and making valuable comments. My gratitude also goes to Vera Mackie, Diana Eades, Chihiro Kinoshita Thomson, Ingrid Piller and Sander Adelaar, who have given me inspiration and encouragement. I am very lucky to have their guidance in my academic work. Emi Otuji, with whom I have shared the joy and misery of academic work for so many years, deserves special thanks for her friendship and patience with my endless whinging. I would also like to thank Jill Hunter and Jeremy Gans for sharing with me their academic expertise in law. My special thanks go to attorneys Yukihiro Masaki, Shun Tanaka and Kiyoshi Yamashita, and artist Mayu Kanamori for their trust in my work. I am also grateful to Monica Pinda, Stacey Steele, Chikako Tsuruta and Caroline Norma for giving me valuable opportunities to share my work with practising interpreters.

This book project would not have been completed without the assistance of the Arts Faculty Grant from the University of Melbourne. I would like to thank the university for the generous support. I would also like to acknowledge that earlier versions of some parts of this book were published in *Journal of Pragmatics* (vol. 43, pp. 2017–2330) in 2011 and *Portal: Journal of Multidisciplinary and International Studies* (vol. 6, no. 1) in 2009. I am indebted to many people for the generous assistance I received for this project, but any faults and shortcomings of this book are my own. I would also like to thank my editorial contacts at Palgrave Macmillan for their generosity and patience.

Finally, my heartfelt thanks go to my family for their support and understanding during this challenging period of time in my career. Very special thanks to my partner John for his love and patience. I cannot thank you enough.

Transcription Conventions

Adapted from Jefferson (1984)

[	point of overlap onset
]	point at which overlap stops
=	latching (no gap or no overlap between stretches of talk)
(0.5)	elapsed time in silence by tenth of seconds
(.)	micropause of less than 0.2 seconds
<u>word</u>	stress
:	lengthening of a sound
.	falling terminal contour
,	a continuing contour
?	rising contour
° °	speech noticeably quieter than the surrounding talk
↑↓	a marked falling or rising intonation
CAPITALS	speech noticeably louder than the surrounding talk
> <	speech produced noticeably faster than the surrounding talk
< >	speech produced noticeably slower than the surrounding talk
.hh	in-breath, the number of 'h' indicating the length
hh	out-breath, the number of 'h' indicating the length
–	a halting, abrupt cutoff
( )	inaudible speech
(why/well)	varieties of transcriptionist doubt
(( ))	non-verbal activity

Introduction: Tripartite Police Interview Interaction

Bilingual police interview discourse

There is no doubt that the police interview is an important part of the legal process. Through it, information relevant to the case is gathered and becomes part of the evidence presented and tested in court. In criminal cases, the interview is considered one of the most important methods available to police for investigating the facts (Gudjonsson, 1992). The police interview therefore has crucial dual roles: evidential and investigative (Baldwin, 1993; Haworth, 2010; Johnson, 2006).

It is also the case that, with globalisation, there has been an increase in the number of people requiring interpreter assistance when interviewed by police. This is especially the case in the USA, the UK, Australia, and EU countries where a high proportion of residents and visitors may not have a full command of the language used in the legal system.

This book aims to foster a greater understanding of the bilingual police interview process. It approaches interviews, through the lens of the discipline of sociolinguistics, as social and institutional interaction, with the interpreter as one of the interlocutors. The book focuses on the interaction dynamics of interpreter-mediated police interviews, specifically, the ways in which an interpreter's participation in the interaction impacts on the interview and on the power relationships in the lay–professional discourse of these interviews. The book positions itself in the broad research field of language and the law, fitting within a branch of research into police interview discourse as a type of legal discourse and, as such, the book looks at what happens to the genre structures and features of police interviews as a legal process, when mediated by an interpreter.

The police interview as a genre in adversarial legal systems

The police interviews analysed in this study were conducted in Australia and mediated by English–Japanese interpreters. Under the common law system, Australia has an adversarial legal process. Since Bennett and Feldman's (1981) description of the discourse processes of adversarial legal systems as a construction of realities, research into legal discourse – and originally applied to courtroom questioning – has drawn on the idea of story or narrative construction (Heffer, 2005; Jackson, 1991; Maley & Fahey, 1991; Snedaker, 1991). The police interview is another discourse process where realities are constructed and competing versions of events are negotiated (Berk-Seligson, 2009; Heydon, 2005; Johnson, 2006; Linell & Jönsson, 1991).

Police interviews and courtroom discourse are also intertwined as sub-genres of the legal process. Johnson (2006) highlights the significance of police interviews and their intertextuality in the legal process, demonstrating how narratives in police interviews run through the legal process from allegation to judgment, with their present, future and imagined audiences. When this kind of institutional discourse is mediated by an interpreter, it 'will be subject to further textualizations' (Johnson, 2006, p. 667). This is one of the issues discussed in this book.

Using this narrative approach, the book examines the impact of interpreter mediation on the construction of varying versions of events in the police interview as a genre, located in the context of an adversarial legal system. According to Johnson (2006), the police interview is 'a hybrid genre and discourse type' in which both lay language and professional legal language are used, and it is 'largely narrative in form with free-narrative and elicited narrative sections' (p. 669). There is a 'mixture of conversational and institutional aspects', although conversational features such as laughter and silences in some respects differ from that of ordinary conversation (Carter, 2011, p. 52). While the police interview is a sub-category of the legal genre (Gibbons, 2003; Maley, 1994), and there are many aspects and issues common to interpreter-mediated courtroom and police interview discourse, these discourses differ in terms of their setting, orientation, organisation of talk and purposes.

Sociolinguistic inquiry into interpreter-mediated police interviews

The study of interpreter-mediated police interviews as discourse belongs to a larger field of sociolinguistic research into language and the law.

Eades (2010) argues that sociolinguistic research into language use in legal contexts should take account of the reciprocal relationship between local language use and the institutional context of communication:

> To understand language usage in any specific legal context is impossible without an examination of structural institutional aspects of the legal system. On the other hand, sociolegal studies of the law can be greatly enriched by an examination of situated language practices in specific legal contexts. (p. 5)

In alignment with Eades's (2010) claim for an integrated approach, a combination of micro-analysis tools such as Conversation Analysis (hereafter CA) focusing on the turn-by-turn orientation to talk and sociolinguistic approaches which consider language use in relation to its social contexts have commonly been used in studies of police interview discourse. Many of these studies have employed micro-analysis of talk-in-interaction to identify discourse strategies used by interviewing officers and interviewees, while at the same time considering police interviews in relation to the institutional structure which informs the discourse practice (for example, Berk-Seligson, 2009; Carter, 2011; Heydon, 2005, 2012; Holt & Johnson, 2010; Johnson, 2002, 2008). Thus, the power dimension associated with the police institutional structure is one of the important contextual factors to consider in the analysis of police interviews – 'a major difference between the interview and everyday conversation stems from the inequality of status and power of the police interrogator and the suspect' (Shuy, 1998, p. 178) – as is the local orientation to talk in the specific institutional context.

The study presented in this book in principle aligns itself with these legal interaction studies, and specifically addresses the following questions: How do the interlocutors' turn-by-turn decisions on communication affect the police interview as a story construction process? What impact does interpreter mediation have in this process? How is the need to construct a convincing version of events realised and negotiated in interpreter-mediated police interviews? How do institutional constraints on police interviewing affect the interlocutors' discursive strategies for constructing their preferred versions of events? And, how does interpreter mediation affect the power of those strategies and the trajectory of interview discourse as evidence?

The present study is distinctive in that the discourse analysed has the following two key aspects: (1) the police institutional practice and (2) the mediated mode of interaction. Interpreter-mediated interaction is a discourse type in itself with its own type-specific features. Previous explorations of these features using a CA approach have shed light upon the mechanism of dialogue-interpreting in institutional settings (Dimitrova, 1997; Müller, 1989; Roy, 2000; Wadensjö, 1998). Similarly, as we will see in the next chapter, research into police interview discourse has also significantly benefited from the insights emerging from CA analysis. The analysis and discussion of police interview interaction data in this book draws largely on CA, relying on its strengths in describing interlocutors' orientations to naturally occurring interaction in specific institutional contexts (Hutchby & Wooffitt, 1988; Psathas, 1995; Sacks et al., 1974).

The 'local' orientation of CA, in which the analysis relies exclusively on the talk itself as the context, is complemented by an approach which allows for the relationship between the language and its institutional context. The book thus also adopts an interactional sociolinguistic approach to communication (Gumperz, 1982), in which the analysis takes into account sociocultural contextual factors such as the role relationships of the participants in the specific institutional setting, and the schema on which the participants rely in making inferences and encoding messages in their interaction (Gumperz, 1982). The main focus of interactional sociolinguistics is to understand the accumulated knowledge required to achieve the goals of the institutional discourse and to ascertain the type of problems that may occur due to any gaps in that knowledge that participants bring to the interaction (Gumperz, 1982). An interactional sociolinguistics approach allows the analysis of police interview interaction discussed in this book to demonstrate how the participants, including the interpreters, achieve or struggle to achieve, the discourse co-construction process in relation to their knowledge, which includes linguistic repertoires.

Although Eades (2008) argues that an interactional sociolinguistics approach falls short in considering roles of power and associated language ideologies, it is nevertheless a powerful tool for analysing issues in intercultural communication in institutional settings, as has been shown by Eades' early work on legal communication involving indigenous Australians (Eades, 1994, 2000). More recently, an alternative with a critical perspective has been adopted by sociolinguists studying language in legal contexts (Eades, 2004, 2008). With regard to police interviews, Berk-Seligson (2009) draws on this critical interactional sociolinguistic approach to offer a powerful analysis of coerced confessions by Latino suspects in the US The analysis reveals both micro-level discursive strategies of coercion and resistance, and macro-level social and institutional structures interacting with the micro-strategies. Interactional sociolinguistics, including Berk-Seligson's (2009) work, has also been adopted for research into interpreter-mediated interaction in institutional settings.

Researchers of interpreter-mediated interaction such as Roy (2000) and Wadensjö (1998) have also drawn on the interactional sociolinguistic approach to examine the process of meaning making and communication issues in interpreted discourse. Both Roy (2000) and Wadensjö (1998) argue for a combination of CA and an ethnographically oriented interactional sociolinguistics approach, pointing out the necessity of examining both the local organisation of talk and broader contexts for a thorough understanding of interpreter-mediated discourse in institutional settings.

An integrated approach to the discourse, drawing on CA, interactional sociolinguistics, and legal narrative theory is therefore adopted by this study in its attempt to deepen our understanding of interpreted police interviewing as a legal process.

Structure of the book

The next chapter, Chapter 1, provides the theoretical and conceptual backgrounds that locate this book in the relevant fields of research. It introduces the institutional frameworks which shape police interviews, as well as sociolinguistic perspectives on police interview discourse as a genre. An overview of research into interpreter mediation as interaction and interpreted discourse in the legal context is also presented.

In Chapter 2, details are provided of the police interview data analysed in the book and the background information relevant to the analysis, including the code of ethics by which interpreters and translators in Australia are expected to abide.

Focusing on discourse strategies for the construction of realities, Chapters 3 and 4 explore issues specific to interpreter-mediated police interviews that are associated with competing versions of events. Chapter 3 discusses the police interview discourse in the information gathering stage from the perspective of the interviewer. Reality construction processes in the tripartite interaction are analysed by focusing on questioning strategies adopted by interviewing officers.

Turning to the perspective of the interviewee, Chapter 4 focuses on the suspects' side of the story by analysing their responses to police interviewers' questions. The analysis examines the management of suspects' resistance strategies as well as their narratives in interpreter-mediated interaction with its type-specific turn-taking organisation. In both Chapters 3 and 4, interaction and power are interwoven in the discussion of story construction processes mediated by interpreters.

Chapter 5 explores how miscommunication is managed in tripartite interview interaction. Drawing on the interaction mechanism of conversational repair, the analysis highlights aspects of miscommunication management specifically found in interpreter-mediated interaction and considers the consequences of certain types of miscommunication management in relation to the narrative construction process.

In Chapter 6, the role of silence, another important aspect of police interview discourse, is examined. The chapter addresses the complexity of decoding and encoding meanings of silence, in particular in relation to the turn-taking organisation of interpreter-mediated interviews.

Finally, in Chapter 7, the key findings of the study are synthesised, revisiting the theoretical and conceptual frameworks introduced in Chapter 1 and discussing the implications, both for the use of interpreters in the legal context and for research into interpreter-mediated legal interaction.

1
Police Interviews and Interpreter Mediation

To locate this book in the relevant fields of research, this chapter gives an overview of research into police interview discourse and interpreter-mediated legal discourse. It introduces the institutional frameworks which shape police interviews, as well as sociolinguistic perspectives on police interview discourse as a genre. The chapter then discusses research into interpreter mediation as interaction and interpreted discourse in the legal context.

1.1 The police interview as a legal process

1.1.1 Purposes of police interviews

One of the purposes of police interviews is to gather relevant facts for an investigation, and another is to confirm what investigators allege to have happened in the crime (Baldwin, 1993; Gibbons, 2003; Heydon, 2005; Hill, 2003). Interviews have been widely seen as problematic, because police interviewers commonly assume the guilt of their suspects during the questioning; they may focus more on confirming guilt or eliciting a confession than on finding out what actually happened (Baldwin, 1993; Heydon, 2005; Hill, 2003; Leo & Drizin, 2010; Shuy, 1998). In recent years, however, overtly coercive questioning tactics have come to be regarded as unacceptable, and legislative changes such as the *Police and Criminal Evidence Act* (PACE) in England and Wales in 1984 have led to the introduction in many parts of the world of official guidelines for investigative interviewing to ensure appropriate procedures and the admissibility of police interviews as evidence (Heydon, 2012; Rock, 2007).

One of the major consequences of this reform in the criminal justice system has been the introduction in 1993 of the PEACE model (see Section 1.2.1 below) of interviewing procedures into the training of

officers in police forces in England and Wales to improve police interview practices and to avoid later exclusion of evidence due to inappropriate questioning. Central to this model is the cognitive interview
technique developed by Gieselman et al. (1984). It involves memory-
enhancing strategies and invitation to free narrative (Milne & Bull,
1999). The PEACE model has been adopted by police forces outside
England and Wales (cf. Rock, 2007), but the uptake has been relatively
recent and limited in Australia (Heydon, 2012). One study claims that
the cognitive interview was introduced to the Victoria state police force
in Australia as early as in 2000, but finds that the actual application of
the approach has not been comprehensive (Buckley, 2009).

Nevertheless, it is important to note that information obtained voluntarily from the interviewee in free narrative style statements is considered the most reliable evidence in many jurisdictions (for example,
Heydon, 2005; Shuy, 1998), including Australia. Thus, analysis of police
interview discourse needs to take into account that the police interviewer's questioning orientation should be guided by this preference
for voluntarily-given free narrative statements. However, if the police
interviewer is under pressure to obtain a confession, especially if other
evidence pointing to the suspect's guilt does not exist, there is a tension
between the need to construct the police-preferred version of events
and the legal preference for voluntarily offered stories (Coulthard &
Johnson, 2007). The interpreter's understanding of these institutional
frameworks affecting the interview could make a difference in the
quality of interpreting and thus in the outcome of the investigation.

The legal requirements and principles of police interviews affect the
ways in which police questioning is conducted (Carter, 2011; Haworth,
2006; Heydon, 2005; Newbury & Johnson, 2006). However, as lay persons, suspects may find some aspects of questioning procedures to be
remote from ordinary conversation and highly puzzling, unless they
are familiar with the discourse conventions and institutional requirements of police interviews (see Rock, 2007 regarding communication
of rights). This puzzlement may increase if the suspect comes from a
minority cultural and/or linguistic background.

1.1.2   Police interviews as evidence

Police interviews are communicative processes, but they are also prod-
ucts because they form evidence which is used and scrutinised in the
trial (Haworth, 2006, 2010). This duality needs to be taken into account
in analysing police interviews. In Australia and jurisdictions such as
England and Wales, police interviews are video recorded and can be

presented in court, as is, as evidence. This means that statements can be confirmed in court in terms of what was said and how the statement was made. However, and importantly, the existence of a future audience and the recording of the interview process itself can affect the way in which police interviews are conducted and questioning tactics are used (Haworth, 2010; Johnson, 2006; Stokoe & Edwards, 2008). Haworth (2010) demonstrates that, unlike police interviewers who are used to pitching their discourse with a view towards future trials, suspects are often unaware of the evidential role of police interviews and could even make incriminating statements. The other consequence of the duality of police interviewing is the police interviewer's need to ensure a recording whose content and quality will be admissible in court. For example, police officers may interrupt the suspect's narrative account, to clarify for the record deictic references made by the suspect or non-verbal aspects of the communication (Stokoe, 2009).

The evidential purpose of police interviewing may affect the process of interpreter-mediated interviews in several ways. One issue is the interpreter's understanding and handling of the legal framing and its linguistic realisation; that is, their understanding of the reasons why questions are constructed and sequenced in certain ways. The interpreter's alignment or lack of it with the police interviewer's institutional orientation, whether intentional or unintentional, may affect the course of investigative interviews and consequently the outcome of the case. Another issue is that the 'interpreter's own speaking space' (Dimitrova, 1997, p. 149) is sometimes constrained, or interfered with, by the police interviewer's need to ensure admissibility of the recorded interview as evidence.

1.2 The police interview as a discourse process

1.2.1 Structure of police interviews

The police interview is a legal genre (Coulthard & Johnson, 2007; Gibbons, 2003; Johnson, 2006), and is 'a staged, goal-oriented, purposeful activity' (Martin, 1984, p. 25). In Australia, there appears to be a focus on standardised legislative elements and a common practice of inviting the interviewee to 'tell their story' before probing (Heydon, 2012). Ord et al. (2011, p. 101), writing for an Australian readership, present a model of interviewing with the following five stages: (1) legal and procedural matters; (2) suspect's account; (3) interviewer's objectives; (4) challenges; (5) interview closure. They also provide guidance on 'Preparation' and 'Evaluation' to investigators, which together with the above five stages aligns the Australian model with the PEACE model. The PEACE model, a top-down approach, includes the stages of Planning and preparation (P) and Evaluation (the last E), which take place outside the interviewing activity itself. The three stages within the interview are Engage and explain (E), Account (A) and Closure (C) (Milne & Bull, 1999, p. 159).

Heydon (2005) identified the following stages of interviewing based on her empirical analysis of police interviews in Australia: Opening, Information gathering, and Closing (p. 73). Heydon also describes the overall goal of each of those stages, with '[a]dhere to legislative requirements' for the Opening and Closing, and '[p]roduce voluntary confession' for the Information gathering stage. This goal of the Information gathering stage is at odds with the recommended approach described in Ord et al. (2011):

> If a suspect is being interviewed, for example, the aim may be to establish whether or not the suspect was involved in the incident or offence, not *to prove* his or her involvement in that incident or offence. (p. 9, italics in original)

Here we see again the tension between 'truth or proof' (Baldwin, 1993) as the aim of police interviewing. This issue is nevertheless partly dealt with through the recommended inclusion of an invitation to the suspect to give their own account of the case in a free narrative style, before specific questions are asked (Gibbons, 2003; Heydon, 2005; Ord et al., 2011). A typical example is 'Tell me what happened on ....' It should also be noted that police officers commonly ask the suspect, in the 'Closing' stage of interviewing, whether the suspect has been coerced into making certain statements (Gibbons, 2003), which is related to a legal requirement for admissibility of the interview as evidence.

The main point concerning the overall structure of police interviews is that there are opening and closing phases before and after the questioning respectively, where communication addressing legal requirements and orientation take place. The questioning itself usually begins with an invitation for a narrative account, followed by specific questioning and probing. In interpreter-mediated police interviews, an awareness of the overall genre structure and the purposes of each of the stages is required of the interpreter since the underlying institutional principles and assumptions are not always explicitly communicated to the suspect.

1.2.2   Opening and closing phases of police interviews

The opening and closing sections of police interviews have been identified as distinctively oriented to 'adhering to legislative requirements'

(Heydon, 2005, p. 73) and as having a participation framework in which the interviewing officers speak on behalf of the police institution (Heydon, 2005). A standardised set of utterances are used to record the time and date of the interview, the persons present, and to communicate the rights of the interviewee (Gibbons, 2003; Heydon, 2005; Rock, 2007). Gibbons (2003) represents Heydon's 'Opening' and 'Closing' stages of police interviews as 'Primary reality framing' and the Information gathering stage as 'Secondary reality framing'. 'Primary reality' refers to the here and now of the legal process (police interviewing procedure) while 'secondary reality' points to the crime, its circumstances and events associated with the crime.

With its semantics and grammar explicitly associated with the legal register, the language used in the opening and closing phases of police interviews is generally more formal than that of the Information gathering or questioning phase (cf. Cotterill, 2000; Gibbons, 2003; Rock, 2007). This is not surprising given that these phases address matters in relation to the primary reality of police interviews as a legal process. Communication difficulties associated with the communication of rights during the Opening phase have been discussed as a serious issue in the legal process (Cotterill, 2000; Gibbons, 2003; Rock, 2007; Shuy, 1997). Nakane (2007) and Russell (2000) discuss how these difficulties might be compounded in interpreter-mediated police interviews.

1.2.3 Questioning and competing versions of events

The information gathering phase, or the 'body' of the interviewing discourse, can be described as questioning proper. The goals of questioning a suspect are, as mentioned earlier, twofold: to elicit information relevant to the investigation of the crime and to establish whether he or she has committed a crime. The orientation of the police, as mentioned above, often tends towards achieving confirmation of guilt (Auburn et al., 1995; Heydon, 2005; Leo & Drizin, 2010; Shuy, 1998).

However, the interviewer's goal and the suspect's interests are in conflict. Suspects often attempt either to deny involvement in the crime or to construct a story with potentially mitigating factors (Haworth, 2006; Linell & Jönsson, 1991; Newbury & Johnson, 2006). This clash of different versions of events is a pivotal aspect of the adversarial justice system, and a significant aspect of police interviews as a legal genre.

As Bennett and Feldman (1981) argue in their seminal work on courtroom discourse, reality is constructed and redefined through the exchanges between the parties concerned. Courtroom discourse in adversarial justice systems has often been discussed in terms of how this reality is constructed through interaction between witnesses and lawyers (for example, Heffer, 2005; Jackson, 1991), and how competing stories are presented and challenged in the courtroom through discursive strategies (for example, Gibbons, 2003; Maley & Fahey, 1991). This competition between different versions of events runs through the litigation process, from police interviews to courtroom proceedings. The credibility of the story and how the story is presented are crucial factors in determining guilt (Gibbons, 2003; Jackson, 1991; Jaquemet, 1996). This book adopts this view of competing storytelling, or the construction of versions of events, as the pivotal aspect of police interviews as a legal genre. The main concern of this book is therefore to explore the dynamics of tripartite interaction involving an interviewer, an interviewee and an interpreter, and the impact on the tensions between forces pulling the story in opposing directions.

Coulthard and Johnson (2007) argue that it is important to recognise the hybrid and dynamic nature of the police interview which is characterised by a combination of 'lay, police and legislative language' (Johnson, 2006, p. 669). In this view, the 'primary reality' is interwoven with the 'secondary reality' in the questioning, with the interviewer bearing in mind the role of the recorded interview as evidence, and both the interviewer and the interviewee evaluating their storytelling. This dynamic hybridity is partly a consequence of police interviewers' professional training and their goal to construct legally acceptable versions of events to build their case. In doing this, however, one aspect of legal requirement is, as mentioned earlier, to obtain evidence through the interviewee's voluntarily provided narrative. This may lead to officers using discourse strategies to invoke a participation framework aimed at eliciting such narratives (Heydon, 2005).

The institutional orientations create a gap in institutional knowledge and repertoires between police interviewers and suspects. As we will see, an important question in relation to this is how interpreter mediation might bridge, close or widen this gap.

1.2.4   Interaction, information and power in police interviews

In her analysis of storytelling in a trial context, Snedaker refers to three key elements: *form, content* and *style. Form* refers to 'the connective structure that gives a pattern and shape to the discourse' (1991, p. 135), and *content* to the ideas presented in the story. The third element, *style*, is about how the story is told, and relates to power and interpersonal relations in interaction. These elements resonate with the functions of language identified by Halliday (1978, 1989): textual, ideational and interpersonal, respectively. Following Snedaker's and Halliday's views of language in the social context, this book examines interpreter-mediated police interviews in relation to these three key elements of discourse, aiming to describe the interaction dynamics of the tripartite interaction (form, or textual), how the dynamics of such interaction shapes police interview discourse as evidence (content, or ideational), and how the layer of interpreter mediation affects the power relations of the participants in the institutional discourse (style, or interpersonal).

1.2.4.1 Form – the textual aspect of interaction

Police questioning is more private than courtroom questioning as far as the immediate context of the discursive event is concerned. There are more instances of co-construction of discourse and the communication is generally more spontaneous than courtroom discourse. The spontaneity of interaction in police interview discourse may pose challenges for the interpreter.

One of the most widely discussed features of police interview discourse is the pre-allocation of turn-types. As the institutional aim of police interviewing of a suspect is to gather information relevant to the case and ascertain whether the suspect has committed a crime, the police interviewer predominantly takes the role of a questioner and the suspect that of an answerer (Fairclough, 1989; Heydon, 2005; Holt & Johnson, 2010). Therefore police interviews typically consist of a large number of Question–Answer 'adjacency pairs' (Sacks et al., 1974, p. 716). The fact that a professional asks questions and initiates the first pair parts (FFPs) of adjacency pairs means that the topic control is also principally with the police interviewer (Heydon, 2005; Holt & Johnson, 2010).

The second pair part (SPP) may be absent or may not always be an answer; for example, if the suspect remains silent or vocally refuses to answer (cf. Coulthard & Johnson, 2007; Fairclough, 1995; Forrester & Ramsden, 2001; Haworth, 2006). Newbury and Johnson (2006), for example, demonstrate the way in which a suspect resisted his interviewer's attempt to elicit relevant information from him by using strategies of contest, correction, avoidance and refusal. A clarification sequence such as repair initiation and repair may be inserted after a question. Heydon (2005) finds that the only interactional context in which suspects may initiate a sequence is when they initiate a repair. The relevance of this aspect of interview dynamics to the present study is that interpreters may have to mediate deliberately misaligned interaction in a hostile and confrontational interview situation.

Simultaneous or overlapping talk is another key feature of police interview discourse. Simultaneous talk may include a cooperative type of overlapping as well as non-cooperative interruptions. In the conversation analysis (CA) tradition, an interruption occurs when a speaker initiates a turn at speaking long before the current speaker has reached the Transition Relevance Place (TRP) in his/her turn in which speaker transition becomes relevant (Hutchby & Wooffitt, 1988; Sacks et al., 1974). Simultaneous talk includes overlaps caused by interruptions but also occurs when speakers speak simultaneously due to their natural orientation towards predicting turn completion and minimising turn-transition gaps (Sacks et al., 1974; Schegloff, 2000). Interruptions in police interviews are often associated with police officers' attempts to stay in control of topics (for example, Heydon, 2005; Momeni, 2011; Shuy, 1998). Some studies report disturbing examples of police officers' interruptions of interviewees' accounts (Berk-Seligson, 2009; Fairclough, 1989). However, we should remember that interviewees also interrupt police interviewers' utterances (for example, Fairclough, 1995; Haworth, 2006). Interruptions are one of the consequences of interlocutors' attempts to construct their own versions of events. However, as we will see later in this book, interruptions and simultaneous talk in general are challenging for police interpreters but also problematic in terms of the police interview as evidence gathered in a legal process (Berk-Seligson, 2009; Russell, 2002).

Finally, silence is another key feature of police interviews. The silence which the suspect may use as their legal right has significance, but literally silent responses and silent pauses also play significant roles in terms of constructing different versions of events. Komter (2003), for example, discusses the use of silence by both a police interviewer and a suspect. One of the ways in which the police interviewer uses the silence is to indicate that the suspect's account is not credible. Silence may also function as a pressuring strategy on the part of the police interviewer (Forrester & Ramsden, 2011; Heydon, 2005) or an invitation to elaborate on answers (Shuy, 1998). In interpreter-mediated police interviews, these functions of silence and the ambiguity of its meaning become serious issues.

1.2.4.2   Content – the ideas in the story

To gather as much relevant information as possible given in a free narrative form, as well as to avoid coercive questioning practices, police interviewers are encouraged to invite suspects to give their own account using their own words (Coulthard & Johnson, 2007; Heydon, 2005, 2012; Ord et al., 2011; Shuy, 1998). Cognitive interviewing is an approach which enhances the quality and quantity of information elicited from interviewees (Heydon, 2012; Milne & Bull, 1999) and various discourse strategies have been recommended as part of this approach (Gudjonsson, 1992; Milne & Bull, 1999). However, as mentioned earlier, cognitive interviewing has not been fully implemented in practice in Australia (Buckley, 2009; Heydon, 2012) but recommendations have been made to police to start with an invitation to narrative, followed firstly by open questions and then by a probing phase with specific questions (Ord et al., 2011).

At a turn-by-turn level of topic control, question types have been discussed in relation to the elicitation of information. Gibbons (2003) provides a description of question types according to the level of 'information control' (p. 103). Discursive strategies other than question types have been identified in relation to constructing a police-preferred version of events. These include formulations (Heydon, 2005; Holt & Johnson, 2010; Johnson, 2006), *and-* and *so-* prefaced questions (Holt & Johnson, 2006, 2010), as well as questions containing repeats of suspects' utterances (Holt & Johnson, 2010). These strategies are used by police officers to construct a prosecution-preferred story not only as a whole but also in terms of incorporating the suspect's own words into the story.

On the other hand, suspects also resist attempts to construct a prosecution-preferred version of events or they put forward their own version of events. Their strategies include silence (Komter, 2003; Kurzon, 1995, 1997) as well as challenge and non-cooperation (Haworth, 2006; Newbury & Johnson, 2006). Auburn et al. (1995) discuss suspects' resistance strategies of 'recasting' through 'removing single agency' and repositioning of the 'perpetrator as victim' (p. 374). Linell and Jönsson (1991) also demonstrate suspects' attempts to mitigate the circumstances in telling their side of the story. However, Linell and Jönsson also make the following observation:

> In the police interrogation the police officer asks questions and the suspect responds on the conditions set by the questions, but the suspect's contributions, of course, also influence the police officer's questioning strategies. On the whole, however the policeman is the one who sets the overall perspective, and with this the suspect has to comply. (p. 96)

An important question for the present study is how interpreter mediation affects both police and suspect strategies when constructing their versions of events, not only in terms of semantic and pragmatic equivalences in the translation but also in terms of the discursive and legal functions of these strategies.

1.2.4.3   Style – the interpersonal aspect of interviews

This aspect of discourse is related to power relations, interpersonal meanings and identity management. In his influential work on 'powerful testimony' and 'powerless testimony', O'Barr (1982) demonstrated that testimony characterised by attributes of power, such as loudness, interruption and fluency, was evaluated positively for qualities such as truthfulness and convincingness. In contrast, powerless testimony with features such as hedges, hesitation and mitigation received negative ratings. This powerful / powerless dimension is likely to apply in the police interview context to a certain degree, although the immediate judge of the suspect's character is the police interviewer. Important findings related to this are that the style of interpreters' speech has been shown to impact on the perceptions held by witnesses when similar studies were carried out on interpreter mediation (Berk-Seligson, 1990; Hale, 2004).

Power in interaction has been analysed by examining question types. While question types are, as mentioned above, associated with the content of the interview, some question types, for example tag questions, put more pressure than others on the interviewee to talk (cf. Gibbons, 2003, 2008; Haworth, 2006; Newbury & Johnson, 2006; Shuy, 1998). This suggests that question types have interpersonal functions.

Modality and politeness are also indicators of interpersonal meaning. The power of questions and answers can be manipulated by modality and other politeness strategies. Newbury and Johnson (2006, p. 229) show a strikingly powerful resistance from a suspect responding to the police with the imperative sentence 'Continue the story'. On the other hand, solidarity-oriented strategies may be used by police interviewers, for example by building common ground through the use of suspects' first language, as discussed by Berk-Seligson (2009). Shuy (1998), drawing on Inbau et al. (1986), mentions some politeness strategies that interrogators are encouraged to use as tactics, which include showing sympathy towards suspects and manipulating forms of address depending on the status of the suspect.

As Berk-Seligson (1990) and Hale (2004) have shown, interpreters' renditions of style-related features impact on perceptions of witness credibility and trustworthiness in trials. This may also be the case for the construction of a suspect's identity in interpreted police interviews.

This overview of the police interview as legal discourse gives us a baseline picture of the discourse which interpreters mediate. The analysis of interpreter-mediated police interviews in this book uses this baseline picture as a reference point. In the following sections we focus on interpreter mediation itself.

1.3   Interpreter mediation as interaction

The mode of interpreting normally used in police interviews is liaison interpreting (Russell, 2002), which is the consecutive mode of interpreting (as opposed to simultaneous) used in most community interpreting settings. This interpreting mode is characterised by dialogic communication between a lay person and a professional (Niska, 1995; Russell, 2002; Wadensjö, 1998).

Previous studies approached interpreter-mediated discourse from a CA perspective and have taken the view that the interpreter is a coordinator of talk in addition to being a transmitter of message content (Dimitrova, 1997; Roy, 2000; Wadensjö, 1997, 1998). Furthermore, 'the interpreter is the centre of the turn taking process' (Dimitrova, 1997, p. 161). Müller (2001) goes as far as to say that:

> [t]he interpreter may thus have a decisive influence on turn length and regulate stages in the progress of conversation. She may allocate turns and regulate who will be [the] next speaker or recipient, initiate 'repairs' or comments, and, in the specifics of her translations, not just influence but co-constitute the talk exchanged by the primary parties. (p. 248)

Indeed, as Roy (2000, p. 67) points out, primary speakers 'are always exchanging turns with the interpreter' and, as a principle, every primary speaker's turn is followed by an interpreter's turn. Thus, while CA has been a useful analytical approach to interpreting as social interaction, there are some aspects of turn-taking rules (Sacks et al., 1974) that deviate from the rules in the CA tradition (Dimitrova, 1997).

One of the distinctive characteristics of interpreter-mediated interaction is the fragmentation caused by the interpreter cutting in to take a turn before his/her memory capacity is overloaded (Dimitrova, 1997; Roy, 2000; Wadensjö, 1998). While '[b]revity of turn is of practical translatory interest to the DI [dialogue interpreter]' (Müller, 2001, p. 263), this can cause awkwardness in interaction and prevent primary speakers from giving narratives. Another distinctive aspect is interpreters' handling of simultaneous talk. Even though there is a normative turn-taking format in which each primary speaker turn is followed by an interpreter turn, overlapping occurs, at times even between the primary speakers. Overlapping talk may result in difficulties in completely rendering all utterances of the primary speakers. To avoid those difficulties, the interpreter at times has to ignore, stop or offer turns to primary speakers (Roy, 2000).

Another significant difference between monolingual and interpreter-mediated interaction concerns miscommunication, which often involves 'repair sequences' (Sacks et al., 1974; Schegloff, 1992). Not only is it challenging to resolve miscommunication through an interpreter but the mechanism of mediated interaction itself may become a cause of miscommunication (Wadensjö, 1998). It should also be noted, however, that problems in interpreted interaction can be created and resolved collectively (Berk-Seligson, 2009; Müller, 2001; Russell, 2000, 2002; Wadensjö, 1998). For example, Roy (2000) shows one of the primary speakers learning to modify turn-taking behaviour for mediated interaction.

1.4   Interpreter-mediated legal discourse

Let us now turn our focus to the legal discourse mediated by an interpreter. Holt and Johnson (2010, p. 23) state that '[c]entral to the nature of legal talk is the system of turn-taking that participants adopt'. The contribution of CA, through its focus on organisation of talk, to the understanding of legal discourse has therefore been significant. This is especially so in the questioning of lay people by professionals in legal contexts such as court proceedings and police interviews. By analysing how the three parties in mediated interviews orient themselves to the interaction, we are able to understand how versions of events are constructed through the information or the 'content' emerging from the interaction. Analysis of interaction dynamics also enables us to understand how versions of events compete against each other, or how the interviewer and the interviewee engage in power struggles over the story that they each wish to put forward.

The present study examines how key elements of police interview discourse as a genre play out when mediated by interpreters. As will be seen, there are interrelationships among form, content and style – or the textual, ideational and interpersonal in Halliday's (1978, 1989) terms. For instance, 'format tying' (Goodwin, 1990) is a strategy which allows police interviewers to exploit the interviewer's own utterance to offer a counter position through the use of the suspect's own wording in questioning (Holt & Johnson, 2010). Wadensjö (1997) demonstrates how this strategy found in police questioning is lost through interpreter mediation. Formulations (Heritage & Watson, 1979) are another strategy to recast and present the interviewee's utterances in a form which assumes the questioner's preferred version of events (Heydon, 2005; Holt & Johnson, 2010; Komter, 2006). An example given by Wadensjö (1997) shows interpreter mediation introducing a formulation despite the original question by the interviewer not being composed as a formulation. These changes affect story construction, but strategies such as format tying and formulation can also be used for interpersonal purposes, or as a 'person targeted strategy' of power (Gibbons, 2003, p. 113) to portray the interviewee as an unreliable criminal (Heydon, 2005).

As mentioned in the previous section, overlapping and interruptions occur in interpreter-mediated interaction. The constraints placed on turn-taking and the organisation of talk by mediation entail a number of problems unique to triadic interaction with an interpreter: first, the information provided by primary speakers may not be shared among all interview participants if there are ignored turns or if not everything is rendered; second, overlapped utterances affect the quality of the recorded evidence (Russell, 2002); third, uninterpreted utterances are not recorded in the language of the court as evidence (Russell, 2002); and finally, the interpersonal function, or the power, of the interruption may not be translatable if mediated by an interpreter (Wadensjö, 1997). The layer of interpreter mediation may twist and complicate the interaction among the 'form/textual', 'content/ideational' and 'style/power' aspects of legal discourse, with varying consequences.

Another potential problem with interpreter-mediated questioning is that, if the interpreter intends to render the interviewee's account in two stages and the interviewing professional asks the next question before the second stage is rendered, the interviewee's account may be cut short. In some cases, the interviewer may not wait for a rendition at all before moving on to the next question. Niska (1995) gives an example of courtroom interpreting where the prosecutor asks a question before the rendition of the defendant's answer to the preceding question. This forces the interpreter to render the previous answer and the question in succession. The rendition of the previous answer becomes part of the evidence, but the story construction process has been disrupted by the prosecutor's interruption.

One important aspect of interpreter-mediated police interviews is how interpreters handle conflicts and tensions between primary speakers. It has been suggested, based on analysis of authentic legal discourse, that interpreters are sometimes inclined to intervene to lessen friction between primary speakers, but in fact should be prepared to let them engage in conflict (Hale, 2008; Komter, 2005; Wadensjö, 1998). Conflict between the police interviewer and the interviewee can be expected since they are often trying to construct competing versions of events. As we will see in Chapter 5, premature interpreter intervention often takes the form of repair sequences (cf. Komter, 2005). Such moves however give interpreters excessive control over primary speakers' narrative construction processes.

How interpreters handle conflict in legal discourse is not only an issue of narrative construction but also of interpersonal power relationships. Komter (2005) and Wadensjö (1998) observe that interpreters offer renditions which serve to mitigate the face-threat posed by primary speakers' source utterances. The interpersonal aspect of police interview discourse may be impacted if the interpreter takes the initiative to address problematic communication. Komter (2005) gives an example of an interpreter referring to the suspect by a third person pronoun to create emotional distance, when an interaction became hostile. This type of repair may make a highly face-threatening challenge interactionally obsolete and 'defuse hostilities or avoid embarrassment' (Komter, 2005, p. 217).

Finally, perceptions of the witness in the courtroom context are likely to be influenced by the style adopted by the court interpreter in rendering witness utterances (Berk-Seligson, 1990; Hale, 2004; see also Section 1.2.4 above). Mason and Stewart (2001) discuss examples of interpreter-mediated courtroom cross-examination and interviews of migrants by immigration officers, highlighting changes in illocutionary force through interpreting. They argue that, in interpreter-mediated questioning, 'it is the power relationship between the interrogator and the interrogated which is at stake' (p. 59) and that changes in illocutionary force could disadvantage either party. In police interview contexts, Komter (2005) gives an example of face-threat mitigated through interpreting in her analysis of Dutch-French police interpreting discourse. In addition to the use of repair (clarification) sequences mentioned above, the interpreter removes the agency clearly indicated in the police interviewer's source utterance to 'mitigate a potential face-threat' (p. 214). Police interpreter respondents of the survey conducted by Ortega Herráez and Foulquié Rubio (2008) in Spain also confirm that interpreters do alter register, for instance by adapting slang.

The participation of an interpreter brings new dimensions to the discourse of police interviews. These new dimensions can be observed in all aspects of discourse including the interaction dynamics, constructed stories, and the power relationships between the interviewing officer and the interviewed suspects. In the ensuing chapters, the analysis of interpreter-mediated police interviews will be guided by these aspects of discourse. The chapters also aim to elucidate the ways form/textual, content/ideational and style/interpersonal interact with one another when police interviews as a legal genre in an adversarial system are mediated by interpreters.

1.5 The role of the interpreter in the legal process

The role of the legal interpreter is a contentious issue which has been discussed widely in the field of interpreting studies. While the role assumed by an interpreter affects the story construction process and the evaluation of a suspect or defendant, taking account of an interpreters' role or stance also gives us a better understanding of interpreter-mediated discourse.

A widely assumed role of the interpreter is that of a 'conduit' (Laster & Taylor, 1994; Niska, 1995; Wadensjö, 1998). The view of interpreters as conduits may come from: first, a misunderstanding of interpreting in which interpreters are regarded as translation machines, and an associated inadequate understanding of the nature of mediated interaction; and second, the impact of the interpreters' code of ethics, which obliges interpreters to maintain impartiality and provide renditions faithful to source utterances (cf. Chapter 2, Section 2.2.3).

Previous studies of interpreter roles, based on authentic legal interpreting and on interpreter interviews or surveys, suggest that interpreters at times go beyond the role of a 'conduit' in reality (Berk-Seligson, 1990; Laster & Taylor, 1994; Leung & Gibbons, 2008; Niska, 1995; Wadensjö, 1998). For instance, they may be asked to offer explanations as an expert on the culture of the witnesses or interviewees, as in Niska's (1995) example of an interpreter being asked to explain the legal status of manslaughter in Italy.

Not only is the interpreter the only official linguistic and cultural expert of the two languages used in the bilingual legal process (Cooke, 1995; Niska, 1995; Laster & Taylor, 1994), but she or he is also at the centre of the turn-taking and is the one who needs to monitor and manage interaction (Dimitrova, 1997; Müller, 1989, 2001; Roy, 2000; Wadensjö, 1998; see also Section 1.4 above). Interpreters are also social beings with their own professional and personal ideologies which could affect their decisions on interaction management and renditions. Leung and Gibbons (2008), for example, demonstrate court interpreters' varying stances towards rape victims, realised in their renditions in rape case trials in Hong Kong.

Discussion concerning the role of the interpreter often involves expectations regarding interpreter loyalty. Drawing on Falck's (1987) study, Niska (1995, p. 297) states that 'immigrants are more prone [than counsel] to see the interpreter as their helper, not strictly as a mediator'. This view is supported by Laster and Taylor (1994), who also point out that interpreters are ambivalent about their loyalty, owing some to those who have assigned them the job.

Legal interpreter role-shifts within a single discourse event have also been discussed. One common trigger of interpreter role-shifts is miscommunication or the anticipation of miscommunication. As the only interlocutor in the legal interaction who can monitor communication in both languages, the interpreter is sometimes the only repairer of miscommunication. Shifts from the task of translating to that of communication management to address miscommunication have been demonstrated by discourse-analytic studies of interpreting (Berk-Seligson, 1990; Komter, 2005; Wadensjö, 1997, 1998). However, eagerness on the part of the interpreter to take up the role of communication mediator could lead to unnecessary interference with the legal process and so interpreters need to be aware of their role boundaries (Hale, 2008; Wadensjö, 1998). Hale (2008) discusses some examples from courtroom interpreting where interpreters try to offer an explanation as a linguistic expert or modify a specialist term to make the concept easier to understand. These examples suggest that there are potential obstructions and risks to due process if the interpreter is too eager to facilitate communication.

The 'facilitator' role could also be incompatible with primary speakers' desires to be indirect or ambiguous. Niska (1995) and Wadensjö (1998) draw on examples from courtroom proceedings and police interviews to show that interpreters may try to clarify the meaning and purposes of primary speaker utterances to avoid problems, even when the primary speakers are deliberately using ambiguity for their own purposes. On the other hand, interpreters themselves may utilise the ambiguity between their role as the conduit and coordinator of interaction to diffuse tension between the primary speakers, as found in Komter's (2005) study of an interpreter-mediated police interview (see Section 1.4).

One way in which role options are commonly realised is through the use of personal pronouns as reference terms. Ortega Herráez and Foulquié Rubio (2008) found that Spanish police interpreters were frequently addressed by the second person pronoun, while the third person pronoun was used to refer to the interviewee. The norm in interpreter-mediated institutional interaction is for primary speakers to address each other directly using the second person pronoun. Ortega Herráez and Foulquié Rubio (2008) contend that the preference for directly addressing the interpreter is due to the setting of mediated police interviews where it is more natural to address the next speaker with the second person pronoun. Interpreters' role-shifts may occur due to the monolingual conversational routines to which primary speakers are accustomed or to conscious decisions on the part of the interpreter or primary speakers to negotiate the interpersonal dimension of the legal process.

One useful approach to the role of interpreters is Goffman's (1981) participation framework. This framework accounts for the turn-by-turn interactional roles available to the interlocutor in social encounters. According to Goffman (1981, p. 226), a speaker is in the role of an *animator* when he or she is 'the sounding box from which utterances come', but when in the role of an *author*, a speaker is 'the agent who puts together, composes, or scripts the turns that are uttered'. A third role is that of a *principal*, 'the party to whose position, stand, and belief [...] the words attest' (Goffman, 1981). This framework was adopted by Wadensjö (1998) in her seminal work on interpreter-mediated interaction, where the 'default' role of the interpreter faithfully rendering the primary speaker's meaning can be described as *animator*. When interpreters edit, create or omit meanings in relation to primary speaker utterances, they are in the *author* role. The *principal* role is assumed when the interpreter communicates their own message instead of offering a rendition. This occurs, for example, when the interpreter asks one of the primary speakers for a clarification to ensure an accurate understanding of the source utterance before rendering it. This framework enables Wadensjö's (1998) analysis to shed light on how interpreters manage the translation and coordination of interaction simultaneously. Leung and Gibbons (2008) also apply this framework to their understanding of court interpreting as a social interaction, to which interpreters bring their ideologies as social beings.

The issue of interpreter role, like other key discourse elements, impacts on the way competing stories are negotiated in the interaction and then presented as evidence. In particular, when the interpreter assumes a *principal* role, there arises a tension between the need to coordinate interaction and the requirement to remain impartial. Interpreter impartiality is important for the admissibility of evidence. The analyses and discussions in the following chapters of this book draw on Goffman's (1981) participation framework and Wadensjö's (1998) approach to interpreter-mediated discourse in which Goffman's framework is adopted.

1.6 Summary

This chapter has given an overview of the areas of research relevant to the discussions in this book. First, some key aspects of the police interview as a legal process were presented. These aspects of police interview affect, and are affected by, institutional discursive practices. They are therefore relevant to the analysis here. Second, the police interview as a legal genre was discussed based on major findings of previous research. The perspective adopted by this book was introduced, which views police questioning as a site of struggle between two versions of events and of power struggles between the interviewer and the interviewee. These struggles are realised through discourse strategies in talk-in-interaction. Following this, key discursive features of interpreter-mediated discourse were discussed and challenges that interpreters face in managing the interaction were identified. The ensuing discussion on issues specific to interpreter-mediated interaction in legal contexts suggested that interpreter mediation has a significant impact on Snedaker's (1991) three key dimensions of legal narratives – form, content and style – and Halliday's (1978, 1989) three key aspects of discourse – textual, ideational and interpersonal. Following this, Goffman's (1981) participation framework was introduced as a useful tool for analysis of interpreter roles.

From the overviews above, it is possible to see that turn-by-turn use of language affects the discourse of mediated interviewing as a social and institutional practice. The institutional structure also manifests itself and may be resisted in any specific context of police interviewing. As mentioned in the preceding chapter, sociolinguistic research into language use in legal contexts should take account of this reciprocal relationship between turn-by-turn language use and the institutional context (Eades, 2010). The study of interpreter-mediated police interviews presented in the remaining part of this book aligns itself with this principle.

2
Setting the Scene: The Police Interviews and the Interpreting

This chapter addresses some of the background information relevant to the discussion of data in the book. It first outlines the source of the police interview data used in the analysis and then gives details of interpreter accreditation procedures, including their code of ethics, and discusses the accreditation levels of the interpreters who participated in the interviews.

2.1 The interviews

The interpreter-mediated police interviews analysed in this book consist of records of four police interviews conducted with four suspects from two criminal cases. The suspects were Japanese nationals alleged to have imported illegal drugs into Australia. Three of the four suspects were arrested in the same case in 1992, when they travelled to Australia as a group. The fourth suspect, who had travelled alone to Australia, was arrested in 2002. Since the drugs were found with these suspects at airports, the investigations were conducted by the Australian Federal Police. All the suspects were prosecuted, but all denied their involvement in the crimes. The suspect in the 2002 case was acquitted, but the suspects from the 1992 case were convicted and, after having served time in Australia, were deported to Japan. The author was given access to the records of four relevant interviews through the defence attorneys from these cases. Audio recordings were made available to the author for all four of the interviews and video recordings were made available for two of the interviews. The interviews in these cases are in the public domain in various forms (for example, Nagao, 2004; Nagano, 2003; Watanabe & Yamada, 2005). Details of this data are given in Table 2.1.

Table 2.1 Police interview data

Case	Interview	Police officer	Suspect	Data format
1992	1	PO1	S1	Audio recording
1992	2	PO2	S2	Audio recording
1992	3	PO3	S3	Video & audio recording
2002	4	PO4	S4	Video & audio recording

Some aspects of this data set require special attention. First of all, the small number of interviews means that the analysis is qualitative. Thus, the findings presented in this book can contribute only one piece of the jigsaw to studies of police interview discourse. Nevertheless, the book is an ambitious attempt to explore a number of important sociopragmatic aspects of interpreted police interview discourse with empirical data.

Secondly, these interviews all come from drug importation cases, which may involve some peculiarities in terms of interviewing as a discourse process. By the time the interviews commenced, the suspects and the interviewing police officers all knew that highly incriminating physical evidence was present. Furthermore, although from the legal perspective they were caught 'red-handed', all suspects denied the allegations. This conflict between two versions of events may have made the work of the interpreters more challenging, as the police officers came into the interviews to search for proof, elicit confirmation of guilt or obtain confessions (cf. Auburn et al., 1995; Baldwin, 1993; Shuy, 1998; Solan & Tiersma, 2005), while the suspects all claimed that they had been innocent mules.

Thirdly, the two cases from which the interview data were obtained were separated by a gap of ten years. The more recent 2002 case complements the 1992 interviews in that cognitive interview protocol had become the norm in many jurisdictions by the time of the later case, following the UK introduction of the previously mentioned PEACE investigative framework (see Chapter 1, Section 1.1.1). It is unlikely that, at the time of the 1992 interviews, the investigating officers would have used the cognitive interview protocol as it seems that it was not until the later 1990s that this protocol was implemented as the norm by state and federal police services in Australia. Victoria Police introduced the cognitive interviewing framework in 2000 (Buckley, 2009), and in 1997 members of the New South Wales Police Force were being taught cognitive interview techniques at the police academy (Stacey & Mullan, 1997). The actual extent of implementation in 1997 could not be confirmed but a newspaper report (Silvester, 2010) on the adoption of the PEACE framework (including cognitive interview techniques) did not include New South Wales or Victoria. The possible differences in the interviewing officers' background training and interviewing approach, taken into account in the analysis here, is a significant factor in investigating the issue of power in police interviews, as the cognitive interview requires interviewers to relinquish more interactional power and control than in a traditional approach. However, it should be noted that there have been reports on UK police practice that police officers' questioning does not necessarily reflect the changes introduced by PEACE (for example, Baldwin, 1993). Buckley's (2009) Australian study also suggests that there are still barriers to officers actually adopting this method and it is unclear whether it has been effectively implemented.

Finally, it should be noted that the interviews analysed here did not take place in the presence of a lawyer. In Australia, unlike the United States, suspects are not entitled to have a lawyer present during police questioning unless they are minors. Although they have the right to contact or attempt to contact a lawyer, the suspects in the data discussed here did not ask for or obtain legal advice during the questioning.

2.2 Interpreting for the police

2.2.1 Legal interpreting and interpreter accreditation

In Australia, when interpreters are required for police interviews, interpreters accredited through NAATI (National Accreditation Authority for Translators and Interpreters) are arranged for most languages. NAATI has four levels of accreditation in interpreting, of which the two lower levels are considered relevant to the particular police interpreting setting discussed in this book: 'Professional Interpreter' and 'Paraprofessional interpreter' (called, respectively, Level III and Level II at the time of the 1992 interviews). The former is the first professional level, at which, 'interpreters are capable of interpreting across a wide range of semi-specialised situations and are capable of using the consecutive mode to interpret speeches or presentations' and target settings include 'banking, law, health, and social and community services' (NAATI, 2013). The latter, paraprofessional interpreters, according to NAATI (2013) 'generally undertake the interpretation of non-specialist dialogues'. Although the minimum level of accreditation required for legal interpreting in Australia is 'Professional Interpreter', it has been suggested that this level of accreditation is not sufficient for the job and that specialist training in legal interpreting is required (Hale, 2004;

Laster & Taylor, 1994; Roberts-Smith, 2007). Paraprofessional interpreters were however arranged for most of the interviews examined in the present research, as this level of interpreter may be used for interviews by the Australian Federal Police (AFP).

2.2.2   The interpreters and their accreditation

The interviews examined in this book were mediated by four interpreters. Details regarding the allocation of interpreters, their accreditation levels, and interview participants' genders are given in Table 2.2.

As can be seen in the table, one of the interpreters was accredited at the 'Professional Interpreter' level (formerly Level III) and two were accredited at the 'Paraprofessional' level (formerly Level II). The accreditation level of IR3 could not be retrieved.

In the 1992/3 NAATI directory of practitioners, 11 interpreters with Level II (Paraprofessional) accreditation and 8 with Level III (Professional) accreditation were listed for Japanese–English interpreting in the state of Victoria. However, in the 1992 case, as there were, unusually, five Japanese detainees to be interviewed in one location at once, the supply of interpreters may have been lacking. Although we are likely to observe better quality police interpreting with interpreters with 'Professional Interpreter' accreditation, most of the interpreting examples examined in this book are not at this level. At the same time, AFP guidelines do allow the use of paraprofessional interpreters, and in 2002, ten years after the 1992 case, a paraprofessional interpreter was also used in Interview 4 in the present research.

It would be reasonable to say that the findings in the present research are not uncommon in practice, as far as Japanese–English interpreting in Australia is concerned. In any case, the data are authentic interpreter-mediated police interviews, and the aim of this book is to investigate the impact of interpreter mediation on the negotiation of power in institutional discourse. The aim is not to compare source text and target language text for an analysis of translation processes, but to investigate discourse processes in three-party interaction in real police interviews.

Table 2.2   Interpreter allocation and accreditation level

Interview	Police officer		Suspect		Interpreter		Accreditation
1	PO1	(M)	S1	(M)	IR1	(F)	Professional
2	PO2	(F)	S2	(M)	IR2	(M)	Paraprofessional
3	PO3	(M)	S3	(F)	IR3	(M)	Unknown
4	PO4	(M)	S4	(M)	IR4	(F)	Paraprofessional

2.2.3 Professional ethics of interpreting

In analysing interpreters in interaction, as they mediate between the inter-viewing officer and the suspect, it is important to recognise that interpret-ers are bound by a professional code of ethics. Specifically, interpreters and translators working in Australia are expected to abide by the AUSIT (The Australian Institute of Interpreters and Translators Incorporated) code of ethics. It is endorsed by NAATI and has been adopted by a number of major organisations such as the Commonwealth Government's Translation and Interpreting Service (TIS), Centrelink Multicultural Services and the Refugee Review Tribunal. NAATI accreditation tests contain a section on the code of ethics to ensure a correct understanding of the professional ethics of interpreting. The general principles, in the pre-2012 version of the code of ethics include the following items (AUSIT, 2010):

1. Professional Conduct
2. Confidentiality
3. Competence
4. Impartiality
5. Accuracy
6. Employment
7. Professional Development

Some sections of the code of ethics are of particular relevance to the study of interpreters as interlocutors:

1. Professional Conduct
   a) v. Interpreters shall encourage speakers to address each other directly.
4. Impartiality
   b) i. A professional detachment is required for interpreting and translation assignments in all situations.
   c) i. Interpreters and translators are not responsible for what clients say or write.
   c) ii. Interpreters and translators shall not voice or write an opinion, solicited or unsolicited, on any matter or person in relation to an assignment.
5. Accuracy
   a) Truth and Completeness
      i. In order to ensure the same access to all that is said by all par-ties involved in a meeting, interpreters shall relay accurately and completely everything that is said.

    ii. Interpreters shall convey the whole message, including derogatory or vulgar remarks, as well as non-verbal clues.

    iii. If patent untruths are uttered or written, interpreters and translators shall convey these accurately as presented.

    iv. Interpreters and translators shall not alter, make additions to, or omit anything from their assigned work.

  b) Uncertainties in Transmission and Comprehension

    i. Interpreters and translators shall acknowledge and promptly rectify their interpreting and translation mistakes.

    ii. If anything is unclear, interpreters and translators shall ask for repetition, rephrasing or explanation.

    iii. If recall and interpreting are being overtaxed, interpreters shall ask the speaker to pause, then signal to continue.

The annotation for Principle 1, a) v. is relevant because it essentially refers to the recommended use of second person pronouns by the primary speakers when they interact with one another through an interpreter. It is associated with the impartiality principle (see Principle 4 above) and the neutral positioning of the interpreter (Berk-Seligson, 1990; Wadensjö, 1998). The use of third person pronouns by primary speakers, instead of referring to each other by the second person pronoun 'you', has been found and discussed in numerous existing studies, despite the fact that the use of the second person pronoun is a well-established standard (for example, Angermeyer, 2008; Berk-Seligson, 2009; Komter, 2005; Wadensjö, 1998). Komter (2005), for example, discusses the use of pronouns by a police interpreter who exploits ambiguous footing by drawing on the notion of recipient design, where there is an expectation that speakers design their turns for particular recipients (Sacks et al., 1974).

Principle 4 concerns the impartiality of the interpreter. Wadensjö's seminal work (1998) mentioned in Chapter 1 (see Section 1.3), highlights the role of the interpreter as a coordinator of goal-oriented discourse, and such a role often contradicts the principle of impartiality. Since such discourse-coordinating work may endow the interpreter with interactional power and control of the discourse, the at-times incompatible forces of the code of ethics and the need to achieve understanding between the two primary speakers will affect the power relationships amongst the participants in mediated police interviews.

The principle of accuracy is linked to that of impartiality. Accuracy of interpreting is crucial in ensuring the human rights of the people who participate in the legal process who do not have a command of the language of the legal system (Hale, 2004). Yet research has shown that it is a difficult task to achieve both semantic and pragmatic equivalence in legal settings (Berk-Seligson, 1990; Hale, 2004, 2008), due to various factors such as language proficiency, cross-cultural gaps, and institutional constraints (Hale, 2004, p. 238). As mentioned earlier, Leung and Gibbons (2008) give examples of courtroom interpreters' renditions that changed the meanings of source utterances in a sexual assault trial, indicating that personal ideology intervened in their work as impartial interpreters. Such renditions obviously go against the principle of accuracy and impartiality in the code of ethics.

The second part of Principle 5 deals with translation mistakes, hearing difficulties and turn-taking issues. These aspects of interaction are significant in the present research since it is concerned with the role of interpreter as a mediator of interaction, and these features of interaction at times have an impact on the trajectory of interaction, which in turn may affect the negotiation of power in police interviews. In terms of interpreter roles, these interactional moves, such as rectifying mistakes, asking for clarification, and intervening when primary speakers' turns become too long in order to ensure accurate renditions, put the interpreter in an identity of the interpreter him/herself instead of the default role of an 'animator' (Goffman, 1981; Wadensjö, 1998; see also Chapter 1, Section 1.5).

The code of ethics has two major implications for the analysis of interpreter-mediated police interviews. First, professional awareness of the code of ethics may guide the interpreter's interactional decisions. Thus, this code of ethics, as an external contextual factor, informs the analysis here. Second, key aspects of the code of ethics interact with the issue of the interpreter's role. As discussed above, the 'invisible conduit' role assumed of legal interpreters is not realistic (Berk-Seligson, 1990; Hale, 2004, 2008; Komter, 2005; Leung & Gibbons, 2008; Niska, 1995; Russell, 2000, 2002; Wadensjö, 1998). The analysis of interpreter-mediated police interviews needs to take account of the challenge of adhering to the code of ethics while participating in turn-taking as the mediator who understands the two languages used. The negotiation of power between the investigating officer and the suspect is likely to be affected by the code of ethics by which the interpreter is bound as he/she engages in the mediation. It should be noted here that, in fact, in the 2012 revised version (AUSIT, 2013), a principle of 'Clarity of Role Boundaries' was introduced along with 'Maintaining Professional Relationships'. This reflects the increasingly heightened attention given to the issue of interpreters acting as discourse coordinators.

2.3   Summary

This chapter has provided background information on the police interview data analysed in this book. The size of the data set and the analytical framework of conversation analysis and interactional socio-linguistics mean that the present research takes a qualitative approach. Information on the interpreters and their accreditation details was given, along with background information on Australia's interpreter accreditation system and the code of ethics which impacts interpreters' decisions on their renditions and their interactional moves as a mediator.

3
Mediated Questioning and Balance of Power

3.1 Introduction

In studies of storytelling in courtroom discourse (Bennett & Feldman, 1981; Jackson, 1991; Maley & Fahey, 1991; Snedaker, 1991), interaction is viewed as a process of 'reconstructing realities', in which competing versions of events are presented (see also Gibbons, 2003). While they may not be so much of a battle as courtroom interaction, Johnson (2006) argues that police interviews contain narrative elements, claiming that there are 'free-narrative and elicited narrative sections' that are co-constructed interactively (p. 669). This chapter explores the impact of interpreter mediation on questioning in police interviews, approaching questioning and questioning strategies as an integral part of constructing police versions of events in relation to alleged crimes. The focus of analysis is on how the mediation affects the level of control that police interviewers have over interview discourse. Construction of realities on the part of suspects will be examined in the next chapter.

3.2 Police questioning and construction of realities

In examining police questioning from the perspective of storytelling, it is useful to recognise different purposes of questions. Gibbons (2003, p. 95) identifies the two main purposes of police questioning as 'elicitation of information' and 'confirmation of a particular version of events'. Questions serving these two types of purposes were found in the data in this study and it emerged from the analysis that problems in communication occurred when interpreters did not appear to be aware of the difference between these types of questions or of the purposes of such questions in particular questioning sequences. Although it is not always easy to draw a clear line between these question types, the discussion will use these categories.

As discussed in Chapter 1, asymmetry of knowledge between the suspect and the interviewing police officer may cause communication difficulties for both parties but especially for suspects as some aspects of police institutional discourse deviate from ordinary conversation (Heydon, 2005). Furthermore, police interviewers' topic-shifts and foci in their questions may cause comprehension difficulties for suspects who lack access to the institutional knowledge and legal requirements which guide police questioning (Heydon, 2005). What is relevant for the police, and thus for the prosecution case in any future trial, may be different from the focus of suspects' storytelling (Linell & Jönsson, 1991). Furthermore, since police interviewers often have access to evidence of which suspects are not aware, there is a knowledge asymmetry that gives power to the interviewing officers (Heydon, 2005). When police interviews are mediated by an interpreter, another layer of knowledge asymmetry is added, although experienced interpreters are likely to have acquired a certain level of knowledge about police institutional discourse and the roles of police interviews in the legal process. Nevertheless, interpreters may not always be aware of what is important for the police and what other evidence has been collected. This may cause distortions of meaning through interpreting, not necessarily at the surface level but at the level of a version of events being constructed through questioning.

The two main purposes of police–suspect interviews are (1) to determine whether the suspect can be charged for the alleged crime(s), and (2) to elicit accounts to construct a version of events, or a story, which will stand as admissible evidence and make a strong case for the prosecution in court. A number of questioning strategies for achieving these goals have been identified in previous studies. One such strategy, or rather, one of the interactional 'resources' (Maley & Fahey, 1991), is topic control. Due to the pre-allocation of turns in the institutional setting of police interviewing, overall, the police officer, as interviewer and questioner, has more power to control topics through turn-taking (Heydon, 2005; Holt & Johnson, 2010; Linell & Jönsson, 1991; Watson, 1990). Heydon (2005) demonstrates that police officers may ignore or interrupt suspects' responses and initiate disjunctive questioning to construct narratives that align with the officers' preferred versions. Nevertheless, a cautious approach is required, as suspects also have interactional resources to resist police control over narrative construction (for example, Haworth, 2006; Newbury & Johnson, 2006; Watson, 1990).

The first part of this chapter discusses problems with mediated information-seeking questioning that may arise if interpreters are not aware of the institutional assumptions affecting the police questioning procedures. The second part of the chapter focuses on the type of questions that are asked for confirmation of a police-preferred version of events. The following three interviewer strategies are analysed: (1) contrast (Drew, 1990), (2) repetition (Maley & Fahey, 1991) and (3) formulation (Heritage & Watson, 1979; Heydon, 2005). Contrast, as discussed by Drew (1990), is a tactic in which lawyers in cross-examination juxtapose witness statements to highlight inconsistencies and emphasise lack of credibility. While Drew (1990) shows how witnesses may counter contrast strategy by directly repairing some elements of lawyers' questions, it is a powerful strategy to create negative images of witnesses. The second strategy, repetition, has been examined in trials by Maley and Fahey (1991), where all or some parts of earlier questions were one of the discursive strategies used by lawyers to construct realities. In cross-examinations, repetitions are often 'unfavourable or adversarial' (ibid. p. 12) and, as is also often the case with contrast strategy, they emphasise the questioner's assumption and attempt to reveal the answerer's inconsistency. The third strategy for effectively constructing police versions of events is 'formulation' (Heritage & Watson, 1979). According to Heydon (2005), who extensively discusses police interviewers' use of formulations:

> [f]ormulations are commonly used to provide a 'summary' of prior talk for the purposes of clarification and necessarily contain different words and phrases from the original as a demonstration of comprehension by the producer of the formulation. (p. 141)

As Coulthard and Johnson (2007) state, formulations are 'a key feature of the asymmetry and a powerful way of transforming the story' (p. 84).

This chapter addresses the way questioning strategies such as formulation, contrast and repetition are maintained through interpreter mediation. It asks, what are the consequences, especially in terms of the power relationships of the police interviewer and the suspect, if the intended effect of such strategies is lost through interpreter mediation?

3.3   Information-seeking questions

This section looks at the impact of mediation on the communication of the purpose of questioning and on the communication of suspect responses to information-seeking questions. The impact of mediation in each of the two types of questions (Gibbons, 2003) is discussed, beginning with questions that have an information-seeking orientation.

3.3.1   Communicating the purpose of the question

In all the interviews analysed, police officers asked questions to elicit information in order to establish the background to the crime they were investigating. These questions, however, are not merely random attempts to collect any information related to the crime in question. In many cases, there appear to be patterns and sequences of actions and arrangements that the law enforcement institution has identified as common features of certain crimes. In the case of the interviews here, there seem to be assumed scenarios of typical drug smuggling that operate at a deeper level of discourse. Knowledge of these scenarios is not always shared by suspects and interpreters, so the point of the police questions may be obscure to them. Such lack of awareness appears to affect the interpreter's ability to produce accurate interpreted versions and the suspect's understanding of the interviewing officer's questions. This problem can manifest itself particularly in mistranslation of the contextualisation cues which signpost the discourse structure.

In the following excerpt, the suspect (S4) is questioned about his travel plans to his hotel from the airport. He responds with the gesture of handcuffed arms to say that he was arrested before he could think of what transport to use.

Extract 3.1 (Interview 4)

```
 1 PO4:  How were you going to travel from the airport
 2        to the hotel,
 3 IR4:  .hh de, (0.4) kuukoo kara hoteru made wa
 4        donoyouni iku yotei deshita ka.
        (And how were you planning to travel from the
        airport to the hotel?)
 5        (0.3)
 6 S4:   Mm mada nanimo kangaetenai tokini kore de heh
 7        heh kore [dattande heh heh]
        (Before I think of it this happened so)
 8 IR4:           [Ah: hah hah hah] the- before I
 9        think about tha:t, I was already arrested.
10        U:hm=
→ 11 PO4:  =No, [sorry],
```

```
   12 IR4:       [I- I ]was already suspended.
   13 PO4:  Ri:ght?=
   14 IR4:  =The- before I (0.2) think about how to get
   15       there.
→  16 PO4:  Okay, but were you intending to meet anyone
   17       who was going to take you: (.) to your hotel?
   18 IR4:  De, .hh kuukoo de dareka mukae ga atte:,=
            (And someone was to come and pick you up at
            the airport and)
   19 S4:   =↑Ya: nai [desu].
            (No no one)
   20 IR4:           [hotel] [ni tsurete]ku˙kotoninatteta˙
            (was to take you to the hotel)
   21 S4:                   [Boku: wa: ] [ma-] mazu basu
   22       saga                                [shite,
            (I well I would first look for a bus)
   23 IR4:  ˙                                   [No]. ˙ [Ah
   24 S4:   yasui no sagashite ikoo tte.=
            (that is cheap and go)
   25 IR4:  =I- I thought that I'm gonna u:m (0.2) look
   26       for the bus going to the the[: town.
```

IR4's filler in line 10 suggests she still had things to say but PO4 cuts in with line 11, indicating that there was a misunderstanding. IR4 repairs her earlier rendition (see also Chapter 5, Section 5.3.2 Extract 5.10 for the analysis of this specific repair). PO4 then tries to clarify the type of information for which he was asking in his original question. The question 'How ...' in lines 1–2 is a less controlling question, and PO4 may have wanted the suspect to voluntarily provide information about a pick up arrangement from the airport without PO4 having to provide specific prompts. However, the unexpected response from S4 constrains his options and he resorts to a polar Yes/No question in lines 16–17.

Looking at the interpreter rendition of this question, the 'but' preceding the question (line 16) is not rendered – instead '*De*' (and) is used in the rendition. Using 'but' would have helped to clarify the purpose of the original question. However, the rendition is interrupted by the suspect who quickly reacts with a negative response (line 19). IR4 continues her rendition of the question in line 20, but this is overlapped by S4's continuation of the response. The rendition (line 23) of S4's 'No' is also overlapped with S4's turn (line 21). IR4 hears this overlapped turn

and renders it in lines 25–26 without incorporating the response in line
19 which denies an arranged airport pick-up.

It is important to note here that neither PO4's 'No' (line 11) nor
his 'but' (line 16) was rendered into Japanese. Thus the purpose and
assumption of the questioning were not clearly communicated to S4.
While there may be other contexts in which rendering these words
verbatim may be unnecessary, in this context of talk they are in fact
'contextualisation cues' (Gumperz, 1982) that signal the assumption
beneath the questions about airport transport – the assumption that a
drug mule would have been given clear instructions as to what to do
once reaching the destination city.

There is also a sense of competing versions of events in the above
excerpt. The suspect's version is of an unplanned arrival and a search
for transport, while the police officer's version is of an organised airport pick-up. The discourse cues which indicated this are lost. Another
noteworthy aspect of this interaction is that the suspect's interruption
of the interpreter's rendition prevents the interpreter from completely
rendering the suspect's responses.

Extract 3.2 gives another example in which an underlying assumption
in the questions is obscured by the interpreter mediation. In the extract,
S3 is being questioned about the process of obtaining a visa.

Extract 3.2 (Interview 3)

```
 1 PO3:  The Australian VISA, where did she get the
 2        Australian VISA from.
 3        (0.4)
 4 IR3:   Oosutoraria no biza kore dokode moraimashita
 5        ka.
        (Where did you obtain the Australian visa
        from?)
 6 S3:    Kore wa, (.) ano Takeshisan ni (0.2)totte
 7        moraimashita.
        (Takeshi got this for me.)
 8 IR3:   U:m Takeshi got that for me.
        ((some exchanges about dates about passport
        and visa))
→ 20 PO3: Why did Takeshi (0.8) obtain the visa for her.
   21     (0.4)
→ 22 IR3: Naze Takeshi wa sono biza: (0.2) o torimashita
   23     ka.
```

```
        (Why did Takeshi obtain that visa?)
24  S3:  Etto: Mareeshia: biza iranai kedo, Oosutoraria
25       wa, biza ga hitsuyoo, (0.5) tte,
        (Um Malaysia, you don't need a Visa, but you
        need a visa for Australia,)
26  IR3: Hai.=
        (Yes)
27  S3:  =Ittemashita.
        (He said that.)
28  IR3: .hh because he said that in Malaysia you
29       don't need a u:hm (0.5) a visa but you need
30       a visa over in Australia.
```

On the surface, the rendition (lines 22–23) of the second question from PO3 (line 20) is accurate, but the response is not aligned with the purpose of the question. PO3's question places the stress on the name of the person who obtained the visa for S3, followed by a 0.8 second pause, which indicates that PO3's focus was on the person's identity and the purpose of the question was to find out about the role that this person may have played. However, IR3's rendition has the stress on 'visa' which is lengthened and followed by a short pause. In addition, 'for her' in the original question (line 20) is not rendered. This projects the purpose of the question as finding out the reason for getting a visa for Australia, instead of why it was this person in particular who obtained the visa for her and why S3 did not get the visa herself. This could have made S3's response appear evasive to the officer. The stress on the name functioned as a contextualisation cue for how to interpret the purpose of the question (see Wadensjö, 1997 for shift of focus due to the interpreter's use of stress). This question also followed a number of exchanges about the circumstances in which Takeshi (pseudonym) helped S3 with her visa application, which also supports the focus of the questioning. The interpreter's use of the case marker 'wa', which is pronounced softly and short, contributed to not foregrounding the focus on the person it marks. To maintain the focus of the question in the source utterance, 'ga' should have been used, since it marks the subject of the sentence as 'new' and focus of the topic, instead of 'wa' which marks the 'given' and 'known' topic (Makino & Tsutsui, 1991; Nariyama, 2009).

What the misunderstanding in this extract means is that S3 interpreted the purpose of this questioning as being to probe her motivation for coming to Australia (and also for going there via another country), rather than the significance of the role that Takeshi played in relation to her coming to Australia in a tour group. While the questioning seeks information to collect necessary evidence and the background for the case, it also has an underlying assumption and entails the possibility of exposing an inconsistency in the suspect's version of events. The interpreter mediation may result in the suspect not getting the agenda behind the questions and responding with information irrelevant to the officer, which then appears as evasive, especially since the officer does not know how the question was communicated. In these cases the suspect may be disadvantaged by interpreter mediation that has not rendered the purposes of questioning hidden beneath the surface level of discourse.

3.3.2   The interpreter as a 'shield' against a potential probe

In the next two extracts the police officers ask information-seeking questions, but the suspects' responses are hesitant or unclear, which could lead to probing questions to challenge the suspect's credibility. The interpreter mediation, however, seems to help them avoid such probing.

In Extract 3.3, the suspect is being questioned about the airline ticket which the officer is showing her.

Extract 3.3 (Interview 3)

```
      1  PO3:  Was this the ti̲cket you used for (0.3)
      2        arriving into Australia.
      3  IR3:  Oosutoraria ni: (.) tsu̲ita toki ni kono
      4        kookuuken o tsukaimashita ka?
              (When you arrived into Australia, did you use
              this ticket?)
      5        (0.3)
      6  S3:   Ie, watashi wa mottemasendeshita.
              (No, I wasn't carrying it with me.)
      7  IR3:  I didn't have the airline ti̲ckets.
      8        (0.2)
      9  PO3:  Who̲ had hold of the ti̲ckets.
     10  IR3:  Da̲re ga motteimashita ka?
              (Who had hold of it?)
     11        (0.3)
  →  12  S3:   Etto: (.) otootosan da to omoimasu.
              (Um I think it was the younger brother.)
  →  13  IR3:  I thi̲nk it was the younger brother.
```

```
    14        (0.4)
→   15  PO3:  What was his name.
    16  IR3:  Ano sono: otootosan no, (0.3) otoo:tosan no
    17        namae wa nandeshita kke.
              (Um the father's, what was the name of the
              younger brother?)
    18  S3:   °Nandattake° (0.7) hi, ro, no, (0.3) [hiro],
    19        mm? =
              (Hi, ro, no, hiro nori?)
    20  IR3:                                        [hiro-]
→   21  IR3:  =hirono, (1.2) I think could I just add
    22        something?=
    23  PO3:  =°Ye[ah°
→   24  IR3:     [Cos of- often in Japanese u:hm (.) with
    25        within family members they often just call,
    26        call (.) younger brothers younger brother (.)
    27        and older brothers older brothers >and don't
    28        call them by their names?<
    29  PO3:  Right.
    30        (0.3)
    31  IR3:  Which is probably why she's not familiar with
    32        the name.
```

When S3 indicates that she did not have the tickets with her on arrival into Australia (line 6), PO3 asks her who held the tickets for her. She identifies this person only as 'the younger brother' (line 12), and the officer asks for his name. S3 is not clear about the name of the brother [of her close friend who invited her on the tour] (line 18). At this point, IR3 speaks to PO3 as a *principal* (Goffman, 1981) (cf. Chapter 1, Section 1.5) to say that, in his own view, S3 is 'not familiar with the name' of the younger brother of her friend as it is common to use kinship terms for forms of reference in Japan (lines 24–28). The brother's name that S3 tentatively utters here is incorrect, but she had earlier stated that she had only met him once before the trip and it is possible that she does not remember the name. However, other than this, there is no other information to determine whether S3 is genuinely unsure about the name. PO3 has not indicated any problems with S3's uncertainty about the brother's name when IR3 intervenes to provide cultural information to justify S3's demonstrated lack of memory. This appears to be a fine line between a reasonable cultural intervention and inappropriately influencing the trajectory of police questioning and narrative construction. In the above case, the interpreter may have provided a kind of 'shield' against a potential probe into the suspect's lack of clarity about the name of the tour leader who had looked after her tickets and passports.

The degree to which interpreters should bridge two cultural and linguistic systems has been one of the issues discussed in the literature on interpreter roles (for example, Berk-Seligson, 1990; Laster & Taylor, 1994; Russell, 2002; Wadensjö, 1998). Russell (2002) discusses how an interpreter intervention to achieve successful communication may not be compatible with the reason behind a primary speaker's problematic linguistic behaviour. In other words, primary speakers may be intentionally making communication problematic for each other, in which case such problems should not be 'fixed' by interpreter mediation since this affects the effectiveness of the interviewing officer's effort to construct his or her version of events. The example discussed above may fall into this category of interpreter intervention.

The next extract (Extract 3.4) shows an example of an interpreter cleaning up disfluencies (see Hale, 2002; Russell, 2002, p. 117). Not only for the purpose of successful communication (Berk-Seligson, 1990; Hale, 2004; Wadensjö, 1998) but also from a fear of appearing to be incompetent (Shlesinger, 1991), interpreters may participate in an interaction as an *author* of the message as well as an *animator* (Goffman, 1981) (cf. Chapter 1, Section 1.5) by rendering the source utterance into a more coherent and tidier version in the target language. In the following excerpt, S1 explains what he did with his overseas contact Mark (pseudonym) when he visited Japan.

Extract 3.4 (Interview 1)

```
 1 PO1: What was the nature of- of your business with
 2       Mark? (0.4) during (0.3) that stay in Japan.
 3 IR1: De sono ano: (0.5) Maaku ga a Nihon ni kita
 4       toki, (0.3) i:>ja suimasen< sono toki no o:
 5       Maaku tono hanashi no nai- shooyoo no naiyoo
 6       wa douiu (0.2) naiyoo deshita ka.
        (And the um when Mark came to Japan, er okay
        sorry what business matters uh did you discuss
        with Mark?)
 7 S1:  Naiyoo wa ano (0.4) Maaku hitori ja nakute,
→ 8       (0.4) ano: (1.2) rokunin ka shichinin de kita
→ 9       ndesu kedo, (0.4) watashi ga, hontoni ano:
```

→ 10   (0.5) *asobide:* (0.3) *kitete,* (1.5) *soide:*
→ 11   *dizuniirando datoka* (0.4) *sooiu tokoro ni*
    12   *nando ka asobini* (0.4) *itte,* (0.5)°*itta*°=
          (It was um it wasn't just Mark alone, um they
          came in a group of six or seven, and I, um
          they came just for holiday, so we went to
          Disneyland and that kind of place a few times
          to have fun, we did.)
→ 13 IR1: =>*tsureteikareta wake desu ka,*<
          (You took them there, is that right?)
    14 S1: *Hai?*
          (Sorry?)
→ 15 IR1: *E, sore isshoni, goit-* (0.3) *go- dookoo shita*
    16   *wake dewa janai wake desu ne?*
          (So it's not the case that you ac- accompanied
          them?)
    17   (0.3)
    18 S1: *Ie, watashi mo isshoni.*=
          (No, I went with them.)
→ 19 IR1: =*Tsuretetta*=
          (You took them with you.)
    20 S1: =*Ha*[*i.*]
          (Yes.)
    21 IR1:   [*Ha*]i. .hhh ((cough)) uh: wasn't just that
    22   Mark=Mark uh brought other uh six or seven
→ 23   people, (0.5) and uh I thought was just uh
    24   they came for holiday, (.) so: we: I took
    25   them (0.2) to uh Disneyla:nd.
→ 36   (12.5)
    27 PO1: Was there any business discussed during that
    28   trip (0.2) in Japa:n, (.) with Mark?

The original response from S1 (lines 7–12) is produced with disfluency. After talking about Mark coming to Japan in a group of six or seven, he starts a new clause with the subject '*watashi*' (I) in line 9, but then, before its predicate appears, he inserts a clause with the verb 'came for holiday' with a confusing omission of Mark's group as the subject of this clause. Then the subject for '*itte*' (went) (to Disneyland) is again omitted in the next clause. This time, the subject could be either 'I' or Mark's group.

This lack of clarity in relation to the subject is a typically observed problem in interpreting Japanese. Unlike languages such as Spanish in which the subject is marked with verb morphology, or English, in which the subject must be stated, in Japanese it is often the context and the speaker's intuition on which the listener depends when interpreting the assumed subject. For this reason, in Japan, it is often recommended to legal practitioners that they explicitly mention the subject when communicating through interpreters in legal settings (Hoosookai, 2003).

Because of this vagueness, IR1 initiates a repair in line 13 to see if S1 took the group to Disneyland. S1 asks for clarification of this repair initiator, to which IR1 gives a paraphrased version (lines 15–16). This second repair initiator is closer to the source utterance because of the meaning of '*dookoo*' (accompany) rather than '*tsureteiku*' (take someone somewhere). S1 says 'together I also ...' in response to the paraphrased repair initiator, but IR1 again brings back '*tsureteitta*' (took them) (line 19), to which S1 gives an affirmative response in line 20. Thus, we can see that in IR1's rendition into English she says he 'took them' to Disneyland. The rendition is more concise and more fluent with fewer pauses, as well as coherent, without the confusing subject–predicate relationships. Given the inexplicitness of subjects in Japanese, it would have been preferable to ask about the subjects to enable translation into English. However, the grammatical relationships are tidied up and cohesion is achieved by 'I ... they' and 'I ... them', and only one specific destination (Disneyland) is mentioned. In fact, IR1 was commonly found in the interview to render the suspect's responses in relatively longer chunks than other interpreters in the data set. This orientation to interpreting seems to clear up disfluencies in the suspect's turn in Japanese and produces tidy renditions in English. As will be discussed in Chapter 4, this interpreter orientation allows for the elicitation of extensive accounts from the suspect and avoids having the suspect's account fragmented or cut off. However, sorting out any disfluency in repair sequences as above may give the officer a false impression of coherent and confident responses. Hale (2002, 2004) claims that omission of hesitations in courtroom interpreting potentially alters the credibility of the witness (see also Berk-Seligson, 1990), since hesitations are one of the features of 'powerless speech' (O'Barr, 1982; Conley & O'Barr, 1990). In this sense, the suspect may be 'empowered' by the type of interpreter mediation shown above, which serves to avert the interviewing officer's potential shift from information-seeking questions to more probing and confirmation-seeking questions. On the other hand, as we will see in Chapter 5 (Section 5.4.1, Extract 5.15, for example), this interpreter strategy may also backfire on the suspect.

3.4 Confirmation-seeking and probing questions

The data set contained some police questioning strategies that, as mentioned above, have been identified and discussed in the literature on monolingual police questioning and courtroom questioning. They are (1) contrast strategy (Drew, 1990), (2) repetitions (Maley & Fahey, 1991) and (3) formulations (Heritage & Watson, 1979; Heydon, 2005). The following sections present an analysis that examines how interpreter mediation may influence the intended effect of these questioning strategies.

3.4.1 Probing using contrast strategies

In the interviews analysed here, all the suspects denied intentional involvement in the case and claimed their innocence. Although the presence of drugs in their luggage was a strong piece of evidence, the police needed a confession and details of the crime and its background to make a strong case to charge the suspects. One of the ways in which confirmation-eliciting questioning was used was to probe the suspects using contrast strategies. Lawyers and police officers may set up relevant facts and evidence and ask questions with the intention of eliciting information that is contradictory to evidence that has been put on record earlier (Drew, 1990; Holt & Johnson, 2010). By using such contrast strategies, the questioner may put pressure on the suspect, exposing inconsistency in the suspect's version of events and potentially leading to a confession.

In the following two excerpts (Extracts 3.5 and 3.6), the suspects are asked why they filled out the Customs and Quarantine Declaration Form without understanding the questions. This probe occurs after they confirmed that they had filled out and signed the form themselves and that they did not understand what the questions on the form meant.

Extract 3.5 (Interview 3)

```
1 PO3: Why did she (0.4) fill out the form without
2      having it explained to her.
3 IR3: Ano: rikaideki, ano setsumee kikanaide naze
4      ano: kinyuushimashita ka.
       (Um why did you fill it out without und- um
       without having it explained to you?)
5      (1.4)
6 S3:  Wakarimasen. Kinyuusureba ii no ka to omotteta
7      kara. Tannaru: ankeeto kato omottandesu.
```

```
              (I don't know. I just thought it just had to
              be filled out. I thought it was just a
              questionnaire.)
    8 IR3:    .hh mm:, (1.5) u:m I just thought it just had
    9         to be filled out and I just thought that it
   10         was like a- like questionnaire type thing.
   11         (2.2)
→  12 PO3:    Does sh- does she usually fill out
   13         questionnaires without understanding the
   14         questions?
→  15 IR3:    Ano,.hh ankeeto kinyuu suru tokini shitsumon
→  16         ga ano: (0.3) wakaranaide kinyuu suru no wa
→  17         futsuu desuka?
              (Um when filling out a questionnaire, is it
              normal to do that without understanding it?)
   18 S3:     .hh ano: futsuuwa, a, watashitachi: u:n,
→  19         (0.3) sono hito niyotte chigaimasu kedo:, (.)
   20         ankeeto tte kaku hito to kakanai hito ga iru
   21         ndesu yo ne? (0.2) [Demo:
              (Um normally, uh we, mm it depends on the
              person, but there are people who fill out the
              questionnaire and people who don't, you see.
              But-)
   22 IR3:                       [Um, it-
   23         everyone's different, sometimes people, you
   24         know: there's some people that don't fill out
   25         questionnaires, (0.4) But,
   26         (0.5)
   27 S3:     Iroiro:, a: shokudoo, (.) resutoran no ankeeto
   28         toka,=
              (Like, uh questionnaires about canteens,
              restaurants, or)
   29 IR3:    =Un
   30 S3:     Ato eega no ne, ankeeto toka: =
              (and questionnaires about movies,)
   31 IR3:    =Un.
              (Yeah)
   32 S3:     Ato: konsaato no ankeeto toka, (0.4)
→  33         kakanakute mo: jiyuu nan desu yo, taitei moo:
→  34         Nihon wa.
```

```
              (and questionnaires about concerts, and so on,
              most of these things, it's up to you to decide
              whether you want to fill it out or not, in
              Japan.)
    35 IR3:   .hhh often in Japan like if you've got u:m
    36        questionnaires about restaurants, movies and
    37        um concerts and that,(0.2) it often doesn't
    38        matter whether you fill it in or whether you
    39        don't fill it in. (.) So you know it's up
    40        to the individual.
    41        (0.4)
 →  42 PO3:   But does she usually fill in questionnaires
    43        without reading, (.) or understanding the
    44        questions.
    45 IR3:   Demo, ano ankeeto kinyuu surutoki ni wa, .hhh
    46        ano: shitsumon o yoma:nakattari: mata ano:
 →  47        rikai dekinakute chekku shitarisuru no wa
 →  48        futsuu desu ka.
              (But um when filling out questionnaires, um is
              it normal to check items without reading or um
              understanding the questions?)
    49        (0.5)
    50 S3:    Sore wa futsuu desu kedo: (0.4) demo: tekitoo
    51        ni: kakeba ii no kana to omotte, (0.7)
    52        [Ko]re ga moshi:
              (It is normal but, but I thought I probably
              didn't have to write it properly. If this-)
    53 IR3:   [A-]
              (Uh)
 →  54 S3:    nyuukoku tetsuzuki da tte wakattereba:, a
    55        janakute, zeekan no: yatsu tte wakattereba:
    56        .hh chanto kiite yatta to omoimasu.
              (If I had known that it was for immigration,
              oh no had I known it was for customs, I would
              have made sure to fill it out after having it
              explained to me.)
 →  57 IR3:   .hh I- if I knew it was so- so important for
    58        customs an- and quarantine then I probably
    59        would have um (0.3) got a proper explanation
    60        then filled it out.
```

```
      61        (0.3)
  →   62  PO3:  Why didn't she think it was important.
      63  IR3:  Naze ano: daiji: da to omoimasendeshita ka?
                (Why um didn't you think it was important?)
      64        (1.4)
      65  S3:   Omoimasen deshita.
                (I didn't think it was.)
      66  IR3:  I just didn't think it was.
```

PO3's question in lines 1–2 – note that PO3 usually inappropriately used the third person 'she' instead of 'you' to ask questions of the suspect – implies an accusation of unreasonableness and irrationality, using a contrast strategy of juxtaposing the suspect's filling out the form without knowing the meaning with an implied rational person who would only fill out a form which they understood. In lines 6–7, S3 justifies her action by bringing in her misunderstanding of the purpose of the form. PO3 picks up on the idea of 'questionnaire' brought in by S3 and again attempts to highlight irrationality by asking her a rhetorical question in lines 12–13. This question is a personal challenge to her rationality and credibility, again using an indirect contrasting strategy, but also a strategy of repetition. However, in the rendition, the subject is omitted as in the previous question. This is probably because in most social contexts in Japanese, it is common to omit the second person pronoun when referring to the addressee of the question. This omission of the subject, coupled with the adverb 'usually', translated as 'normal' in the rendition (lines 15–17), appear to result in S3 not understanding the focus and force of the original question. S3's response (lines 18–20) indicates that she understood it to be about the norm in Japan as we can see from 'we' ('*watashitachi*'), 'it depends on the person' (line 19 '*sono hito ni yotte chigaimasu*'), 'there are people ...' (line 20 '*kakuhito to kakanai hito ga iru*') and 'it's up to you ... in Japan' (lines 32–34).

This response was not acceptable to PO3, as, even with his contrasting strategy, he was unable to get S3 to admit her response was not credible. He then pursues by recycling the question, the initial 'but' in line 42 indicating a problem with S3's response. The rendition again omits the personal reference to S3 'she/you', but this time, the rendition maintains the 'but' from the original question, and the repetition of the contrast strategy seems to lead to S3's defending her own action. After responding to the non-rhetorical meaning of the interpreted question first in line 50, she also provides an excuse as a defence strategy in lines 51–52 and 54–56.

This excuse is rendered with an addition 'it was important' (line 57), and PO3's question in line 62 following this rendition picks up on this. This is an attempt to use 'format tying' (Goodwin, 1990), where a speaker strategically recycles a 'phonological, syntactic and semantic surface structure feature of prior turn at talk' (p. 117). Format tying 'may be used as a powerful counter, because the prior speaker's words can be turned and used against her/him' (Church, 2009, p. 24). Holt and Johnson (2010, p. 29) identify a strategic use of this in police interviews, calling it a 'repeating question'. However, in this example the counter effect which such a strategy could produce is lost through interpreter mediation, since S3's original contribution did not contain 'if it was so important' and for her there is no effect of format typing. This loss of the 'powerful counter' effect was also found in Wadensjö's (1997) study of police interpreting in Swedish and Russian. Thus, while, for the interviewer, the mediation created an opportunity for a powerful interaction strategy, for the suspect, who is not aware why PO3 uses 'important' in his question (line 62), the question is rather vague and unspecific, which may have resulted in the pause in line 54 before she gives an unconvincing reply in line 65.

The following excerpt shows a similar question through which another suspect is probed for the reasons he filled out the form without understanding the questions on it.

Extract 3.6 (Interview 2)

```
 1  PO2:  What did he think this form (.) was for.
 2        (2.3)
 3  IR2:  E: n, kono (0.4) sho- e: (0.3) shoshiki desu
 4        ne:
 5        (Uh mm this fo- uh form, )
 6   S2:  Hai,=
        (Yes)
 7  IR2:  =Kore wan nan no tameni, (0.5) e::: kaku mono
 8        da to omoimasu ka?
        (What do you think uh this is filled out for?)
 9        (1.2)
10   S2:  N, (0.8) a:: (0.6) wakannai.
        (Mm uh, don't know.)
11  IR2:  No, I don't know.
12        (0.4)
13  PO2:  Ask him does he usually fill out forms, (0.5)
14        and then answer questions that he doesn't know
```

```
     15           what he's answering to?
     16           (1.0)
  →  17  IR2:    Ee Takada san, anata wa (0.4) e, dooiu u-
     18           shoshiki ka wakaranaku temo, (0.4) e: jibunde
     19           kinyuusuru koto ga, (0.5) [jibunde] (.) futsuu
     20           kinyuu shimasu ka?
                  (Um Mr Takada, do you uh fill out a form even
                  if you don't understand what it is, do you
                  usually fill it out by yourself?)
     21   S2:                            [°A hai,]°
                                         (Uh right)
  →  22           °Ah° (2.5) °(chotto)°
                  (Uh)           (well)
     23           (1.2)
     24  IR2:    Yes.=
  →  25   S2:    =hhh (0.4) iya s- u:n (0.5) sore wa:, (0.2)ya-
  →  26           ya sooiu wake janai kedo:, (.) [kotoba ga
  →  27           wakaranai]?
                  (Well, um that is, not really, but I don't
                  understand the language.)
     28  IR2:                                   [(
     29                  )] all the time, (0.4) but I didn't
     30           understand (.) the language.
```

The suspect (S2) has answered that he did not know what the form was for in line 10, so then in lines 13–15 the interviewer uses the contrasting strategy of pointing out the fact that the suspect had filled out the form without understanding the questions. Both S2 and S3 had ticked 'no' to all questions, including the one which asks whether the passenger is bringing prohibited drugs into Australia. Therefore the officers attempted to elicit confessions that the suspects had selected 'no' intentionally, knowing that their suitcases contained an illegal substance. In the above extract, the rendition contains both the name of the suspect and the second person pronoun *anata* 'you' (line 17), maintaining the powerful tone of the contrasting strategy, unlike the example above. The suspect is taken aback, as shown by a pause and hesitations in line 22. He continues with a series of hesitations and pauses, before responding with a negative (line 26), making PO2's strategy successful. More rhetorical questions indirectly accusing the suspect of not being forthcoming with his responses follow, as we will see in the discussion of recycled questions (Section 3.4.2).

Extract 3.7 below shows another example of an officer's contrasting rhetorical strategy. The suspect (S4) has told the police officer (PO4) that the travel agent who arranged his trip to Australia contacted him through his acquaintance, who had told S4 that there was some temporary work in Australia.

Extract 3.7 (Interview 4)

```
   1 PO4: Okay, (.) um so, did you meet him through a
   2       friend? Or did you just meet (.) at (0.2) the
   3       restaurant, (.)by coincidence.
   4 IR4: Hai, .hh de, e: guuzen ni okaishita ndesu ka
   5       sono resutoran de, soretomo sono resutoran no
   6       naka de tomodachi ni shookaisareta toka (.)
   7       tte koto desu ka?
         (Okay .hh and um did you meet him at the
         restaurant by chance, or were you introduced
         to him by a friend at the restaurant or
         something?)
   8       (0.3)
   9 S4:  .hh e:tto moo sore wa (.) guuzen desu.
         (Umm it was rather by chance.)
  10 IR4: Yeah, just coincidence.=
→ 11 PO4: =Just coincidence? Okay. U:m (.) ha:s (0.3)
→ 12       when did this person, (.) u:m (0.3) give
  13       you or i- (0.3) say suggest that you should
  14       get in contact with this travel agent.
  15       (0.5)
  16 IR4: Ah=
  17 PO4: =Sorry (I think you[   )   ]
→ 18 IR4:                   [ De ] (0.5) kono kata ga,
  19       (0.3) e: kono ryokoosha ni renraku o shime-
  20       shita hoogaii tte iu fuuni itta ndesu ka?
         (So did this person tell you that you should
         contact this travel agent?)
  21       (0.5)
  22 S4:  Iya (0.5)[soo] janakute
         (No     he didn't)
  23 IR4:          [No ]
  24 IR4: °Mm°
  25 S4:  Kare ga renraku ga kakattekuru kara, kocchi
  26       kara, (0.4) mattenasai tte.=
```

```
                (He told me to wait for them to contact me)
      27  IR4:  =Ah ah, .hh he asked me to wait,=
      28  PO4:  =mm hm,=
      29  IR4:  =until the they- (.) these people c- contacted
      30        him.
→     31  PO4:  But um what (.) how did this (.)come about-
→     32        were you (0.3) u:m intending to tr- were you-
      33        have you been intending to travel to
      34        Australia?
      35  IR4:  .hhh de sono mae ni wa Oosutoraria ni kuru
      36        yotee toka atta ndesu ka?
                (And had you had any plans to come to
                Australia before that?)
      37   S4:  Nai desu.
                (No I hadn't)
      38  IR4:  No.=
→     39  PO4:  =No? um (0.5) w:hy (.) would have (0.2) uh
      40        your friend suggested that (0.2) this (.)
      41        travel agent (.)contact you.=
      42  IR4:  =mm. .hh dooshite kono kata ga, (0.2) kono (.)
      43        ryokoosha ga, (0.2) e: Mori san ni
      44        renrakushimasu yo, tteiu fuu ni itta ndeshoo
      45        ka.
                (Mm why did this person tell you that that
                travel agent uh would be in touch with you?)
      46        (0.6)
      47   S4:  M, (.) dooshite tte iu ka ma: (.) chiketto
      48        toka: (0.2) okane toka iu sono dandori,
      49        shuppatsu no maeni nittee ga mada (0.2)
      50        hakkiri shitenakatta nde, (.) nijyuukunichi,
      51        (0.3) no hi mo mada wakannakatta nde,
                (Why...well rather, the planning steps like
                tickets and payment, because the dates were
                not finalised before the departure, these
                things were not certain even on the 29th, so)
      53  IR4:  Hai.
      54        (Yes)
      55   S4:  De: (0.6) sanjyuunichi no hi ni, (0.3) sono
      56        toojitsu ni, (0.8) a, >chigau chigau,<
      57        niyuukunichi ni wakatta ndesu yoru osoku.
```

```
               (And on the very day, the 31st, oh, no no on
               the 29th late in the evening I found out)
58   IR4:   Hai, .hh the on the 29th of the (.) um
59          Hi[kooki no chiketto toreta [noga
               (that they managed to get the airline
               tickets.)
60   IR4:   [J-                        [June,
61   PO4:   Mm hmm,
62   IR4:   U:m (2.8) that all the t̲icket was re̲a̲dy.
```

The police officer questions S4 about how he came to receive an offer of
a job in Australia. PO4's question in lines 11–14 about the travel agent
getting in touch with S4 contains a couple of self-repairs. In lines 18–20,
a polar question is rendered instead of the more repaired version (when-
question). In lines 22 and 25–26, S4 denies that he was told to contact
the agent, saying he was told to wait to hear from the agent instead.
While unaware that the 'when' question was not rendered, PO4 does
not attempt to elicit when S4 was told that he would be hearing from
the agent, but instead questions openly in line 31 how it came about
that S4 was selected as a mule, saying 'how did this come about', with
his sense of misalignment suggested by 'but'. However, this question
was also immediately followed by a more specific polar question asking if it was because he already had a plan to travel to Australia (lines
32–33). This contrasts S4's 'coincidence' account with a more rational
course of events where S4 would be approached because he had been
planning to go to Australia. IR4 this time renders the second question
and drops 'how did this come about'. It is possible, however, that this
first question was not in fact to be 'repaired' but a legitimate component of the turn which contained two questions. In many cases in the
data set, interpreters do not render false starts and abandoned questions
that are repaired. While most of these cases do not affect the course of
investigation, this instance of omission may have prevented the suspect
from understanding what the officer wanted to probe. The 'but' in the
original is also dropped, and instead *de* (and) appears at the beginning
of this turn. Thus, PO4's suspicions of S4's version of events realised
through the contrast strategy are not conveyed. When S4 responds with
'No', PO4 repeats it with a rising intonation 'No?' (line 39) – a classic
format-tying which highlights the significance of the fact that S4 went
along with the out-of-the-blue offer to go to Australia. Combined with
this format-tying 'No?', the ensuing question with the modal 'would'

encodes PO4's critical stance towards S4's story. However, neither the meaning of 'No?' nor of 'would' is rendered, and S4 does not make any attempt to justify his version of events. The rendition was also likely to have been misunderstood, due to the word order in Japanese, to mean 'Why did this person, this travel agent, tell you that he would be in touch?' – with a self-repair of 'this person' with 'this travel agent'. Thus, S4's response focuses on the dates of flights, indicating that his interpretation of the question was that he was asked to explain why he had to wait to hear from the agent, rather than the unusual circumstances in which he had been approached by the acquaintance.

Another way of looking at the lack of interactional alignment is that interpreter mediation may license evasion, a licensing that cannot occur in unmediated interviews. If the interpreter is unaware of the schema in which the police questioning discourse is embedded and does not render contexualisation cues, this may allow suspects to be evasive without flouting the maxim of relation in terms of interactions in their own language.

3.4.2   Repetitions and recycled questions

This section examines the impact of mediation on questioning that appears to be used for the purpose of confirming the police version of events. The officers make an attempt to put on record that the suspects knew that they were importing illegal drugs. However, key information that incriminates the suspect needs to be offered voluntarily by the suspect for the record of interview to be accepted as an appropriately obtained piece of evidence. This was not easy in the present study as the suspects denied the allegation and did not volunteer incriminating information when asked an open question or when invited to talk about key aspects of the case.

One of the strategies used to elicit such key information was to repeat or reformulate questions. This strategy may be used to highlight inconsistencies in suspects' narratives or to indicate that suspect answers are not what they should be from the police perspective (Maley & Fahey, 1991). This strategy was seen frequently in the police officer's questioning in Interview 2 (PO2). It should be noted that accusatory questions assuming the suspect's guilt were more common in the 1992 interviews (Interviews 1–5) than in the interview from the 2002 case (Interview 4). This is most likely to be due to the introduction of approaches to investigative interviews such as PEACE, and more specifically, cognitive interview techniques (see Chapter 2). PO2's strategy of recycling questions retained its power through interpreter mediation when the questions were straightforward (for example, repeating the question 'What do you think that is?' pointing at bags of heroin). However, when the question was intended to elicit a criminal intention indirectly and was rephrased a number of times, as will be demonstrated, the interpreter did not seem to understand the intended purpose of the chain of recycled questions, thus appearing to cause confusion and frustration between the primary speakers.

Before the beginning of Extract 3.8, PO2 had been asking S2 about his understanding of the customs and quarantine declaration form, on which he had ticked 'No' for all questions, including the one about bringing narcotics into Australia. S2 claimed that he had not understood the questions on the form but another passenger had suggested ticking 'No' for all questions. PO2 repeatedly asks S2 about his understanding of the purpose of the form, intending to pressure S2 to admit that he ticked 'No' knowing that he was intentionally bringing a narcotic substance into Australia. In line 1, the question about the purpose of the form is repeated.

Extract 3.8 (Interview 2)

```
  1 PO2:  What did he think this form was fo- what do
  2        y- what did you think this form was for.
  3        (1.0)
  4 IR2:  .hhh ja: anata wa, (0.2) kono shoshiki ga
  5        nanno tame ni (.) aru mono da to omoimasu ka?
  6        (0.2) Nan no tame no monodato omoimasuka?
           (So what do you think this form is for? What
           do you think it's for?)
  7        (2.8)
→ 8  S2:  N::: (1.3) wakarimasen, ano: dakara,
  9 IR2:  I don't know. =
→ 10 S2:  =Saisho, (.) ano ima, kite:, yatto: nanka
→ 11       (0.2) imi ga wakattekimashita.
           (First, now, as I was listening, now I sort of
           came to understand the meaning)
  12 IR2:  I- I now know what it is, (.) I'm beginning to
  13        (.)understand what it is. (0.7) after hearing
  14        (0.4) what you said.
  15        (2.4)
→ 16 PO2:  I put it to you you know, (.) or you knew what
  17        this wa:s, when you filled it in.
  18        (1.1)
→ 19 IR2:  Ja: shitsumon shimasu.=
```

```
              (Now, I ask you)
      20  S2:  =Hai,=
              (Yes)
  →   21  IR2: =Anata wa (0.6) kore o kinyuu shita toki ni,=
              (When you filled this in)
      22  S2:  =Hai,=
              (Yes)
  →   23  IR2: =Shi- (0.4) shittetan desu ka, (0.5) soreteomo
      24      ima,
              (Di- Did you know it, or now,)
      25  S2:  Hai,
              (Yes)
  →   26  IR2: Sorry what was the question again? (.)(Why)
      27      you knew and
  →   28  PO2: I put it to you, (.) you knew (.) what this
      29      form was for, (0.2) when you filled it in.
      30  IR2: °Okay yep°. (0.5) Ja: mooikkai
      31      shitsu[monshimasu.
              (Now I ask you again).
      32  S2:       [Hai.
              (Yes)
      33      (1.2)
      34  IR2: Ano:, anata wa (.) kore o kinyuushita toki ni
              (Um when you filled this in)
      35  S2:  Hai.
              (Yes)
  →   36  IR2: Shitteimashita ka.
              (Did you know?)
      37  S2:  Shiri- shirimasen.
              (I d- don't/didn't know).
      38  IR2: I didn't know.
      39      (4.6)
  →   40  PO2: What do you understa:nd that form to be now.
      41      (0.3)
      42  PO2: What is your understanding.
      43  IR2: Ja: =
              (Now)
      44  S2:  =Hai=
              (Yes)
      45  IR2: =Kono kono shoshiki no koto o [ima] (.)
```

```
46           shitteimasu ka?
             (Do you know now about this form?)
47    S2:                              [Hai].
                                       (Yes)
48    IR2:   Kore wa (.) nan da to omoimasu ka?=ima nan da
49           to omoimasu ka?
             (What do you think this is, now what do you
             think this is?)
50           (0.3)
51    S2:    A: ken'eki toka? Ima (.) itta, (   ) no koto
52           desu ne, ken'eki to ato:
             (Uh quarantine, and (       ) you just said,
             is it? Quarantine and)
53    IR2:   It's quaranti:ne,
54    S2:    Ato zeekan
             (and customs)
55    PO2:   (              ) °right°
56    IR2:   Customs?
57           (0.6)
58    S2:    teyuu yoona (.) naiyoo no koto desu ne?
             (that sort of thing)
59    IR2:   Uh things like (.) that. (0.4) Just what you
60           said.
61           (1.0)
→ 62  PO2:   And what does that mean to him, what does that
63           mean to you. (2.0) What does that mean to you.
64           (1.0) (do you)
65           (0.4)
→ 66  IR2:   Sorry, (  )(difficult to translate)(  )
67    PO2:   Uhm
68           (1.0)
→ 69  PO#:   What is the purpose, (0.2) of this form, now
70           he has (.) now you have a new understanding.
71           (2.8)
72    PO#:   Do you understand that?
73    IR2:   Um: (2.6) are you asking [the reason why
74    PO#:                            [No, I'm a:sking]
75           him. (.) No I am asking him, (0.3) he's just
76           said now that now he knows what the form is.
77           Yes?=He has an idea.
```

The suspect (S2) denies that he had known the purpose of the questions on the form (line 8). However, as it is already the second time that the same question is being asked of him and PO2 has already mentioned that the form is for customs and quarantine, S2 states that he has begun to understand the purpose of the form (lines 10–11). Then, in lines 16–17, PO2 issues a strongly accusatory challenge by using the projection frame 'I put it to you ...'. The projection frame is used in courtroom examination but, as Heydon (2005) shows, it appears to be used in police interviews when the interviewer is unable to receive a desired response from the suspect after attempts with preferred and less coercive open questions. This phrase is loaded with presumptions associated with the sociocultural context in which it is used. It is embedded in the context of the adversarial legal system where two narratives, or versions of events about the crime in question, are contested (Bennett & Feldman, 1981; Jackson, 1991) This projection frame indicates that PO2 is presenting her side of the 'story', and given S2's denial of previous knowledge about the purpose of the discussed form, this challenge suggests that S2 is not telling the truth and puts pressure on him to confess. However, the translation of this phrase 'I put it to you ...' is difficult because the sociocultural and institutional assumptions which inform its meaning and pragmatic force are absent in the Japanese legal system. The projection frame is rendered in line 19 as 'Now I ask you', which does not carry the same pragmatic force or 'context of culture' (Halliday, 1978) as the source utterance. IR2 does not seem to be aware of the sociocultural and institutional assumptions, yet seems to be aware that this rendition is somewhat problematic. He then asks PO2 for clarification (lines 26–27). PO2 repeats the challenge in lines 28–29 using the same projection frame, but its rendition is again 'I ask you'. S2's response is 'I don't know'. Although S2 keeps to his story that he did not know the purpose of the form and began to understand it only when PO2 mentioned customs and quarantine, the legal framework evoked and carried with the phrase 'I put it to you' – often described using the metaphor of a 'battle' between the defense and prosecution – is not communicated through interpreter mediation. This deprives the suspect of the opportunity to fight his battle effectively.

After confirming S2's current understanding of the purpose of the form in broad terms, PO2 asks, in lines 62–63, what that understanding means to S2. The underlying version of events here is that S2 intentionally imported narcotics and, when he filled in the form, intended to deceive the authorities by ticking 'no'. However, the interpreter does not seem to be aware of this underlying story, and is unable to translate

PO2's question (line 66). As PO2 cannot paraphrase 'What does it mean to you?' another officer in the room (indicated as PO# in the extract) reverts to the earlier question 'What is the purpose of this form?' which does not imply an assumption of S2's guilt, and the story PO2 is attempting to build up is sidetracked.

In this example, police tactics for putting pressure on a suspect by using various question forms were not as effective as is possible in monolingual interviews for eliciting versions of events that are damaging to the suspect. This may have been due to the lack of shared understanding between the police interviewer and the interpreter with regard to the nature of police questioning strategies and the legal framework in which these questions are embedded.

3.4.3 Formulations

Formulation is another police questioning strategy used to construct a police-preferred version of events (Heydon, 2005; Holt & Johnson, 2010; Johnson, 2002). The intended effect of this strategy can also be reduced through interpreter mediation. In Extract 3.9, PO2 asks S2 if he indeed did nothing despite having seen, in a car boot, damaged luggage that belonged to him and his fellow travellers. Earlier, S2 had told PO2 that their luggage was damaged in transit and he and his fellow travellers were provided with new luggage, which contained the illegal substance.

Extract 3.9 (Interview 2)

```
 1 PO2:  So: you saw all damaged (.) luggage in the
 2        back of the car, (0.2) and you did nothing
 3        about it, is that correct.
 4 IR2:   .hhh ja: anata ga iu niwa: (0.2) sono:
 5        kowasareta nimotsu desu ne:,
        (So you are saying that the luggage that was
        damaged)
 6 S2:    Hai,
        (Yes)
 7 IR2:   Sore o ma: kuruma no ushiro: no nakani aru no
 8        o mite, =
        (You saw it in the back of the car and)
 9 S2:    =Hai,
        (Yes)
10 IR2:   Sorede nannimo shinakatta toiu wake desu ka?
        (and you didn't do anything about that, is
        that right?)
```

```
        11      (0.8)
→       12  S2:  °N:° (1.1) nannimo shinakatta, (.) dakara:
                 (mmm didn't do anything, well,)
                 ((further exchanges on the luggage))
        30  S2:  Gaido no (.) hito ga, (0.2) ano wakatta rashii
        31       tteiu hanashi wa (0.2) °kikimashita°. =
                 (I heard that they heard the guide had found
                 out about it.)
        32  IR2: =I was told that (0.5) u:m tour guide, (1.2)
        33       uh:m (0.4) found it out.
        34       (1.4)
→       35  PO2: And you didn't tell anyone (0.2) about the
        36       luggage in the boot, (0.3) the damaged luggage
        37       in the boot, is that correct.
→       38  IR2: .hh ano ja: sono toranku no nakani oiteatta
        39       kowasareta nimotsu nandesu kedo:,=
                 (Um so about the damaged luggage placed in the
                 boot,)
        40  S2:  =Hai,
                 (Yes)
→       41  IR2: Sono koto ni kanshite:, darenimo nannimo
→       42       iimasendeshita ka,
                 (You didn't mention anything about it to
                 anyone?)
                 ((further exchanges on the luggage))
→       65  PO2: The question that I asked was, (0.4) did you
        66       tell anyone about the damaged (0.2) luggage
        67       that you saw in the boot of the car.
        68  IR2: °Okay°, ano: watashi ga tazuneta shitsumon toiu
        69       no wa: .hh ano: sono toranku no nakani
        70       ireteatta (0.5) kowasareta nimotsu desu n[e:,
                 (Um the question I asked you is um the damaged
                 luggage that was placed in the boot,)
        71  S2:                                          [Hai.
                                                         (Yes)
        72  IR2: uh sore ni tsuite dareka ni nanika iimashita
        73       ka.
                 (Did you say anything about it to anyone?)
        74       (1.4)
        75  S2:  Dareka ni, tteiu no wa sono watashi: ga desu
```

```
       76         ka?
                  (To anyone, do you mean did I tell anyone?)
                  (0.5)
       77 IR2:    You mean, (.) I ?
       78 PO2:    Yes. [(yeah).]
       79 S2:          [Watashi] ga desu ka,=
                       (Do you mean I?)
       80 IR2:    =Hai.
                  (Yes)
   →   81 S2:     Iya watashi wa iwanai desu, (0.2) darenimo.=
                  (No I didn't, to anyone)
       82 IR2:    =Well uh I didn't [sa:y], (0.2) to anybody,
       83 S2:                       [Hai.]
                                    (No)
       84         (0.4)
   →   85 PO2:    And this, (0.2) you did not (0.3) want to tell
       86         (0.2) anybody. (0.2) You did not think to tell
       87         anybody, (0.2) Is that correct. (1.5)
   →   88 IR2:    °(Did you think-)[(sorry)] °
   →   89 PO2:                     [Did you]think to tell
       90         anybody about the damaged luggage [that you
       91           saw] in the boot?
       92 IR2:                                      °[ah all
       93         right].°
       94 IR2:    .hh ano: dakreka ni: sono:: kowasareta nimotsu
       95         ni tsuite:,
                  (Um anyone, uh about the damaged luggage)
       96 S2:     Hai,
                  (Yes)
       97 IR2:    Nanika iou to iufuuni wa: omoimasendeshita ka,
                  (Didn't you think to say something?)
```

In the stretch of interaction above, PO2 probes S2 four times as to whether he did anything or notified others when he saw the stolen and damaged luggage that belonged to his tour group (lines 1–3, 35–37, 65–67 and 85–87). In the first instance, PO2 uses a 'formulation' that provides a gloss of 'what we are talking about (or have talked about) thus far' (Heritage & Watson, 1979, p. 149). By saying 'So you saw all damaged luggage ... and you did nothing about it' (lines 1–3) as a formulation, PO3 attempts to present an account that presents S2's behaviour as suspicious and suggests that S2 did not do what he should have done. The formulation here is 'so-prefaced' (Holt & Johnson, 2010; Johnson, 2002). 'So-' and 'And-' prefaced questions are often used in formulations and are powerful strategies to allow police interviewers to construct narrative sequences through turn-taking with suspects (Holt & Johnson, 2010, p. 27). Heydon (2005) gives a very similar example of questioning by an interviewing officer and argues that the police officer 'constructs a version of events where [the suspect] is remiss firstly in evading the suggested course of action', and 'secondly in failing even to consider that such a course of action may have been appropriate' (p. 137). The so-prefaced formulation in the above extract challenges the suspect by foregrounding problematic aspects of his statements. Additionally, the question 'is that correct?' tries to get S2 to make this negative account his.

The rendition in lines 4–10 accurately renders the pragmatic force of the source utterance, with *'Ja'*, the equivalent of 'so', and the projection frame *'anata ga iu niwa … toiu wake desu ka'* (what you are saying is... is that right?). To this, however, S2 does not answer with yes or no, but explains that the tour group heard that the guide had found the culprit. While IR2's rendition may have prevented S2 from providing a further account to make his response more coherent, this response does not appear to be a direct response to PO2's question. PO2 thus ignores S2's response and recycles the question using 'and' as a preface (lines 35–37) to restore the narrative construction initiated in lines 1–3. The rendition of this second formulation (lines 38–42), however, does not carry the same pragmatic force as the first. The rendered question starts with a hesitation 'Ano (Um)', and the confirmation-seeking 'is that correct?' is lost. This confirmation-seeking question is an attempt to officially make S2, the answerer, responsible for the version of events constructed through PO2's formulation. Thus, the loss of this confirmation-seeking question has an impact on the evidential value of this exchange. The changes that came about through the rendition may have contributed to S2's irrelevant response (not presented above) focusing on the damaged luggage instead of on the challenged inaction on his part (regardless of any intention on the part of S2 to provide this response). This irrelevant response prompts PO2 to ask the same question again in lines 65–67, this time clarifying it and using an affirmative question ('did you tell anyone?'), without 'is that correct?' SO2 says (line 81) that he did not tell anyone about the damaged luggage, a response which aligns with the interviewer's version. However, in lines 85–87, PO2 changes the angle of the question by swapping 'you didn't say' with 'you didn't want to tell, think to tell …' prefaced by the narrative constructing 'and'

and followed by the question 'is that correct?' The same set of strategies are used, but this time SO2's intention behind 'not telling anyone'
is challenged, as PO2 introduces 'want' and 'think' instead of 'say' to
construct a story that SO2 *intentionally* avoided telling anyone about the
luggage, which would suggest his involvement in a crime. IR2, however,
does not begin his rendition for a couple of seconds, and asks for a clarification (line 88). Given the similarities of PO2's question to the preceding ones and the familiarity of the newly introduced verbs (want and
think), it is possible that IR2 is confused by the repetitiveness of PO2's
questioning. A similar situation was observed in Extract 3.8 above, in
which IR2 remains silent and PO2 repairs the question for IR2's comprehension. It appears that IR2 is not aware of the pragmatic functions
of the discursive strategies used by PO2, and is therefore unable to
follow the trajectory of PO2's construction of narrative through turn-
taking. This may have led to omissions of some key linguistic features
of the narrative construction such as the turn-initial 'and' and 'so', and
the confirmation-seeking question. The consequence of this may have
been that S2 was less able, than a suspect in a monolingual interview,
to grasp the pragmatic force of PO2's questions. On the other hand, it is
possible that failure to render the pragmatic force of the questions may
have allowed the suspect to evade relevant responses and avoid having
to participate in constructing the police-preferred version of events.

3.5 Conclusions

This chapter has discussed the ways in which interpreter mediation may
impact on the power and control exercised by police officers through
their use of questioning strategies. The changes through interpreting
were not always caused by obvious cases of mistranslation but appear to
be associated with questioning strategies that are part of the process of
constructing realities (Bennett & Feldman, 1981), or certain versions of
events. This is where focusing on the ways in which the participants
orient themselves to the talk can offer insights into the peculiarities
of interpreter-mediated police interviews (cf. Komter, 2005; Roy, 2000;
Wadensjö, 1997). Distortions of story-construction processes due to
problems in maintaining the force of discursive strategies have been
discussed in previous studies of court interpreting (Hale, 1997, 2004,
Hale & Gibbons, 1999; Leung & Gibbons, 2008; see also Krouglov, 1999
for police interpreting), and the above analysis suggests that police questioning entails the same risk. Furthermore, it is possible that interpreter
mediation can not only reduce the impact of questioning strategies, but

can also introduce strategies that were not present in the interviewer's source utterance. Wadensjö's (1997) study of police interpreting shows an example in which an interpreter unwittingly incorporates a formulation into her rendition, changing the trajectory of the questioning.

The impact of mediation on questioning strategies and interview discourse examined in this chapter also points to the peculiarities of police interview discourse, which are the consequences of the legal framework of the police interview, and the fact that the two primary speakers orient to varying versions of events. Some of the questioning strategies discussed in this chapter would be regarded as unnatural in social interaction in other contexts, but violations of the maxims of the Cooperative Principle of conversation (Grice, 1975) tend to be motivated by the need to construct preferred versions of events. Therefore the familiarity of interpreters with regular violations of the maxims by primary speakers in police interview discourse would be one of the key background knowledge areas required in addition to specialist legal terms.

While the analysis suggests that interpreter mediation may reduce the effectiveness of the interviewing officers' probing and pressuring strategies, it also reveals that it can lead to suspects' divergent interpretations of the intention and focus of the source utterance. This means that suspects are disadvantaged if they provide irrelevant or off-topic responses, as officers may view these as avoidance strategies. This in turn could reinforce the officers' assumptions of guilt. Thus, the types of interpreter-mediated exchanges discussed in this chapter which deprive suspects of the contextualisation cues needed to understand where they stand interactionally, and legally, may have the effect of reducing suspects' power. In the next chapter, we turn to suspects' perspectives and explore how interpreter mediation may affect their attempts to tell their side of the story.

4
Mediated Responses and Balance of Power

4.1 Introduction

This chapter explores the impact of interpreter mediation on suspects' tellings of their versions of events. Since all the suspects in the data set denied the allegations against them, conflicting versions of events are manifest in the interview discourse. However, the way in which the versions of the events are constructed is at times made more complex by the process of interpreting. How this occurs is demonstrated in this chapter by focusing on turn-taking in tripartite interaction and suspect-resistance strategies.

4.2 Suspects telling their versions of events

A record of police interview is more convincing as evidence if information is obtained from the interviewee's voluntary statements and in free narrative forms (Berk-Seligson, 2009; Heydon, 2005; Shuy, 1998). However, even when free narratives are encouraged by the interviewing officer, what is regarded as relevant by the officer may differ from the suspect's focus in the narrative (Berk-Seligson, 2009; Linell & Jönsson, 1991). Police interviews, as stated in the previous chapter, include both free narratives and 'elicited narrative sections' (Johnson, 2006, p. 66; also Gibbons, 2003; Gudjonsson, 1992; Heydon, 2005) and in the elicited sections, interviewers can use various forms of questioning, whether deliberately or not, to elicit their preferred versions of events, or to co-construct them with the suspect (Berk-Seligson, 2009; Milne & Bull, 1999).

One of the ways in which attempts to construct different versions of events come into conflict in police interviews is through competition for the floor (Berk-Seligson, 2009; Heydon, 2005; Russell, 2002; Shuy, 1998). Even when the interviewing officer invites the suspect to tell their story, if an aspect of their story emerges that the officer finds necessary to probe, an opportunity for an uninterrupted free narrative can be lost (Berk-Seligson, 2009). The strategies used to hold the floor over multiple TCUs (Turn Construction Units) to allow for story-telling in ordinary conversation (Goodwin, 1984; Jefferson, 1978; Sacks, 1974) may not work the same way in police interviews due to the institutional goals of the interview and the default preallocation of question turns to the police interviewer (cf. Carter, 2011; Heydon, 2005).

In interpreted interviews, suspects' lengthy turns would overload interpreters' memory capacity, which means that suspects' accounts need to be rendered in multiple turns with manageable lengths. Although their studies do not focus on police interview contexts, the analyses of turn-taking in dialogue-interpreting by Dimitrova (1997), Müller (2001) and Wadensjö (1998) demonstrate that the turn-taking mechanism in interpreted interaction entails an inherent risk that the flow of story-telling may be disrupted and the interlocutors may 'lose the thread' (Wadensjö, 1998, p. 235). In police interviews, fragmentation of suspects' turns due to interpreter rendition creates a 'legitimate' space for interviewers to question the suspect on any one aspect of the story-so-far. Interpreters also play significant roles as they deal with overlapping talk in police interviews (Russell, 2002). The analysis which follows will demonstrate that interpreters' handling of turn-taking and overlapping as well as primary speakers' turn-taking all impact on the way in which narratives are co-constructed and contested.

Another important aspect of suspects' telling their versions of events is their use of resistance strategies. When the suspect denies allegations, we see their resistance manifested in various forms (for example, Haworth, 2006; Heydon, 2005; Newbury & Johnson, 2006). Two resistance strategies discussed in Newbury and Johnson (2006), and found in the data set, are correction and contest. The chapter explores (Section 4.4) how these suspect resistance strategies work in interpreter-mediated police interviews.

As the present research adopts interactional sociolinguistic as well as conversation analysis (CA) perspectives, suspects' resistance in mediated police interviews is analysed as embedded in the context of the ongoing discourse and the institutional and cultural contexts, instead of focusing solely on semantic and pragmatic changes in translation. In other words, the main focus of the book is the management of roles and of the tripartite interaction. Therefore, translation-induced semantic or pragmatic changes will be discussed in relation to the roles which interpreters play (cf. Wadensjö, 1998; Berk-Seligson, 1990) and to the way the three parties in the police interview manage interactions in which competing versions of events are constructed.

4.3 Turn-taking and suspects' versions of events

4.3.1 Timing of interpreter rendition and its impact

When an interpreter is involved in an investigative interview, suspects' turns sometimes have to be segmented, or put on hold, to allow for interpreter renditions because of the memory capacity of interpreters who must retain the information in the source utterance. While long primary speaker turns with an excessive amount of information may jeopardise the accuracy of renditions (Dimitrova, 1997; Müller, 2001; Roy, 2000), frequent segmentation of discourse may also affect the reliability of communication in the legal process as interpreters may need to guess what will be said next, for example when translation involves two languages with different sentence structures (Nakane, 2007). Similarly, if interpreters wait for the suspect to complete a lengthy response, the accuracy of the interpreting will be at risk. On the other hand, if interpreters cut into suspect turns too early to provide accurate renditions, this may also lead to problems. Importantly, in the 'information gathering' phase of the police interview (Heydon, 2005, p. 47) in which suspects' accounts related to the allegation are to be elicited, fragmentation of the suspect's turns may cause misunderstanding and reduce the amount of information that is rendered and recorded as evidence for the trial. Such fragmentation may occur if the interpreter initiates renditions before the suspect's response is completed.

In Extract 4.1, the suspect is being questioned about the cash (more than $2,000 Australian dollars) which is present in the interview room and which he was carrying with him at the time of his arrest. The assumption behind the officer's questioning is likely to be that this money was payment for being a mule.

Extract 4.1 (Interview 4)

```
1 PO4:  uh: (1.6) did you think, why did you think
2       you were being given this money.
3 IR4:  .hh a: dooshite kondakeno okane o moraeta to
4       omoimasu ka?
        (.hh er why do you think you received so much
        money?)
```

```
      5       (1.4)
      6  S4:  E: iya (0.3) kore ano: (1.0) hoteru no okane
  →   7       mo haitte mase[n shi:]
              (U:m no this u:m does not include the hotel
              cost and)
      8  IR4:              [Ah : :]
      9  S4:  hoterudai mo harawa nakyaikenai shi:
              ([I've] got to pay for the hotel and)
     10  IR4: So m uhm it's not include the uh (.)
     11       accommodation= I have to pay the
     12       accommoda[tion]
  → 13  PO4:           [you ]have to pay your
     14       accommo[dation].
     15  S4:         [ Sore ]kara: ichinichi no: (0.5)
     16       yakusoku ga (0.4) ichinichi ni nihyaku doru de
  → 17       yu:esu doru de. [ ma: ] oosutoraria doru
              (And then the agreement for each day is two
              hundred dollars in US dollars. Well Australian
              dollars)
  → 18  IR4:                [so uh]
     19  S4:  [desukedo]
              (though)
  → 20  IR4: [I (    )] uh (0.5) I was told they (.)
     21       they promise to pay two hundred in the US
     22       dollars,=
     23  PO4: =mm hmm?=
     24  IR4: =per day.
  → 25  PO4: Okay, (0.4) uh how were you going to be paid
     26       that money.
     27  IR4: .hh Sorede sore (.)dooiufuuni sono nihyakudoru
     28       tteiruno o harau (0.2) yotee data ndesu
     29       ka=beedoru de nihyakudoru.
              (.hh and that how were they going to pay those
              two hundred dollars, 200 US dollars?)
  → 30   S4: Ya kore mata mochikaette, oosutoraria doru o
     31       mochikaette, (0.4) Tai de mata (0.4)
     32       ryoogaesuru toiu,
              (No, I take this back with me, in Australian
              dollars, and I was to exchange it in
              Thailand.)
     33  IR4: mm so (then I) bring these Australian
```

```
34        money,=
35 PO4:   =mm hmm,
36 IR4:   back to Thailand,
37 PO4:   right?=
38 IR4:   =exchange to the US dollars.
```

S4's initial response is contradictory if a normative interpretation is applied; the money for the hotel accommodation was *not included* (*'haittemasen'*) in the money referred to by PO4 as 'this money' in line 2. A coherent response to the question would be that the hotel cost *was included* in the cash in question, but IR4 renders the response, although ungrammatically, based on the meaning of the source utterance. (However, there is a deviant but possible implication in this response that the hotel payment has not been *deposited/received yet*.) The second part of the response, 'I have to pay for the hotel', would suggest that the hotel payment should be made from S4's own pocket, not from the Australian dollars given to him in cash. This response is not a coherent answer to the question, but PO4 nevertheless acknowledges the second part of it in lines 13–14. S4 however self-selects his turn in line 15, overlapping with PO4's turn with *'sorekara'* (and), disclosing that he was promised US $200 per day for his work in Australia (earlier in the interview he had said that he was told to interview Thai workers about their work conditions in Australia and report back). PO4 picks up on this payment agreement in line 25 and asks S4 how that payment was to be made. The response from line 30 does not directly refer to the method of payment. Overall, S4's utterances do not appear to produce a coherent account in response to PO4's original question.

Looking at the turn-taking, IR4's rendition starts (line 10) straight after S4's utterance ending with the conjunction *'shi'*, which is an emphatic 'and' meaning 'and what's more' (Makino & Tsutsui, 1991). Thus, it is possible that the turn transition did not strictly occur at a TRP (Transition Relevance Place). However, *'shi'* can also occur at the end of a sentence to 'weaken the sentence and obscure the cause' (Makino & Tsutsui, 1991, p. 396). The timing of the rendition suggests that IR4 either took up the latter function of the *'shi'* ending or tried to render the utterances there for the sake of accuracy. However, S4 self-selects his turn in line 15, starting it with *'sorekara'* (and), and continuing with his accounts. After giving up her turn when S4 continues with this response despite reaching a TRP in line 17 ('in US dollars'), IR4's next rendition (line 20) is overlapped with the end of the TCU *'desukedo'* (though) (line 19) which adds extra information. Although *'oosutoraria'* (Australia) in line 17 is not overlapped with IR4's rendition, this last TCU 'Well Australian dollars though' is not rendered. S4's original utterances and self-selection in lines 15–17 give rise to an alternative interpretation of his utterances, that is, that the Australian dollars in cash that he was questioned about included the hotel cost and his remuneration of US $200 per day. In line 25, PO4, however, treats the new information about the payment in US dollars as a new and voluntarily provided piece of information which is not part of the response to his original question about the cash in Australian dollars. While there is a translation error of using an active sentence for a passive 'be paid' (line 28 '*harau*'), S4's reference to 'this' and 'take the Australian dollars back' in lines 30–31 also supports the above alternative interpretation of S4's response to the question.

What the above analysis suggests is that the suspect's explanation is affected by the interpreter's decisions about the point at which renditions are to be initiated. While in this example the suspect's utterances are generally confusing and liable to be misunderstood even as they are, and it is possible that the suspect may have been being deliberately vague in his responses, the segmentation of his utterances in the interpreter turns may have prevented a more coherent account, or may have given the officer opportunities for a different line of questioning. In this segment, instead of pauses at potential TRPs in S4's utterances, instances of overlapping (for example, lines 17–18 and 19–20) are found. Turn-taking also affected renditions of discourse devices important for story-telling. The conjunction '*shi*' (and) was not rendered by IR4 in line 12 partly due to PO4's overlapping start of his turn, and '*sorekara*' (and) in line 15 was not rendered, again partly due to overlapping. As Dimitrova (1997, p. 149) says, overlapping and interruptions by the interpreter may be expected if the primary speaker's utterance is too long. However, what is deemed as 'too long' may vary amongst interpreters and frequent segmentation by the interpreter may entail problems.

In some interviews, the suspect's turns were interrupted by the interpreter initiating a rendition long before the TRP. In the following Extract 4.2, S2 is being questioned about why airline passengers have to submit a customs and quarantine form on arrival.

Extract 4.2 (Interview 2)

```
1   P2:  What (0.8) does he mean by those >customs and
2        quarantine<=what (1.2) what do you mean by
3        (0.3) rela- what is related (0.2) to customs
4        and quarantine.
```

```
    5        (0.6)
    6 IR2:  Sono: zeekan toka, ken'eki ni kansuru
             (So, related to Customs and Quarantine)
    7 S2:   Hai,
             (Yes,)
    8 IR2:  Mono da toiu no wa (0.3) tsumari dooiu imi de,
    9        hanashiteru ndesu ka? (0.2) Dooiu imi de
   10        kankee shita mono da to omoimasu ka.
             (which you are saying it is, what do you mean
             by saying that? In what sense do you think it
             is related to those?)
   11 S2:   A: ken'eki dattara, u- watashi ga byooki o
→  12        motteru ka dooka toka,
             (Uh with quarantine, u- for example if I am
             carrying a disease, or)
→  13 IR2:  Well, if it is the quarantine, I guess it's
   14        asking if I have any (0.4) disease (0.2) or
   15        not.
   16 S2:   Sorede zeekan: dato, =
             (And with customs,)
→  17 IR2:  =If it is the [customs],
   18 S2:                [sono mo]no nanka ne, (0.2) ano:
   19        okane toka sooiu sooiu:
             (You know, things like you know um for example
             things like, like money,)
→  20 IR2:  Money-
   21 S2:   Sooiu
             (things like that)
   22        (0.3)
   23 IR2:  things like [money,]
   24 S2:               [sore o]kikarete chekkusuru toiu
   25        koto desu ne,
             (We are questioned about it and they check,
             that's what it is, isn't it.)
   26        (0.4)
   27 IR2:  those things will be asked.
   28        (2.0)
→  29 PO2:  What else.=
→  30 S2:   =sono gurai, sono gurai [da to]
             (that's about it that's about it I think)
```

```
  31 IR2:                              [Sono ] hokani wa
  32        arimasen ka?
           (Is there anything else?)
  33        (1.8)
  34 S2:    Un mochiron: kore: watashimo >[bikkuri]
           (Yeah of course this, myself I was)
→ 35 IR2:                                   [I was- ]
  36 S2:    shimashita kedo,<
           (surprised, but)
  37 S2:    [sono baggu no] naka ni haitteru tteiu no desu
           (uh the fact that it was in the bag you see,
  38 IR2:   [I was surprised],
  39 S2:    ne, (.) wakatta kara bikkurishitemasu kedo:
→ 40        Soo[iu mono mitsukeru].
           (I am surprised about what was found but
           it is to find that kind of thing.)
  41 IR2:    [I was surpri:sed] (0.2) that stuff was in
  42        my ba:g,
  43        (0.4)
→ 44 PO2: What [stuff].
  45 IR2:      [I gue]ss (0.9) I guess uh (0.5) to check
  46        that sort of stuff (.) that sort of stuff. (.)
→ 47        Ja sono(0.3)sooiu mono tteiu no wa nandesuka,
           (Then that 'that kind of thing,' what is it?)
  48        (0.4)
  49 S2:    Ano: sono ba[ggu]
           (Um uh the bag)
  50 IR2:              [Well]
  51        (0.4)
  52 S2:    no sono:(0.3)nandesuka sono etto mayaku desu
  53        ka.
           (er what is it, er um is it narcotics?)
```

In line 12, S2's response has not reached a TRP, but IR2 renders this turn following the conjunction *'toka'* (or) (line 12) given by S2 with a continuing intonation, which signals 'more to come'. Accordingly, S2 self-selects a turn in line 16 to continue with his response, but as soon as he says 'And with the customs', IR2 latches onto the utterance to render it. S2's turn was terminated prematurely, and his next utterance (line 18) overlaps with the rendition. Again, before the turn reaches a TRP, a rendition starts in line 20. This short rendition 'Money-' is followed by S2's self-selected turn, which is a single word '*sooiu*' (like), but when this is followed by a short pause (line 22), IR2 again offers a rendition before S2 produces the predicate of his fragmented sentence. At this point (line 29), the officer asks another question 'What else', most likely to be intended to elicit a reference to drugs, but before this question is rendered, S2's turn 'that is about it' (line 30) latches onto it. IR2 however renders PO2's question, overlapping the end of S2's turn. This nullifies S2's attempt to end this particular sequence regarding the purposes of the customs and quarantine form. The response which comes after 1.8 seconds of pause is also interrupted by IR2's attempt (line 35) to initiate a rendition before any meaningful response is provided and long before a TRP is expected. S2's response as a whole to 'What else' (line 29) is rendered in fragments with three instances of overlapping. Moreover, the main clause of this response '(it is) to find things like that' (line 40) is mostly overlapped by IR2's rendition of the preceding subordinate clause 'although I was surprised because (something) was found (there)'. The attempt by IR2 to reinterpret the overlapped main clause may have resulted in the ensuing 0.4 second pause (line 43). However, this pause allowed the interviewing officer to pick up on the rendered part of S2's response and ask 'What stuff?' (line 44). This question is overlapped by IR2's rendition of the main clause of S2's response, but it occurs between 'What stuff?' (line 44) and its immediate rendition in Japanese (line 47). Thus, the rendition ('I guess …') starting in line 45 does not give PO2 any space for reaction to the last part of S2's response. The focus of the sequence from line 47 remains the narcotics that were found in S2's baggage.

This extract shows that fragmentation of suspect turns by interpreter renditions may risk premature intervention by the interviewing officer before the suspect is able to get to the point of their response. PO2 appears to have capitalised on such fragmentation, since the partial rendering by splitting up the suspect's account gave PO2 opportunities to foreground the discovery of the narcotics in the suspect's luggage.

This tendency to provide renditions in shorter segments was commonly found in Interview 2, where IR2's renditions often overlapped with S2's utterances. In another extract (Extract 4.3) from this interview, S2 attempts to stop IR2 from rendering his uncompleted response.

Extract 4.3 (Interview 2)

```
1 PO2: So you saw all that damaged luggage (.) in the
2      back of the car (.) and you did nothing about
3      it=is that correct.
```

```
      4  IR2:  .hh ja anata ga iu niwa: (0.3) sono: (.)
      5        Kowasareta nimotsu desu ne:=
               (.hh so what you are saying is that the
               damaged luggage, you know,)
      6  S2:   =Hai,
               (Yes)
      7  IR2:  Sore o ma: kuruma no sono ushiro no naka ni
      8        aru no o mite, =
               (you saw it in the back of the car but)
      9  S2:   =Hai,
               (Yes,)
     10  IR2:  Sore de nannimo shinakatta toiu wake desu ka?
               (then didn't do anything, is that right?)
     11        (2.5)
  →  12  S2:   °N:° (2.0) Nannimo shinakatta, (1.8) dakara:
               (Mm)        ('didn't do anything', so)
     13  IR2:  Well,
     14        (1.2)
  →  15  S2:   Dakara: (0.4) iya [chotto: CHOTTO: ]
               (So)             (no, hang on, hang on,)
  →  16  IR2:                    [by saying, that, ]I did
     17        nothing [a:nd]
     18  S2:           [U::n]
                       (Mmm)
```

In the above interaction, S2 is asked a 'so-prefaced' question (Johnson,
2002; see also Chapter 3, Section 3.4.3) that functions as a formulation
by PO2, which projects S2's behaviour as being of a suspicious nature
because of the assumption that he did not do anything when he saw
his own stolen and damaged luggage in the boot of the van. The pauses
in lines 11 and 12 cast him in a negative light, as he is not forthcoming
with an explanation for his non-action. There is a repetition of 'did
not do anything' by S2, but because the copula is not in a polite form
which S2 has been using consistently in his responses, it is likely to be
a monologue reflecting on the question in line 10. After a 1.8 second
pause (line 12), '*dakara*' (so), which prefaces an explanation, is produced, and IR2 renders this immediately, but a pause follows (line 14).
S2 starts again with '*dakara*' in line 15, but sensing that what he said
in line 12 is going to be rendered, S2 raises the volume of his utterance
in line 15, repeating '*chotto*' (hang on) to block IR2's rendition. Before
S2 produces any explanation or yes/no response, IR2 starts rendering

the utterances in line 16. However, IR2 does not render S2's resistance attempt in line 15. This may be because IR2 may have regarded it as resistance against *his own* interactional move to start a rendition there. After line 18, S2 gives an indirect explanation for his lack of action.

The turn-taking phenomena exemplified in the above two extracts suggest that, if the interpreter attempts to initiate renditions too early, suspects may be pressured to respond without being allowed to take the time to produce a coherent account. The intention of such premature renditions may well be to secure accuracy, but early interventions by interpreters raise the possibility of fragmented narratives (Dimitrova, 1997; Wadensjö, 1998) and coercive questioning (Berk-Seligson, 2009).

In contrast to the above examples of fragmented renditions, in Interview 1, the suspect often gave his responses containing multiple TCUs in a single turn without having them rendered in short segments, as can be seen in Extract 4.4 below. The interpreter (IR1) was, unlike most other interpreters in the interview data of the present research, accredited at NAATI level 3 (professional).

Extract 4.4 (Interview 1)

```
 1 PO1:  Uh (.) under what (0.2) circumstances did you
 2        meet Mark,
 3 IR1:   Donoyoona jookyoo: de e Mark ni aimashita ka,
         (Under what circumstances did you meet Mark?)
 4 S1:    E:to (0.3) ano: (0.6) nihon ni ano: betonamu
 5        kara imin shite kita, ano tomodachi ga, (0.4)
→ 6       shiriai ga iru ndesu kedo, (2.1) sono hito
 7        no:: (0.3) tomodachi: shiriai tte koto de
 8        awashite moratta ndesu. (.) sorega hajimete
 9        desu. =
         (Um er in Japan I have uh a friend, or
         acquaintance, who migrated from uh Vietnam and I
         was introduced to him [Mark] as this
         person's friend, or acquaintance. That was the
         first time.)
→ 10 IR1: =I met Mark for the first time, uh: because I
 11        had a- some u:h (0.3) a Vietnamese friend in
 12        Japan, (.) and I was told Mark's u::h the
 13        person's friend.
 14        (0.3)
 15 PO1:  And what were your (0.2) friend's names.
```

```
        16          ((10 turns regarding the friend))
        17  IR1:    Mr. Satoo brought Mark uh: to me.
        18          (0.3)
        19  PO1:    And why did he bring Mark to see you.=
        20  IR1:    =De dooshite tsuretekita wake desu ka,
                    (And why did he bring him to you?)
        21          (0.3)
        22  S1:     E:to (0.5) kooiu koto desu ano: (1.0) Satoo
        23          (0.4) tteiu hito ga ano:: ikkai mareeshia
        24          asobiniitte, sorede sono Mark tteiu no to
   →    25          shiriai ni natta rashii ndesu ga, (3.0) ano:
        26          (1.1) n ano: (0.4) >shiriai ni natta rashii n
        27          desu kedo,< .hh sono: (.) mareeshia kara (0.3)
        28          kondo Satoo ntoko ni asobi ni kita ndesu yo
   →    29          ne? (1.5) sooiu are de: atashi ntokoro ni ano:
   →    30          mukoo no tomodachi dakara tte itte: (0.2)
        31          shookai shite moratta ndesu.
                    (Um it was like this, uh that person called
                    Satoo uh, went to Malaysia for a holiday and
                    I heard that he'd met a guy called Mark and,
                    um mm um I heard that he met him, .hh er he
                    then came to visit Satoo from Malaysia, you see.
                    That was how- to me, uh I was introduced
                    to him who was Sato's friend from overseas.)
        32          (1.0)
   →    33  IR1:    Well (0.2) I think uh Mr. Satoo uh went to
        34          Malaysia, (0.3) on a trip one day, .hh and uh
        35          he uh met Mark in Malaysia, (0.2) and the next
        36          time uh: Mark uh: came to Malaysia, (0.2) uh
        37          came (.) came to Japan from uh Malaysia to see
        38          Satoo, (0.4) Mr. Satoo, (.) and that's how we-
        39          er: how Mr. Satoo brought Mark to see me.
        40          (0.3)
        41  PO1:    Was there any specific reason why he brought
        42          Mark to see you?
```

As a response to a wh- question by PO1, S1 gives a response that contains two TCUs. The first TCU contains a clause which refers to the existence of a Vietnamese migrant friend who introduced S1 to Mark. However, with the ending of this clause '*kedo*' (lit. but) in line 6, which marks background or preliminary information, more is expected to follow explaining how this friend led to S1's meeting with Mark. While grammatically speaking the TRP has not been reached yet, it is possible to render this first clause, while signalling there is more to come with 'and'. Instead, IR1 waits for 2.1 seconds for S1 to produce the second clause. Furthermore, IR1 waits until S1 signals the end of his response with 'That was the first time [I met him]', before initiating a rendition (line 10). The source turn is rendered as a full and coherent response. Although video recording was not available to confirm this, it is likely that IR1 utilises effective note-taking skills. The 2.1 seconds of pause in line 6 may have been used for note-taking and IR1 may have also been waiting for the rest of S1's response. Throughout the interview, IR1 showed a tendency to render longer chunks of suspect utterances, asking clarification questions before renditions where necessary.

A similar pattern in IR1's turn-taking is found in line 33. The clause in S1's original turn from line 22 'I heard that someone called Satoo went to Malaysia for a holiday and met a guy called Mark' ends with '*ga*' (lit. but) in line 25, which makes the clause a 'preface' to the statement provided in the subsequent clause. The 'preface' can be rendered into English at this point, but IR1 does not take a turn. A three second pause ensues, followed by further hesitations by S1. S1's sentence finishes with 'came to visit Satoo on holiday, you see' (lines 28–29), but IR1 still does not initiate a rendition, possibly because S1's turn so far has not provided an answer to the question of how S1 came to meet Mark. While it is difficult to know whether S1 wanted to wrap up his response there, he continues his response to say that he was introduced to Mark as Satoo's friend. Following this, a pause of one second occurs (line 32) before IR1 initiates the rendition of the whole response. A coherent and complete narrative is rendered in response, without problematic overlaps which may prevent a full narrative being produced. Overlapping in interpreter-mediated police interviews also entails a risk of utterances not being captured on recording, and therefore of evidence for trial not being preserved (Russell, 2002). Rendering suspects' responses without fragmentation appears to reduce such risks. As a response to the question in line 19, the rendition in lines 33–39 is coherent and full, albeit less specific (as reflected in PO1's expansion in lines 41–42).

It should however be pointed out that this approach to turn-taking entails a risk of reducing interpreting accuracy. In the renditions above, the propositional content 'as his friend from overseas' (line 30) is dropped. While almost all other propositional content which directly answers the question is rendered, the opening of the narrative 'This is the case' is rendered as 'I think', and the repetition of 'I heard that he met [him]' is dropped in the rendition. The original 'the person called Satoo' is rendered as 'Mr Satoo', and 'a guy called Mark' is rendered as 'Mark'. These changes conceal from the interviewer S1's attempt to imply his social distance from these men. The ending of the sentence with the interactional particle '*ne*' ('you see') in line 29 is not rendered, but instead, the rendition combines this sentence and the subsequent one with the conjunction 'and' (lines 37–38).

This approach to interpreting, in which the interpreter waits until a multi-unit turn is completed, seems to involve a trade-off between a better flow of communication and '"filtering" the answer by omitting repetitions, hesitations, and tags, by raising register and by adding a cohesive phrase' (Hale, 2008, p. 113; see also Hale, 1997, 2004). Extract 4.5 gives an example where IR1's role includes that of an *author* (Goffman, 1981), adding information to the source utterance for effective communication. At the beginning of the extract, PO1 asks S1 if he can remember exactly when he had a meeting with his Malaysian contact in Tokyo.

Extract 4.5 (Interview 1)

```
    1 PO1: Where was that meeting.
    2 IR1: A, sore wa dokode aimashita ka.
           (Uh this, where did you meet?)
    3  S1: Tookoyoo desu.
           (It was in Tokyo.)
    4 IR1: That was in Tokyo.
    5      (5.5)
    6 PO1: Does he know when in May that meeting was?
    7      (0.3)
→   8 IR1: E, gogatsu no nannichi ka oboetemasu ka?
           (Uh do you remember what day in May it was?)
    9  S1: Choodo renkyuu,(0.2) ano (.) gooruden uiiku no
   10      toki datta to omoimasu.
           (Just at the time of consecutive holidays, um
           I think it was during the Golden Week.)
   11 IR1: I think was uh during the th:e (.) what we
   12      call Golden Week, c- Golden Week, continuous
   13      uh 1- it's a long holiday week(.)end.
   14      (2.4)
→  15 PO1: Do you know what date that was
```

```
      16        appr[oximately]?
      17  IR1:     [Ee ::: de] sono renkyuu (0.2) wa gooruden
      18        uiiku wa nannichi desu ka, oyoso daitai.
                (Uh and the consecutive holidays, the Golden
                Week, what dates were they approximately?)
      19        (2.5)
      20  S1:  Nihon no desu[ka],
                (The Japanese one?)
      21  IR1:              [Ha]i.
                (Yes.)
      22        (3.4)
      23  S1:  hhh °Chotto muzukashii°,[ N i j u u :::: , ]
                (hhh it's a bit difficult. Twenty-)
      24  IR1:                          >[It's quite difficult]<
  →   25  S1:  nijuukunichi ga ten'noo tanjoobi desu yo ne?
                (The 21st is the Emperor's Birthday isn't it?)
      26        (0.3)
  →   27  S1:  Sonde,(0.7)sanjuu ga are de (0.3) ato mikka
      28        to itsuka.
                (And the 30th is that and then the third and
                the fifth.)
      29        (0.4)
      30  IR1: Uh the je- public holidays in Japan, uh: is
      31        29th of April, it's uh (0.2) Emperor's
      32        birthday? (0.2) and the third is u::::h
  →   33        Constitution Day, (.) and fifth is uh
  →   34        Children's Day. (.) So uh round about that
  →
  →   35        time (0.2) was the uh long weekend.
```

While PO1's question in line 15 asks for the date of the meeting, the rendition (lines 17–18) requires S1 to give the dates of 'Golden Week' (consecutive holidays in Japan from 29 April to 5 May, containing four public holidays). S1, after a pause, asks for clarification (line 20), to which IR1 responds. After a 3.4 second pause, S1 indicates his difficulty in remembering the dates, which IR1 renders with '(It's) quite difficult' (line 24), overlapping the beginning of S1's answer '*Nijuu ...*' (Twenty ...). Then S1 gives the 29th (of April) as the Emperor's birthday (line 25), with a rising intonation and the interactional particle '*ne*' (isn't it). The rendition does not start until all the dates have been mentioned, with some pauses (lines 27–28). In the rendition, the public holidays which S1 mentioned only by date are described by name at IR1's discretion. Furthermore, there is a closing statement which is not provided by S1 in the source utterances which wraps up the response. After this (not recorded in the transcript), PO1 does not pursue S1 concerning which date S1 had the meeting in question but moves on to ask about the nature of the meeting. The closing statement refers to the 'long holiday weekend', which appeared in IR1's rendition in line 13. S1 had only mentioned '*renkyuu*' (consecutive holidays) and '*Gooruden uiiku*' (Golden Week), which usually lasts beyond a three day long weekend, but this reference to 'long holiday weekend' in the rendition in English narrows down the meeting date to one of three possible dates rather than during a period of seven days. The suspect's account is presented as more coherent and definite because of (1) the use of 'so' in line 34 which signals that what follows is a conclusion, and (2) the mention of the 'long weekend' that corresponds to the rendition of S1's response before PO1's question requesting a specific date. If the rendition had concluded after 'Children's Day' (line 34), a follow-up question may have been asked, to clarify the specific date of the meeting.

IR1 was the only interpreter in the data set who tended to wait for multi-unit responses to be completed. The 'filtering' and editing of source utterances found in the example above may not be practised by other interpreters who also have this orientation toward waiting for the completion of multi-unit turns. However, to a certain extent, rendering suspect turns in longer chunks seems to entail a risk of 'tidying up' suspect responses and making them more coherent than the original responses. This is a sensitive and highly important aspect of legal interpreting, since difficulties in collecting evidence – such as lack of coherence, hesitations, and (un)willingness to provide relevant information – are themselves also part of the evidence, especially in cases in which two competing stories are being told.

4.3.2   Primary speakers' turn-taking

In interpreter-mediated interaction, the default rule of turn-taking, or what Knapp and Knapp-Potthoff (1985, p. 457) term 'normal format' (quoted in Wadensjö, 1998, p. 143), is for primary speakers to wait in silence while the other primary speaker finishes his/her turn and the interpreter renders his/her utterance. However, studies of turn-taking in interpreter-mediated interaction have shown that primary speakers do not always follow this pattern of turn-taking (Roy, 2000; Russell, 2002; Wadensjö, 1998). Dimitrova (1997) goes so far as to say that regarding turn-taking, 'the interpreter is the interlocutors' competitor' (p. 162). Furthermore, deviation from the default turn-taking format may result in overlapping of primary speakers' utterances, which puts the interpreter in a difficult situation (Russell, 2002). According to Roy (2000, p. 85), the interpreter's four options when faced with overlapping talk are as follows:

1. An interpreter can stop one (or both) speakers and allow the other speaker to continue. If an interpreter stops both speakers, then either the interpreter indicates who speaks next or one of the primary speakers decides who talks next.
2. An interpreter can momentarily ignore one speaker's overlapping talk, hold the segment of talk in memory, continue interpreting the other speaker, and then produce the 'held' talk immediately following in the end of a speaker's turn.
3. An interpreter can ignore overlapping talk completely.
4. An interpreter can momentarily ignore overlapping talk and upon finishing the interpretation of one speaker, offer the next turn to the other speaker, or indicate in some way that a turn was attempted.

Overlapping talk is commonly found in the data set for the present research, where examples of the first three options above are found. While the above options say what an interpreter 'can' do, there are cases in which the rapid turn-taking and frequent overlapping make it difficult for the interpreter to manage turn-taking. This has implications for the suspect's telling of their version of events. The interpreter's decisions as to whose turn is to be rendered first, or preserved, may affect the trajectory of interaction, and may lead to one party's version of events being given prominence. Some salient examples of interruptions by the primary speakers are discussed in terms of their impact on the construction of each speaker's version of events.

In Extract 4.6, the suspect (S3) is asked what baggage she was carrying when she arrived in Australia. She refers to a dark-red suitcase and a bag that are in the interview room, but realises a plastic bag which she had with her upon her arrival in Australia is missing.

Extract 4.6 (Interview 3)

```
1 PO3: What items of baggage was she carrying when
2      she arrived (0.3) [in Australia].
3 IR3:                   [Tsuita toki ], tsuita toki
4      ni nimotsu nani o mottemashita ka?
```

```
              (When you arrived, when you arrived what
              luggage were you carrying?)
     5        (1.4)
     6  S3:   Ano:(.) enji no kaban to:,
              (That dark red bag and)
     7  IR3:  Nani- nan no kaban?
              (What- what bag?)
     8  S3:   Ano: wain reddo no [kaban to, (0.3) kono bakku.
              (That wine-red bag and this bag.)
     9  TR3:                     [Hai,
                                 (Yes)
    10  S3:   to: (1.2) ato: tabako haitteru: fukuro.
              (And um a bag with cigarettes in it.)
    11  IR3:  .hhh so I had the wine-red bag over there,
    12        (.) I had this bag here,
 →  13  S3:   A-,
              (Oh)
    14        (0.5)
 →  15  PO3:  What one was she [carrying] when she first
 →  16  S3:                    [ Are::: ]
                               (Hmmm?)
    17  PO3:  arri[ved]=not (0.2) [what she] picked up I've
 →  18  IR3:      [Ano]           [ ichio- ]
                  (Um)            (So just-)
    19  PO3:  asked [her] about that.
 →  20  S3:         [A- ]
                    (Oh)
    21  IR3:  Tsui- ano tsuita toki ni:=
              (Arri- um when you arrived,)
 →  22  S3:   =Kore (0.3) bakkku to:(.) tabako no,
              (This)      (bag and cigarettes)
    23        (0.3)
    24  IR3:  So I had a ba:g? (.) an I had um:
    25  S3:   [Ta]bako ga haitt[eru]
              (one with cigarettes in it)
    26  IR3:  [A]              [ a ] plastic bag with c-
    27        cigarettes in it.
 →  28  PO3:  What bag is she referring to,
    29        (0.2)
    30  IR3:  Nan no: fukuro desu ka.
```

```
              (What bag is it?)
        31  S3:  .hh biniiru: no, (0.2) fukuro desu.=
              (.hh it is a plastic bag.)
        32  IR3: =It was a: plastic bag.
        33  PO3: Which ba:g (0.3) was she carrying.
        34       (0.4)
        35  IR3: Don- no: fukuro o motte imashita ka.
              (Which bag were you carrying?)
        36       (0.4)
        37  S3:  Tesage desu.=
              (A carry bag).
   →    38  PO3: =Is she referring to this bag on the bench?
        39       (0.3)
        40  IR3: Kono(.)kono fukuro desu,(.)kono=
              (This, it's this bag, this)
        41  S3:  =Kono baggu to: ato: mareeshia de: tabako o
        42       katta ndesu yo ne?=
              (This bag and also in Malaysia I bought
                           cigarettes, you see.)
        43  IR3: =Hai=
              (Yes)
        44  S3:  =Sono tabako o ireta fukuro,
              (The bag in which I put those cigarettes.)
        45  IR3: Hai,
              (Yes)
        46  S3:  Biniiru no.
              (A plastic one.)
        47  IR3: No, (.) um I had this bag and I had a um a
        48       plastic bag=I bought some cigarettes in
        49       Malaysia (.) and it was full of c- cigarettes.
        50       (1.9)
        51  PO3: What other (.) items of baggage did she
        52       have to collect from the baggage carousel.
```

The rendition of S3's response (lines 11–12) refers to two items of luggage, but before IR3 has mentioned the third item (a bag with cigarettes in it), S3 interrupts IR3 with '*A*' (oh) in line 13 as if she had remembered something. However, hearing 'wine-red bag' in line 11, and probably without knowing that the rendition has not been completed, in line 15, PO3 ignores S3's interjection and takes a turn, narrowing the scope of the question. However, in the middle of PO3's question, S3 produces another interjection '*Aree*' (Hmm?) (line 16). IR3 attempts to start rendering PO3's question, overlapping closer to its TRP (line 18), but PO3 continues his turn. IR3's further attempt to render the question can be found in another instance of overlapping talk ('*ichio*', a part of '*ichioo*' [so just]) in line 18.

Note that this particular interpreter frequently used the expression '*ichioo*' ('actually', 'so just', or 'just in case') at the beginning of the rendition before a question, which often made the Japanese rendition unnatural. It seems to have been used as a tentative discourse marker such as 'so' or 'well'. Therefore the back translations provided here may vary according to the discursive context.

Despite the police officer's control over turn-taking at this point and IR3's attempt to render the question, S3 overlaps PO3's question once again with '*A*' (oh). IR3 ignores this, starting to render the question in line 21, but this is interrupted by S3, whose repeated interjection and subsequent utterances suggest that she has realised that the plastic bag with cigarettes purchased in Malaysia is not with her. This forces PO3 to temporarily put aside the question he just asked, and follow on with a question (line 28) that aligns with the focus of S3's responses (that is, a lost plastic bag with cigarettes). However, in line 33 PO3 brings the focus of questioning back to what she was carrying upon her arrival. S3 is vague in her response (line 37 'carry bag'), but this response is ignored as PO3 quickly takes a turn in line 38 before letting IR3 render S3's turn.

The lack of alignment is in fact traceable back to line 13, when S3 produced an interjection and the reference to a plastic bag was not rendered. In this sense, even though S3 exercised power through interruptions in some parts of this interaction, her account was not effectively told. This is also because further on in the interaction PO3 did not relinquish his turns when interrupted but pushed ahead with his questioning without having S3's turn rendered. In the extract, the utterances lost due to primary speakers' overlaps and interruptions are not rendered by IR3 either by retrieving those lost turns or by active management of turns from a *principal* role. The police officer did not attempt to retrieve S3's accounts lost because of interruptions. These factors seem to have resulted in disruption and a misunderstanding of the suspect's account. The extract also demonstrates that primary speakers interrupting each other impairs their ability to tell their versions of events (Dimitrova, 1997; Russell, 2002). This is not to say that the interviewing officer and the suspect do not also interrupt each other in monolingual interviews (see Carter, 2011), but the fact that the primary speakers usually do not understand each other's utterances in interpreter-mediated interviews may make them less sensitive to interruptions and overlapping, and the presence of the mediator who may also be vulnerable to interruptions makes mediated interviews a site for complex struggles for competing versions of events. A serious issue in interpreted interviews is that overlapping talk causes greater loss of communication than in monolingual interviews, because the primary speakers do not share a common language.

Suspects' accounts may be interrupted by interviewing officers when specific aspects are perceived as relevant to the police-preferred version of events (and therefore also to the prosecution case), as shown in Berk-Seligson's (2002) analysis of a police interview in the US. Interruptions may also occur when interviewing officers need to record evidence in a manner acceptable as admissible evidence. In Extract 4.7, the suspect (S4) is being questioned about the bottle of alcohol containing stimulant drugs that he has allegedly imported. His attempts to tell his account are met with the police officer's preoccupation with following obligatory institutional procedures.

Extract 4.7 (Interview 4)

```
   1  PO4:  Uh so: (0.7) what were you: when you come to
   2        Australia, what were you: (0.2) um told to do,
   3        (.) with this bottle. =
   4  IR4:  =Hai, .hh de oosutoraria ni kitara, .hh kono
   5        (0.2) mottekita uh osake no bin wa douiu fuu
   6        ni shiro tte iu fuu ni shiji sarete mashita
   7        ka.
            (Ok. .hh and what were you instructed to do
            when you arrived in Australia, about the
            bottle of uh sake that you brought?)
   8        (0.3)
   9  S4:   E:to kono: (0.2) shorui no
            (Uhm on this document)
→ 10  PO4:  =>Sorry just for the purpose of the tape< Mr.
→ 11        Mori is (0.2) u:m pointing to: (0.2) three
→ 12        pieces of paper?
→ 13  S4:   Kono hito ni (.) omiyage de watashi[te  ]
            (I was told to give it to this person
  14  PO4:                                   [ma-]
→ 15  S4:   ku[re, (.) tte.]
            as a souvenir.)
```

→ 16 IR4: [(pass that)]
→ 17 PO4: J-JC slash zero zero zero: one? U:m he has
   18   referred to a piece of paper, (0.3) which has
   19   hand-written notes? (0.2) u:m (0.3) on this
   20   note there's =
   21 IR4: = 'to this person.'=
   22 PO4: = Okay, (0.2) u:m (0.8) Mr. Mori this person
   23   he:re? I cou- (0.3) to me that says omiyage,
   24   oo em a:i [wa:i e]i gee,
→ 25 S4:   [*omiyage*].
                    (souvenir)
   26 PO4: omiyage? .hh gee ee (It's) to: u:m (0.6) that
   27   appears to be a (0.2) telephone number?
   28 IR4: *Kore wa denwa bangou desu ka,* 'koko ni kaite
   29   *aru no wa*'.=
                    (Is this a telephone number, what is written
                    here?)
   30 S4: =*to omoimasu.*
                    (I think so.)
   31 IR4: Ye[ah,]I think so=
   32 PO4:   [yes?]
   33 PO4: =Okay, u:m=
→ 34 S4: =*ma boku ga kakeru koto wa nai* [(*daroo kedo*).
                    (well I don't think I'll be calling that
                    number myself.)
→ 35 PO4:   [and that
   36   numb[er-
→ 37 IR4:   [but (.) I don't think I will call him=
   38 PO4: =All r(h)ight (0.2). okay now that number is
   39   zero zero uh: (0.4) possibly a one or a
   40   slash? oo four oo one, zero three seven, nine
   41   six two. The name underneath that telephone
   42   number, is uh Mr. JEF, spelled jay ee eff.
   43   (0.2) Who wrote (0.4) that, (.) on that
   44   document.
   45 IR4: 'Hai' de koko no kami ni kakareteiru kore
   46   nandesukeredomo dare ga okakininarimashita ka.
                    (Okay, and about this written on this paper,
                    who wrote this?)
   47   (.)

```
      48   S4:   Wakanaranai desu sore [wa:]
                 (I don't know about that.)
      49   IR4:                      [ah ]I don't know.
      50   PO4:  When were you given this (0.6) piece of paper?
      51   IR4:  Kono kami wa itsu moraimashita ka,
                 (When did you receive this piece of paper?)
      52   S4:   E chiketto to issho ni
                 (Uh with the ticket)
      53   IR4:  Ah with the (.) the ticket.
      54   PO4:  With the tickets? And with the bottle?
      55   IR4:  Sontoki ni osakeno bin to.
                 (At that time with the sake bottle?)
      56   S4:   Ee botoru to issho ni.
                 (Yes, with the bottle.)
      57   IR4:  Hai.
                 (Right.)
      58   PO4:  Okay. and when were you told to ca:ll, this
      59         person.
      60   IR4:  De, .hh itsu koko no hito ni renraku o toru
      61         you ni tte >iwarete imasu ka.<
                 (And when have you been told to contact this
                 person here?)
      62         (0.4)
→     63   S4:   Ya, renraku ga nakereba.
                 (No, if he/she doesn't contact me.)
      64         (0.6)
      65   IR4:  So if: (1.0) if I don't get any (0.4) uh:: the
      66         contact.=
      67   PO4:  =uh huh?
      68         (1.2)
      69   S4:   Soudesu renraku ga nakereba kakete:,
                 (That's right, I'm to call if he/she does not
                 contact me and)
      70         (0.4)
→     71   IR4:  So if- (0.2) [if nobody ] contac- [contact
→     72   S4:                [da- komakai]        [komaka-
                               (so- in detail      in det-)
      73   IR4:  me:, I have to call.=
      74   PO4:  = call Mr. JEF.=
→     75   S4:   =da-,[ komakai hanashi nante ] nai ndesu yo
```

```
                    (so, I haven't been given details,)
  → 76  IR4:        [sono misutaa jefu ni (    )]
                    ((     ) that Mr JEF.)
  → 77  S4:  soko no hen wa.
             (about that sort of stuff).
    78  IR4: Ah, I d- did't uh informed any details,=
    79  PO4: =Ri[ght.]
    80  IR4:    [at a]ll.
```

In the above interaction, we see frequent overlapping, latching and interruptions. The turn-taking pattern deviates from 'normal format'. These features of interaction make accurate and complete renditions of the source utterances difficult. In fact, some of the source utterances are not rendered fully.

The institutional context requires that the investigating officer has to have everything verbally recorded, which also includes verbal clarification of deictic expressions pointing to materials or people in the statements. This causes disruption in turn-taking in the above extract. The suspect's response in line 9 refers to a document in front of them with 'kono shorui' (this document). Before this turn reaches the TRP, PO4 interrupts S4 (line 10), to put on the recording what exactly S4 is referring to as 'this document'. A similar phenomenon of interviewing officers inserting 'for the benefit of the tape' and clarifying the referent of indexical terms has been discussed by Stokoe (2009) for monolingual interviews in the UK. S4 nevertheless continues with his response in line 13, but his turn is also interrupted briefly by PO4 (line 14) who continues with the 'recording for evidence' discourse. The competition for the floor between the primary speakers makes it difficult for IR4 to take a turn. She is forced to interrupt S4's turn to render parts of his response at line 16, but then PO4 comes in at line 17 to ensure that details of the document mentioned by S4 remain on the recording. There is substantial information in PO4's turns so far, but IR4 disregards it and latches on to PO4's turn in line 21, interrupting PO4, to complete the rendition of S4's response. As for the suspect's source utterances, IR4's rendition does not contain 'on this document' (line 9), 'I was told' (line 13) or 'as a souvenir' (line 13).

In this interaction, PO4 seems to be preoccupied with following required police interview procedures as evidence-gathering legal processes. This preoccupation with putting evidence on record for a future audience leads to the questioning of details on the card, which may be an attempt to elicit evidence pointing to the organised nature of the crime. Probing the circumstances in which S4 was given instructions regarding the number on the card may not only lead to further arrests but also to proving the intentionality of the crime (cf. Edwards, 2008; Stokoe, 2009). Stokoe (2009) shows that the phrase 'for the benefit of the tape' could function as a strategy for formulation and for putting on record the police-preferred version of events.

While formulation is not used in conjunction with the officer's move to divert the interaction for the sake of the recording, due to institutional priorities, PO4 does not give space for IR4 to deliver renditions. S4's self-selection of his turns also puts pressure on IR4 to manage turn-taking. A large proportion of the content of PO4's utterances in this extract concerns details of the material evidence being discussed, and the clarification of these details is directed towards a future audience of the ensuing stages of the legal process. IR4's disregard for PO4's procedural utterances could be explained by the tendency for interpreters to drop 'primary reality' references (Hale & Gibbons, 1999). Thus, it is possible that, because of the nature of PO4's utterances, IR4 did not render most of the content directed at the future audience but remained with that directed at the suspect. It is only when PO4 directs a question to S4 in line 27 that IR4 renders his utterance (lines 28–29).

In line 34 there is another instance of S4 self-selecting his turn, which is overlapped with PO4's 'and that number-'. PO4 again does not give space for S4's turn to be rendered, but the interpreter cuts in, rendering the suspect's turn. The police officer finds this response funny (note the laughter in 'All right' in line 38) perhaps because it was interpreted as S4 being sarcastic ('now that I am detained I won't be calling him'). However, S4 is not being sarcastic here, since later (line 63) he says that he was instructed to call the person if nobody contacts him. In fact, S4 could have continued with an explanation in line 34 if he had not been interrupted by PO4. 'I won't be calling him' in line 34 on its own implies that he is knowingly involved in the drug importation crime, while combined with the explanation provided later, it suggests a passive involvement of S4 in the crime. If a longer account had been allowed, an alternative interpretation of this utterance may have resulted. Thus in this case the suspect's account was cut off by the police officer prioritising the legal framework, which forced the interpreter to fragment the suspect's account further by cutting in with her rendition. As a consequence, the suspect's attempt to tell his account was further disturbed by the police officer, who is 'entitled' to take a turn after interpreter rendition.

Towards the end of this extract, S4 continues to try and provide explanations by self-selecting his turns (lines 69, 72, 75 and 77). The interpreter tries to render his utterances in short chunks and the police officer in line 74 also latches onto the rendition to clarify or to put on record to whom the phone call would have been made by S4. Both the police officer and the suspect fail to wait for interpreter rendition (at lines 10, 13, 14, 34, 35, 72, 75) in this extract. Where the primary speakers are competing for the floor like this, the interpreter is put under considerable pressure when attempting to render everything.

It should also be pointed out that the meaning of '*omiyage*' (souvenir, line 13) remained unclear to the police officer for a while because of the overlapping talk, despite its importance in the case. The Japanese word was written on the piece of paper that PO4 had in front of him as labelled evidence, but his utterances in lines 22–24 suggest that he does not know the meaning of the word. PO4, despite the repetition of the word, follows his line of inquiry ignoring the term. The term '*omiyage*' in this case has significance as the bottle in which the drug was found, as S4 claimed, was brought as a souvenir, and the giving and receiving of souvenirs is an important Japanese custom.

In this example we can see power negotiated vigorously by all interlocutors including the interpreter. The police officer exercises his institutional power by cutting in for the sake of putting all interview processes verbally on record. The suspect's account is ignored as the officer concentrates on probing the material evidence that may support intentionality and the organised nature of the crime. However, this effort is in a way not rewarded due to the interpreter's tendency to focus on the secondary rather than the primary reality (Hale & Gibbons, 1999), thus reducing the police interviewer's power. The interpreter on the other hand struggled to render the suspect's utterances and had to resort to interruptions and forceful intonation. It is also interesting to see here that the suspect seems to make the best of opportunities such as silent pauses (see Chapter 6 for further discussion) to self-select a turn and provide his side of the story.

4.4   Suspect resistance and interpreter mediation

In this section, the impact of interpreter mediation on suspect resistance is discussed. As mentioned, because all suspects in the data set denied the allegations of importation of narcotics, their versions of events are often in conflict with those of the police, and resistance strategies are used by the suspects. Based on their analysis of interviews from a notorious murder case in the UK, Newbury and Johnson (2006, p. 231) provide the following response types for resistance:

Contest: for example, answering 'no' when the question expects yes.
Correction: for example, saying 'No'; 'This happened/is the case'.
Avoidance: for example, saying 'I don't remember'; 'Continue the story'.
Refusal: for example, saying 'I have nothing to say'; Remaining silent.

In the data set for the present research, there were no instances of refusal and none in which the suspects invoked their right to silence. Responses such as 'I don't remember' or those that were not directly relevant, which may be regarded as avoidance strategies, were found, although they may have genuinely indicated a lack of memory or the misunderstanding of questions. However, it was found that the suspects used 'contest' and 'correction' strategies to resist police power in order to construct their version of events. This section examines these suspect resistance strategies and explores the ways in which interpreter mediation may impact on the force of such resistance moves by suspects.

4.4.1   Correction strategy

The following extract (Extract 4.8) shows a suspect's use of the correction strategy. After a series of questions regarding S3's arrival into Australia, PO3 asks S3 when she packed the bag (that is, the suitcase) that she had brought from the place where her tour group had a stopover on the way to Australia.

Extract 4.8 (Interview 3)

```
    1 PO3:  When did she pack that bag,
    2        (0.4)
    3 IR3:  Itsuni: ano: sore tsumemashita ka?
           (When um did you pack it?)
    4        (0.8)
→   5 S3:   Tsumete atta ndesu.
           (It was already packed.)
    6 IR3:  E?
           (Sorry?)
    7 S3:   Tsumete atta ndesu.
           (It was already packed.)
    8 IR3:  Um: (0.2) It was already packed.
    9        (2.2)
```

```
  →  10  PO3:  What does she mean it was already packed.=
     11  IR3:  =Tsumete atta to iu to,
                (What do you mean by it was already packed?)
     12        (0.9)
  →  13   S3:  Desukara: (0.3) ano: Mareeshia de, (0.4) bakku
     14        ba nusumareta ndesu. =
                (So um in Malaysia, my bag was stolen.)
     15  IR3:  =Hai.=
                (Yes.)
  →  16   S3:  =Sorede:(.) tsugino hi no asa ni,(0.2) juuji
     17        goro ni.hh Kono bakku no naka ni watashi no
                nimotsu ga haitte: todoita ndesu.
                (And then the next day in the morning, around
                ten o'clock, .hh this bag, with my things in
                it, was delivered to me.)
     18        (1.0)
     19  IR3:  So what actually happened was in Malaysia,
     20        (0.3) um my: suitcase was stolen, (.) and the
     21        next morning, (0.4) u:m (0.7) it my suitcase
     22        came= an another suitcase came back, and it
     23        had all of my clothes and everything all all
     24        packed in it (2.5) >and that was about ten
     25        o'clock.<
     26        (1.0)
  →  27  PO3:  In the morning,
     28        (0.5)
     29  IR3:  Asa deshita ka, gozen no juuji desuka,=
                (Was it in the morning, 10 o'clock in the
                morning)
     30   S3:  =Hai.
                (Yes.)
     31  IR3:  Yes.
     32        (1.1)
  →  33  PO3:  Can she describe to me what she (0.3) packed
     34        in the (.) the suitcase.
     35        (0.4)
     36  IR3:  Nimotsu ni nani o tsumeta no ka, (.) setsumee
     37        shite moraemasu ka?
                (Can you describe what you packed in your
                luggage?)
```

```
       38        (0.4)
→  39  S3:   Tsume=((breathy))
               (Pack-)
   40  IR3:  =Suutsukeesu no naka ni nani o tsumeta[no ka],
               (What you packed in your suitcase.)
→  41  S3:                                          [Tsume]
   42        te atta no ka.
               ([What] was packed.)
→  43  IR3:  Uhm but it- it was already actually packed
   44        into the suitcase.
   45        (0.9)
→  46  PO3:  What- (0.6) what's inside the suitcase.=
   47  IR3:  =A,(0.2) suutsukeesu no nakami wa nan desu ka._
               (Uh what is in the suitcase?)
   48  S3:   Watashi no: (0.3) irui to: (0.4) ato:, shanpuu
   49        rinsu komono desu.
               (My clothing and also shampoo, conditioner and
               other small things.)
               ((several turns))
   59  IR3:  U:m, clothes, (0.4) shampoo and rinse, (0.2)
   60        dryer, (0.2) u:m underclothes, socks body
   61        shampoo toothbrush toothpaste towel tissues
   62        shoes.
   63        (1.0)
→  64  PO3:  What happened after she picked up the bag,
   65  IR3:  Ano nimotsu o ano totte kara nani ga
   66        arimashitaka = nani ga okori mashita ka?
               (Um what was there after um you picked up the
               luggage = what happened?)
   67        (0.9)
   68        Naniga arimashi[ta ka]?
               (What was there?)
   69  S3:              [totte]kara tte dooiu imi desu
   70        ka?
               (What do you mean by 'after you picked up'?)
   71  IR3:  A:no: (0.4) what do you mean by after she
   72        took the bag.
→  73  PO3:  .hh (0.2) would- did did she hand another
   74        form to customs?
   75        (1.0)
```

```
    76  IR3:  Ichioo, (.) nimotsu o totte kara: ano: zeekan
    77        ni hoka no shorui o dashimashita ka,
              (So just, did you hand other documents to the
              customs after u:m you picked up the luggage?)
    78        (4.6)
→   79  S3:   °Imi ga wakannai desu.°
              (I don't understand what you mean.)
    80  IR3:  I'm not un- not sure what you mean.
```

IR3 renders PO3's question accurately in line 3, except for the redundant use of the particle *ni*. In line 5, however, S3 repairs the rendered question, saying that the bag was already packed by someone else. This is an important aspect of the investigation, and of the suspect's version of events because who packed the suitcase relates to the narcotics found in it. This correction takes IR3 by surprise, and S3 repeats the repair in line 7. When PO3 asks S3 for clarification (line 10), S3 explains how she came to receive an already packed suitcase in Malaysia. Thus, S3's correction of PO3's question leads to her opportunity to tell her story (that the tour group members' suitcases were stolen, then swapped with replacement suitcases with heroin hidden in them during their stopover). While PO3 seems to be following S3's narrative by asking a follow-up question in line 27, his subsequent question (lines 33–34) indicates that S3's repair and ensuing story – resistance through correction – did not have any impact on his (the police officer's) perception of what had happened. That is, PO3 reverts to the pre-repair assumption realised by the syntax of the question in which 'she' (S3) is the person who 'packed' the suitcase during the stopover.

Indicating her exasperation over PO's apparent indifference to her repair, S3 says '*Tsume-*' (pack-) with an outbreath in line 39. IR3 however seems to take this a request for clarification of PO3's question and repairs 'luggage' into 'suitcase' in line 40. As soon as she hears the repetition of '*tsumeta*' ([you] packed), S3 repairs the question directly in lines 40–41. The emphasis which she adds to '*atta*', an auxiliary verb indicating the action had been done, also suggests a desperate effort of resistance on her part. The intensity of this resistance is somewhat reduced through the mediation. The interpreter's rendition (lines 43–44) is a comment inviting correction rather than a direct correction. The force of the source utterance is also weakened by the introduction of hesitation (uhm) and the adverb 'actually'. While PO3 takes account of this rendition and repairs his question by removing S3 as an animate subject (line 46), PO3 did not use the expression 'what was packed' as provided in S3's correction. It is also confusing when PO3 uses the abbreviated form 'what's', which leads to IR3's rendition in present tense. This is especially the case because the suitcase in question is present in the interview room. By avoiding the adoption of S3's correction directly, PO3 covertly rejects the version of events presented in S3's correction. The analysis above supports the findings of previous studies of monolingual police interviews that suspect resistance (for example, Haworth, 2006; Newbury & Johnson, 2006) and suspect persistence in their own narrative perspective (for example, Linell & Jönsson, 1991) do little to the power asymmetry at the institutional level and do not have an impact beyond shifts in power dynamics at the local level of interaction.

4.4.2 Contest strategy

Suspects may also resist police interviewers' repetitive attempts to elicit confirmation of a version of events that supports the interviewers' allegations (Berk-Seligson, 2009; Heydon, 2005; Shuy, 1998). The questioning sequence in Extract 4.9 was preceded by a tense interaction in which the suspect was asked repeatedly why he had written an occupation different from his actual one on the arrival card for Australia. He had also indicated that a Japanese tourist near his seat had showed him what to write on the form. The interviewing officer knows that S2 had had a holiday in the Philippines.

Extract 4.9 (Interview 2)

```
 1 PO2:  When (0.2) you travelled to the Philippines,
 2 IR2:  Anata ga (.) Firipin ni ryokoo shita toki ni,
         (When you had a trip to the Philippines,)
 3 S2:   Hai,
         (Yes,)
 4 PO2:  Did you fill out a (0.6) form like this?
 5 IR2:  .hh Anata wa kooiu yoona shoshiki o kinyuu
         shimasahita ka?
         (.hh did you fill out a form like this?)
 6 S2:   Kinyuu shimas- (0.2) shimasen.=
         (I did not fill [one] out.)
 7 IR2:  =No. I didn't.
 8       (1.4)
→ 9 PO2:  Is he sure? (0.2) Are you sure?
10 IR2:  Honto desu ka?
```

```
                    (Is that true?)
      11   S2:  Yes,
  →   12   IR2: Tashika desu ka,=
                    (Are you sure?)
      13   S2:  =Hai.
                    (Yes.)
  →   14   PO2: Positive?
  →   15   S2:  Yes,=
      16   IR2: =Hontooni (0.2) zettai daijoobu desu [ ka?]
                    (Are you really absolutely sure?)
      17   S2:                                        [hehe]
      18        (0.5)
  →   19   S2:  Kore: kaita koto nai desu. (.) kooiu ofisaa to
      20        ka. Un, (0.6) machigai nai desu.°(ima made ni)°
                    (I haven't written this before. Things like
                    'officer'. Yeah, no doubt. (before.))
      21        (0.6)
  →   22   IR2: °The (0.3) grammar is quite difficult° in
      23        Japanese,=
      24   PO2: =O:h [(   )]
  →   25   IR2:     [ when] he says ye:s. (0.2) I agree. (0.4)
      26        It didn't- it doesn't mean (0.3) yes I did.
      27        (0.3) I- yes I wrote.
      28   PO2: All right.
      29   IR2: Yes so (    )
      30        (0.6)
      31   PO2: So you did fill out a form (0.3) when you
      32        travelled to the Philippines.
      33        (0.3)
      34   IR2: Ano: Firipin ni ryokoo shita toki ni,
                    (Um when you had a trip to the Philippines,)
      35   S2:  Hai,
                    (Yes,)
      36        (0.3)
      37   IR2: Kooiu yoona shoshiki o (.) kinyuu shimashita
                ka,
                    (Did you fill out a form like this?)
  →   38   S2:  Kinyuu shinai desu.
                    (I didn't fill [one] out.)
      39   IR2: No no, I didn't fill in.
```

In line 6, S2 denies that he filled in the form which required passengers to write their occupation. PO2 presses on in line 9 to ask for a confirmation ('Are you sure?'), and S2 responds directly with 'Yes' in English. IR2, mirroring PO2's double questions in the source utterance, renders '*Tashikadesuka*' (for sure?), to which S2 responds with '*Hai*' (Yes) in Japanese (line 13). This affirmative response is not rendered, since PO2 takes a turn, paraphrasing the previous question with 'Positive?' S2 yet again responds immediately with 'Yes' (line 15) before IR2 manages to render PO2's paraphrased confirmation question. The persistent questioning, despite S2's repeated 'contest' clearly denying having filled out a form similar to the Australian one, makes S2 giggle (line 17), perhaps suggesting that he is now finding the repeated confirmation questions absurd, and in lines 19–20 he elaborates on his minimal responses to assert his denial. However, instead of rendering this elaborated version of S2's 'contest' against the coercive line of questioning, IR2 shifts his role from that of an *animator* to a *principal* (Goffman, 1981), and in line 25 starts to explain that 'yes' and 'no' responses in Japanese do not always correspond to those of English, since 'yes' in Japanese shows agreement to the whole proposition rather than the predicate. However, PO2 interprets this to be the other way around, as implied in the next question (lines 31–32) 'So you did fill out a form ...'. However, this still receives a negative response from S2.

While PO2 put unusual pressure on S2 to admit that he had filled out a similar form (and therefore intentionally tried to deceive the authority regarding his occupation when he entered Australia), IR2 may have begun to have doubts about the motivation for this unusually persistent questioning. Bilinguals proficient in Japanese and English are aware of the grammatical pitfall of negative questions in English for Japanese speakers. Since the clarification questions were asked about S2's negative response rendered as 'No I didn't' (line 7), it may have occurred to IR2 that S2's affirmative responses in English following the confirmation questions may have been understood by PO2 as 'Yes, I did fill out a form'.

Nevertheless, this move by IR2 to explain the grammatical pitfall was not only unnecessary but it was also produced instead of the rendition of S2's explicit clarification in lines 19–20. In other words, IR2's explanation sidetracked S2's consistent contesting stance in this questioning sequence. It is also worth pointing out that PO2, despite IR2's attempt to elicit a response in Japanese (line 12), did not wait for the rendition of '*Hai*' before she pushed on yet one more time with 'Positive?'. If interviewing officers take for granted the meaning of minimal affirmative responses such as '*Hai*' and proceed with questioning without having them rendered, it may have serious consequences (cf. Nakane, 2007). In this case, IR2 may have felt an urge to step in as PO2 kept pressuring S2 without finding issue with the fact that the suspect had used English (line 11). In other words, PO2 seemed unaware of the problems which could result from not having the suspect use Japanese and, as a result, of no translation being provided.

Hale (2008) gives an illuminating example of a courtroom interpreter whose intervention as a communication facilitator fails, making the courtroom communication more confusing. The above instance may be an equivalent example in the police interview setting. While repeated questioning to elicit a preferred answer from the suspect is a typical coercive strategy (Berk-Seligson, 2009; Heydon, 2005; Newbury & Johnson, 2006), IR2 may not have been familiar with the contesting discourse and felt an urge to repair what he may have perceived as 'problematic' communication, but the realities of conflicting perspectives in legal interaction mean that the contested nature of this 'interrogation' should have been maintained in the interpreting.

Suspects' resistance can also be communicated through a more subtle form of contest. The analysis of interaction in Extract 4.10 illustrates problems arising from difficulties in maintaining the illocutionary force of this form of resistance. The problems are compounded by the competition for the floor amongst the three interlocutors. PO4 asks S4 whether he will be contacting 'Pat' in the next few days, the person who had accompanied him to the airport and who had entrusted the liquor bottle to him before his departure for Australia.

Extract 4.10 (Interview 4)

```
       1 PO4: U:m, are you intending to be in contact with
       2      Pat (.) in the next (0.2) few days?
       3 IR4: De.hh korekara ni san nichi no aida ni, patto
       4      san ni renraku suru yotei wa arimasu ka.
              (And .hh do you have a plan to contact Ms Pat
              In the next few days?)
       5      (0.4)
    →  6 S4:  Moo renrakushinai to komarimasu yo ne, kore.
              (Well I must contact her, don't I, all this.)
       7 IR4: Mm: I I I guess I have to talk- talk to her:,
    →  8 PO4: °Mm hm?° (0.4) Okay, (0.5) U:m (1.2) I just ask
       9      now if Federal Agent (0.5) XXXX has any
```

```
         10          ques[tions he would like] to ask?
→ 11     S4:         [Moo demo kore mo ta]berenai kara komatta
         12          mon desu yo ne.
                     (But we can't eat this any more so that's not
                     good, is it?)
         13          (0.6)
→ 14     XXX:        I do,
         15          (1.0)
→ 16     S4:         (Sore wa) boku ga tsukamacchatta tte iu shika
         17          nai deshoo.
                     ((Of course) I have no choice but to tell her
                     I have been arrested, don't I.)
→ 18     IR4:        Uh so: I I I think I have to tell her that I I
→ 19                 I'm su- suspe(hh)nded at the airport.
         20          (0.5)
→ 21     PO4:        U:m (0.3) well is that- (.) Did she give you
         22          any instructions (0.2) if you were (0.3)
         23          detained,
         24     IR4: Mm mm.
         25     PO4: That (wh- of) anything that you were supposed
         26          to do?
         27     IR4: A sorede, eapooto de tukamattara, douiu n:
         28          kooiu koto shinasai tte iu fuuni wa,
         29          shi[ji sarete]masu ka.
                     (Uh so have you been given instructions for
                     what do to if you are caught at the airport?)
→ 30     S4:         [iya:,son-]
                     (No, su-)
→ 31     S4:         Sonna,konna,[ze-]
                     (Such, like this, n-)
         32     PO4:             [No?]
         33     IR4: [No.]
→ 34     S4:         [Son]na hanashi, kore ga daitai,.hhh (0.2)
         35          sono (.) kusuri ga haitteru nante no wa kootte
         36          shirabete,(0.3) ↓joodan↑deshoo [tte].
                     (Such a story, this in the first place, .hhh
                     like, check if there're drugs in it like this,
                     and I went, 'this must be a joke!')
         37     IR4:                              [Mm ] mmm. .hh
         38          so I didn't know anything about the narcotic
```

```
        39            substance in it, [at all
        40  PO4:                      [Okay], we- we'll
        41            still have to have the bottle u:m examined by
        42            our foren[sic department] [.hh um]
        43  S4:               [(Dakara) komaru]
                              ((So) I'm at a loss)
→       44  IR4:                           [ Demo ]koremo mata
        45            chotto kore so- atodemo(0.2)chanto shirabe
        46            naito ikenai desukeredo mo=
                      (But with this we still have to kind of, this,
                      s- we have to examine it properly later.)
        47  S4:       =Fuu kicchatta kara iino kana kore demo kore
        48            (0.2) hito no mon dakara, ii no kana hh [teiu]
        49            no omottende.
                      (This, the seal has been broken, but this is
                      Also for someone else, so I am worried if it
                      will be okay.)
        50  IR4:                                              [mm: ]
        51            ah:, (.) I the- I am worried about this
        52            because it is not belong to me:,=is supposed
        53            to be given to [somebody] °else°
        54  PO4:                     [ Okay, ]
→       55  PO4:      No problem, .hh this signature that appears
        56            >sorry just re referring to the< third page of
        57            (0.2) exhibit JC slash zero zero one, .hh can
        58            you read that name in full? =oh sorry, >first
        59            of all< are you able to read the English
        60            writing that's on that page.
```

S4's source utterance starts with the adverb '*moo*' (well) which indicates frustration, and contains a combination of interactional particles '*yo*' and '*ne*', which yields 'the meaning "I assert S, don't you agree?"' (Makino & Tsutsui, 1991, p. 545), and then '*kore*' (this) at the end of the sentence. It is not possible to ascertain what proposition is omitted in this ellipsis, but judging from his accounts as a whole in this segment, this turn is most likely intended to communicate 'Well I must contact her, don't I, because of all this', expressing exasperation. It would be unlikely that a suspect who intentionally imported an illegal substance would readily admit that he/she will have to contact the person who conspired in the crime. However, S4's response is translated without the sense of exasperation or of indirect blaming of whoever put him into trouble. In addition, the illocutionary force is weakened by the addition of the hedging 'I guess' (line 7) in the rendition. There are also false starts in this rendition, and the image of 'a drug mule in trouble' seems to satisfy PO4 ('Mm hm? Okay,') for now.

PO4 then proceeds to ask another investigator present in the room if he has any questions (lines 8–10). However, S4 ignores this turn, interrupting in the middle of a question, and continues his accounts, expressing his frustration and concern. This utterance again ends with the interpersonal particles '*yo*' and '*ne*' (line 12), reinforcing the message. This interruption, however, puts IR4 in a dilemma as she needs to decide whose turn to render, and whether to ignore one of the turns. The assisting police officer at this point takes a turn (line 14), providing a second pair part for PO4's invitation. The clash between the police officers' procedural exchange and the suspect's emotionally charged discourse continues as IR4 remains silent through the two pauses (lines 13 and 15), possibly unable to decide what to do.

S4's accounts in lines 11–12 and 16–17 suggest that because the foodstuff is wasted and will not reach the people who are to receive it, he has to explain to 'Pat' about his arrest. The reasons given would indirectly deny S4's intentional involvement in the crime. However, S4's talk in lines 11–12 is not rendered and communicated to the officers at all, as it is between the police officers' question–answer adjacency pair parts. For the officers, S4's initial response confirmed their version of events that S4 was Pat's accomplice, and no further account related to the question is necessary. As for S4, he has not finished the story yet. When he self-selects his turn in line 16, IR4 chooses to ignore the police officers' exchange and renders S4's turn. This is an example of interpreter mediation supporting the suspect's opportunities to have their side of the story heard.

The rendition however not only retains lines 11–12 but also weakens the illocutionary force of S4's utterance. It uses 'I think' as a projection frame for 'I have to tell her …', but the source utterance was again a statement with rhetorical impact, ending with the auxiliary verb '*deshoo*', indicating his assertion. This leads to PO4's literal interpretation of S4's response and the next question (lines 21–23) concerns the 'instructions' which Pat possibly gave to S4. S4 vehemently denies receiving such instructions (line 30), and in line 34, he shifts the focus of his account to his reaction to the discovery of narcotics ('I went, "This must be a joke"'), and therefore to his claim of innocence. The subsequent rendition in lines 38–39 however lacks the modality of S4's utterances, expressed in the use of dramatic pitch changes and the use of the term 'joke', and explicit references to 'such a story' and 'in the first place, this [event]'. PO4 then quickly shifts the discourse according to the framing of forensic evidential procedures, putting it on record that the 'narcotic substance' is yet to be forensically confirmed (lines 40–42). The police officer's attention is now to put on record that the suspect was *not* told that the substance was definitely narcotic, in order to ensure that the investigative procedures have been followed appropriately. Again, the institutional orientations to interview discourse seem to warrant the interviewing officer's control (cf. Carter, 2011; Stokoe, 2009), fragmenting the suspect's account. In Heffer's (2002, p. 232) terms, there appears to be a clash of 'narrative' and 'paradigmatic' modes of discourse, with the police discourse pulled towards the paradigmatic mode to fit it into the institutional framework.

However, PO4's turn is overlapped towards the end by what appears to be S4's continuation of his explanation from the previous turn and a reiteration of '*komatta*' (concerned) from line 11 when he had mentioned wasted food. It seems to be an attempt by the suspect to frame the account as that of an innocent victim who is concerned about the food brought for his work contacts. But S4's overlapped utterance is not rendered at this point, as in lines 44–46, IR4 first renders PO4's turn. S4 however again self-selects (line 47), latching onto IR4's rendition of PO4's turn and expressing concern about the foodstuff. In lines 51–53, S4's overlapped and uninterpreted utterance in line 43 is incorporated with 'I am worried' from the subsequent rendition, although the 'worry' (original '*komaru*' in line 43, meaning 'I'm at a loss') was linked with a causal conjunction ('*Dakara*', meaning 'so') to the discovery of the illegal substance that he thought was 'a joke' – his side of the story was cut off at line 37 by a rendition – and the link between the utterance in line 43 and S4's emotional reaction to the discovery of the drug expressed in lines 34–36 is lost.

The last part of the rendition of S4's account suggesting his innocence is overlapped by PO4's 'okay' (line 54) and then immediately after the rendition, PO4 responds to S4's explanation with 'No problem'. The first pair part of this 'No problem' is a statement expressing concern, but PO4 does not offer to assist S4 in relation to those concerns. Instead, PO4 moves on quickly to questioning S4 about another piece of material evidence (the signature on one of the exhibits) that is not related to S4's preceding accounts. 'No problem' seems, along with the 'okay' in line 54, to be used as a boundary between S4's story and the next phase of questioning, 'accepting' that his account has been put on record but not taking up the core claim.

While S4 seems to gain some power interactionally by taking the floor through self-selection, assisted by the interpreter prioritising more than once S4's utterances over those of the officers, in the end the officers have power to evaluate, and dismiss, the suspect's versions of events. Thus, when S4's statements are interpreted as incriminating, PO4 picks them up and probes further; but when S4 produces an explanation which implies his innocence, his attempt to continue his side of the story is quickly blocked. Furthermore, the suspect's utterances have also lost their pragmatic force through the loss of sarcasm in the rendition, which reduces the interactional power of his accounts.

This section has discussed the impact of interpreter mediation on suspects' resistance. The tripartite structure of interaction may give the advantage to the suspect in interpreter-mediated interviews as the power to manage turn-taking largely rests with the interpreter. However, interpreters' decisions as to whose turn to render when primary speakers' turns overlap suggest that they depend on the context and flow of questioning and do not prioritise one party over another.

Furthermore, in interpreter-mediated interviews, not understanding the police officer's language may make it easier for the suspect to interrupt the officer's turn, despite the 'normative format' of turn-taking organisation in which the primary speakers are expected to wait till the interpreter has rendered the previous speaker's turn.

In addition to the complex issues related to turn-taking, the reduction of the illocutionary force of suspects' resistance strategies through interpreting may affect suspects' power to tell their side of the story. This may be an issue of maintaining pragmatic equivalence at a turn-unit level (cf. Hale, 2004), but there is also a discursive or sequential level at which the force of resistance may be skewed through interpreting.

4.5 Conclusions

This chapter has explored suspects giving their versions of events in interpreter-mediated police interviews. As all the suspects in the data set denied their involvement in the crime for which they were charged, the interviews provided rich data for analysis of the ways in which suspects' versions of events and their resistance strategies to support those versions were communicated in interpreter-mediated interviews.

The timing of the interpreter's turn-taking played an important role in the suspects' tellings of their versions of events. A tension between fragmentation of suspects' accounts and interpreters' needs to ensure accuracy was identified, especially when there is competition for the floor and deviation from the normal format of turn-taking. The impact of interpreter mediation discussed in this chapter echoes what Müller (2001, p. 264) has described as the 'fragmenting effects which translatability and its cumbersome and costly machinery may have on the natural flow of conversation', referring to Sacks' (1972, 1995) notion of 'lousy conversation' characterised by 'lack of structures and topic coherence' (Müller, 2001, p. 264).

Interpreters' moves in relation to whose turns are to be rendered first (or at all) influenced the trajectory of the investigative interviews and the constructions of versions of events. As shown in the analysis, the interpreter's mediation at times prioritised and supported suspects' attempts to tell their side of the story. However, the analysis showed that police interviewers ultimately had control over the overall narrative construction process, as their interactional role as questioner, with their institutional resources, allowed them to be selective about aspects of suspects' responses. Two ways in which this selectivity can be manifested were found in the data. First, it was manifested through not confirming or ratifying the suspect's account using a sequence-closing third (Schegloff, 2007), which may be used as an 'evaluative third part' to either 'support or challenge answers to questions' in legal settings (Gibbons, 2003, p. 124). Police officers may use an evaluative third part to signal that the defendant's/suspect's accounts are officially for the record (Stokoe & Edwards, 2008). However on the other hand, by not offering the third part or by signalling a closure of the sequence with 'okay' and moving to the next question, suspects' accounts are not officially confirmed or ratified on the record by the interviewing officer. Second, the selection of interruptions and topic shifts may be warranted for interviewing officers when the institutional requirements make it necessary for them to put certain details of the evidence on the record without delay. However, the analysis showed examples of this move in Interview 4 leading to fragmentation and loss of the suspect's version of events.

The analysis of primary speakers' turn-taking has also shown that primary speakers' deviations from the norm of turn-taking and interruptions (cf. Roy, 2000; Russell, 2002; Wadensjö, 1998) affect the extent to which suspects' versions of events are heard (and recorded as evidence). The lack of a shared linguistic code between the interviewer and interviewee may make interrupting each other less intrusive, but such competitions for the floor bring a challenge to interpreters. It seems that in interpreter-mediated police interviews, as has been found in monolingual interviews (for example, Berk-Seligson, 2009; Heydon, 2005; Johnson, 2006, 2008), versions of events are elicited through specific questions and co-constructed by the interviewing officer and the suspect, but the interpreter is also at times an active participant in the construction of the story.

The chapter also examined suspects' resistance as one of the vehicles for giving their versions of events. It was demonstrated that rendering and maintaining the illocutionary force of the resistance may be challenging for the interpreter, as previous studies of court interpreting have also shown (Berk-Seligson, 1990; Hale, 1997, 2004). Mason and Stewart (2001) found in their analysis of two lay–professional legal interactions that changes in illocutionary force through interpreting 'disempowered' the interrogated party (p. 59). The present research also found that the illocutionary force of the suspect's resistance was weakened through the interpreting process. However, as we saw in Chapter 4 and in the analysis of the final extract in this chapter, police interviewers' illocutionary force is at times also weakened through interpreting. This however may work against suspects, since they may not be able to defend themselves against interviewers' strategies to discredit them if the illocutionary force in the realisation of such strategies is weakened or changed.

The analysis also suggested that the rendition of illocutionary force in suspects' resistance is interwoven with the negotiation of power through all parties' turn-taking and interpreters' participation in discourse management. Thus, interpreters' awareness of and familiarity with the police interview genre, especially where narratives are in conflict and where tension arises from such conflicts, is essential in maintaining the illocutionary force realised in the discourse.

The analysis in this chapter suggests that the nature of mediated tripartite interaction endows interpreters with power to influence suspects' attempts to make their side of the story heard. The impacts of interpreting may or may not be produced intentionally, considering the moment-by-moment pressure to ensure accurate renditions as well as to manage interaction. The fact that there are impacts has already been argued by previous studies of liaison interpreting in legal contexts (for example, Berk-Seligson, 1990, 2000; Hale, 1997, 2004; Hale & Gibbons, 1999; Russell, 2002; Wadensjö, 1998). To minimise the impact of the interpreting process on the trajectory of interviews, interpreters need both an awareness of the nature of police interview discourse and the ability to handle interpreting *discursively* beyond the level of sentences or turns. This is partly because each party in interpreter-mediated police interviews has their own interests. This seems to make the mediated interaction a site of power struggle among the three parties, including the interpreter who is caught in the middle.

5
Miscommunication and Repair

5.1 Introduction

This chapter addresses how miscommunication is dealt with by the three participating parties in police interviews. 'Miscommunication' is defined by Wadensjö (1998, p. 198) as 'lack of fit between the sense aimed at by one interlocutor, and what is displayed by another as the sense made of the current message'. This definition effectively captures the type of phenomena which interpreters, within their professional capacity, may feel a need to prevent or rectify. The term 'miscommunication' is therefore used to refer to the phenomena discussed in this chapter and the concept of 'conversational repair' is adopted as the a key analytical unit, as repair is an attempt to address threat to interactional alignment such as problems of understanding (Sacks et al., 1974; Schegloff, 1992; Schegloff et al., 1977). By examining repair sequences, this chapter aims to explain how interpreter mediation may impact on the trajectory of interview discourse when a problem is perceived and addressed by the interlocutors. The following sections explore the factors that make repair a precarious interactional activity which is susceptible to further miscommunication or to problematic influence on the construction of evidential accounts.

5.2 Miscommunication and interpreter mediation in police interviews

The ways in which miscommunication is dealt with in police interviews as a discourse process has not been extensively discussed. Heydon (2005) claims that most of the repair sequences in her police interview data in English were two-part insertion sequences, after which the predominant question–answer exchange pattern between the inter-viewing officer and the suspect resumes. As we will see, in interpreter-mediated interviews, repair sequences do not always lead to such a swift resumption of the main question–answer sequences. The layer of interpreter-mediation in the process of dealing with miscommunication and the possibility of miscommunication occurring due to the transla-tion process may make repairing communication problems a complex process vulnerable to further miscommunication.

Komter (2005) demonstrates how trouble sources that trigger repair sequences (Schegloff et al., 1977) play out in her analysis of problems in a Dutch–French interpreter-mediated police interview. In her data, the interpreter oscillates between the 'normal format' of interpreting (Knapp & Knapp-Potthoff, 1985, p. 457) and 'asides' (Komter, 2005, p. 208). In the former mode, the interpreter's rendition turn occurs after every turn taken by one of the primary speakers, and the rendi-tion turn is followed by the other primary speaker. When one of the primary speakers initiates a repair, in the 'normal format', it is treated as directed towards the other primary speaker and rendered as such. In this mode, the interpreter can be assumed be participating as an *animator* (Goffman, 1981). On the other hand, in the 'aside' sequences, the inter-preter engages in exclusive interaction with one of the primary speakers in 'side sequences' (Jefferson, 1972), in which the ongoing interaction is temporarily suspended for conversational repairs to address mishear-ing or miscommunication. In Jefferson's (1972) view, side sequences are also used to provide relevant contextual pre-conditions for structuring the main sequence. Svennevig (1999), however, distinguishes between 'asides' and 'side sequences' in that asides are not related to or depend-ent on the main sequence, and, in Komter (2005), the terms are used interchangeably.

The significance of these sequences is that one of the primary speak-ers is excluded from this sequence without access to what is going on. The interpreter participates in a *principal* role, either initiating a repair themselves or responding to offer a repair turn directly of their own accord (Berk-Seligson, 1990; Müller, 1989, 2001; Wadensjö, 1998). The oscillation between these two formats of interaction brings further com-plications to the miscommunication between the interviewing officer and the suspect.

As Wadensjö (1998) states, the interpreter is the only person who can 'let (mis)understanding become a common issue' (p. 210). This also means that when mediated by an interpreter, interaction can go on without miscommunication being recognised as such by primary speakers. Wadensjö (1998) points out that the interpreting process itself entails 'trouble sources' such as 'the non-standard turn-taking and fragmentation of discourse', 'the non-standard dependence on a mediator's understanding' and 'the non-standard position of understanding on others' behalf' (p. 234). Komter (2005) also observes that, for the purpose of alleviating face-threatening situations, the interpreter exploits the 'sequential ambiguities' (p. 212) in which interpreter turns can be regarded as either a rendition of a primary speaker turn or the expression of the interpreter's own voice. Thus, repair sequences are discursive contexts in which interpreters may shift role to facilitate communication. The danger here is that police questioning strategies have divergent assumptions and interpreters may consciously or unconsciously align to such goal-oriented institutional frameworks, 'promoting and occasionally reinforcing a prototypical asymmetric pattern between officer and layperson' (Wadensjö, 1998, p. 211).

The analysis of repair sequences in this chapter will look at the repair types from two angles. Firstly, from the point of view of the format used by the three participants; that is, whether normal turn-taking format is followed or whether asides are used, either primary speaker-initiated or interpreter-initiated. This allows us to examine how miscommunication may be handled by interview participants when interpreters maintain their *animator* role, and how an interpreter's direct approach to miscommunication as a *principal* may affect the trajectory of the interview. The second way of looking at repair types draws on interaction dynamics and power negotiations among participants. It considers the 'initiator' versus 'repairer' of the repair sequence. Repairs may be initiated by the primary speakers or the interpreter. When these two points of view are cross-referenced, we arrive at three types of repairs based on turn-taking organisation (Table 5.1).

In repair sequences between primary speakers in the normal format of turn-taking, the initiator is either the police officer or the suspect,

Table 5.1 Types of repair sequences

Type of format	Initiator	Repairer
Normal	Suspect	Police officer
	Police officer	Suspect
Asides: primary speaker-initiated	Police officer	Interpreter
	Suspect	Interpreter
Asides: interpreter-initiated	Interpreter	Police officer
	Interpreter	Suspect

and the interpreter participates as an *animator*. Repair sequences occurring as asides are categorised according to whether the interlocutor who initiates the repair is a primary speaker (police officer or suspect), or the interpreter. Either way, the interpreter in these sequences acts as a *principal* with a turn that is not a rendition of a primary speaker's turn. In the first type of aside, the interpreter responds directly to the primary speaker's repair initiation without conveying the repair initiator turn to the other primary speaker. In the second type of aside, it is the interpreter who initiates the repair to act on current or potential miscommunication between the two primary speakers. Each type of repair sequence has its own issues.

5.3   Repairs initiated by primary speakers: normal turn-taking format

5.3.1   Repairs initiated by suspects in a normal turn-taking format

In this section, suspect-initiated repairs in the normal turn-taking format are examined first, followed by an example of police officer-initiated repairs. Before the complex aspects of interpreter-mediated repair sequences are discussed, a 'successful' repair sequence following the 'normal format' of turn-taking organisation is presented in Extract 5.1, as a baseline example. One of the primary speakers, in this case the suspect, asks a clarification question, which is a repair initiator.

Extract 5.1 (Interview 2)

```
    1  PO2:  What did you do with this, (0.2) form? (0.6)
    2        when you filled it out.
    3        (1.4)
    4  IR2:  Kono shoshiki o kinyuu shita toki ni, (1.0)
    5        kono shoshiki ni tsuite nani o shimashita ka?
    6        = Kono shoshiki o (.) doo shimashita ka?
          (When you filled out this form, what did you
          do to this form? What did you do with this
          form?)
    7        (1.5)
→   8  S2:   Ah (0.3) °ah° moo ikkai, (0.3) moo ikkai,
          (Ah? Again, again.)
→   9  IR2:  Could you repeat the question again.
   10        (1.4)
```

```
→ 11  PO2:  After you filled this form out, (.) did you
   12        give it (0.2) to anyone.
   13  IR2:  .hhh kono shoshiki o kinyuu shita ato ni, (.)
   14        dareka ni (.) watashimashita ka?
             (After you filled this form out, did you give
             it to anyone?)
   15        (1.7)
   16  S2:   Watasanai °desu°.
             (I didn't give it (to anyone))
   17  IR2:  No, I didn't.
```

Here, we see an example of a four-part repair sequence by the primary speakers starting with PO2's question. Although IR2 quickly self-repairs in line 4 for a better translation of 'what did you do', S2 appears to find the question confusing, as he initiates a repair in line 8 after a pause. This repair initiator is rendered in line 7, and PO2 repairs the rather vague question (lines 1–2). S2 then responds to the interpreted repaired question in line 16. It is possible that PO2 was aware that the initial question was vague and made it more specific (lines 11–12) despite the fact that the repair initiator requested a repetition rather than a specification (miscommunication caused by questions modified through repairs by interviewing officers will be discussed in Section 5.5.2). As far as the interpreter is concerned, the *animator* role (Goffman, 1981), in which he speaks in the first person *as if* he is a primary speaker, is maintained throughout this sequence. This is the 'default' role expected of legal interpreters who are expected to maintain impartiality and accuracy. The above extract shows a successful repair sequence following the normal turn-taking organisation of interpreter-mediated interaction.

5.3.1.1 *Shifting from the normal format to institutional intervention*

Repair sequences may expand if miscommunication is not resolved after a single attempt at repair. Extract 5.2 gives an example in which the suspect does not understand one of the terms used in the rendition of a question. It occurs towards the end of Interview 2, when the interviewing officer asks S2 if the answers he has given were voluntarily provided, of his own 'free will'. The interpreter, except for the first repair, attempts to adhere to the *animator* role, and the miscommunication is only finally resolved by an explanation offered by a second police officer who intervenes by interrupting the interpreter.

Extract 5.2 (Interview 2)

```
 1  PO2:  Have the answers you have given du- have the
 2         answers you have given, (.) during this
 3         interview, (.) been made of your own free
 4         will,
 5         (0.6)
 6  IR2:  .hhh ee, kono desu n[e:]
            (Uh, you know,)
 7  S2:                      [Ha]i.
                              (Yes.)
 8  IR2:  Ano: jijoochooshu: intabyuu (.) noaidani,=
            (Um during this interview- interview,)
 9  S2:   =Hai.
            (Yes.)
10  IR2:  .hh ano: (0.2) kotae o (.) iimashita ne,=
            (.hh um you gave answers you know)
11  S2:   =Hai.=
            (Yes.)
12  IR2:  =Shitsumon kikarete,
            (when you were asked questions.)
13  S2:   Hai.
            (Yes.)
14  IR2:  Sore anatano jiyuuishi ni yoru mono desu ka?
            (Is that in your free will?)
15         (1.1)
→ 16  S2:   Jiyuu- jyu[u-],
            (Free- free-)
→ 17  IR2:            [Ji]yuuishi ni yoru mono desu ka?
                      (Is that in your free will?)
18         (1.3)
→ 19  S2:   Jiyuuishi tteiimasu to:, °chotto wakannai°=
            (What do you mean by free will, I don't quite
            understand.)
→ 20  IR2:  =What do you mean by f[ree will. ]
21  S2:                        [°Jiyuuishi] tte°,
                                (What's free will?)
→ 22  PO2:  Have you given answers freely of your own
23         choice.
24  S2:   Jiss[ai]
            (In reality)
```

```
25  IR2:     [An]o: tsumari [jib]unde: (0.2) erande
             (Um that is, it means you chose,)
26  S2:                    [Hai].
                           (Yes.)
27  IR2:  desu ne,
          (you know,)
28  S2:   Hai.
          (Yes.)
29        (0.3)
30  IR2:  Ano jiyuu ni kotaeta to.
          (your answers and responded freely.)
31        (0.5)
32  S2:   Sore [wa ji]-
33        (Does that mean re-)
34  IR2:       [Sokuba]ku naku kotaeta to[iu koto desu
          (Is it the case you answered without
35  S2:                              [Sooiu wake ja
                                     (It's not really
36  IR3:  ka]?
          being influenced?)
37  S2:   na]ku te, jissai atta koto o .hh watashi wa
          (the case but I told what happened in
38        (.) itte[masu.]
          reality.)
→  39  IR2:           [I just] told [you] what had happened.
40  S2:                           [Hai].
                                  (Yes.)
41  S2:   Sooi[u:]
          (That)
42  IR2:    [an]d what happened.
43        (0.2)
44  S2:   hanashi [o, sh- shita] tsumori desu.
          (I believe I've told you that sort of thing.)
45  IR2:         [The fact ( )].
46        (0.4)
47  IR2:  °Well° I just think I uh I told you.
48        (0.6)
→  49  PO2:  °Yes°. So your answers were given of your own
50        free will.
51  IR2:  Ah tsumari: anatano jiyuuishi ni motozuite
```

```
      52            yatta toiu koto desu ne,.hh
                    (Uh so it is the case that you did it on a
                    voluntary basis, isn't it.)
  →   53   S2:      Jissai yoosuruni ano: atta koto o nobeta tte
      54            koto wa, (.) sooiu koto desu ka,
                    So um that I stated what happened in reality,
                    is that what it means?)
      55            (0.5)
  →   56   IR2:     Well u:m
      57            (0.5)
  →   58   POa:     The explanation, (.) did anyone make (0.4) him
      59            answer the way he answered or was it by his
      60            own choice (.) that he answered how he
      61            answered.
      62   IR2:     .hhhh ano tsumari desu ne: dareka ga sono
      63            kooiufuuni kotaenasai toka, (.) iufuuni
                    (.hhhh um so you know, someone uh pressured you
                    like 'you should answer this way')
      64   S2:      Ah ah ah [ah ah],
                    (Oh right right right right.)
      65   IR2:              [Anata] ni atsuryoku o kaketa toka,
                    (or something like that)
      66   S2:      Hai hai.
                    (Yes yes.)
      67            (0.4)
      68   IR2:     Sooiukoto wa (0.5) arimasuka = [soretomo
                    (was that the case? Or did you)
      69   S2                                      [ya >sooko-
      70   S2:      sooiu wake janai desu].<
                    (No, it wasn't like tha- that.)
      71   IR2:     s- s- sono jibunde] (0.2) jibunde (0.2)
      72            jibunkara kotaeta [ndes]u ka?
                    (uh uh uh answer by yourself by yourself
                    voluntarily?)
      73   S2:                        [Hai,]
      74            jibunkara kotaeta.
                    (Yes, I answered voluntarily.)
```

At line 16, the suspect has trouble either understanding or picking up the word '*jiyuuishi*' provided as the translation of 'free will'. IR2 seems to regard S2's partial repetition of the term as S2 not having caught the word in full, and repeats the last part of the rendition containing the word '*jiyuuishi*'. This is an example of an 'aside', in which the interpreter directly engages in solving the miscommunication with one of the primary speakers rather than translating the repair initiator (Komter, 2005). S2 then asks for a definition of the word in line 19. This time, IR2 renders the repair initiator as an *animator*, and PO2 repairs in lines 22–23. In the institutional framework of police interviews, the answer expected here is a simple 'yes', but S2 does not respond immediately (line 31). This seems to prompt IR2 to elaborate on the notion of 'answering freely' and adds 'answered without being influenced' (line 34) to the rendition. This addition may be considered as a self-repair of the translation in the preceding turn in line 30, but can also be regarded as IR2's attempt to *explain* the word rather than *translate*, especially given that S2's turn (line 32) was interrupted by this turn.

However, S2 gives an answer in lines 35–38, which shows that he still has not understood the question and the legal framework in which it is embedded. From this answer it may be deduced that he may have interpreted 'answering from his free will' as 'making up his own stories as he pleases'. Since S2's answer does not satisfy the legal requirement for admissibility of evidence, PO2 initiates a repair in lines 49 and 50, repeating the core part of the original question containing the trouble source term 'free will'. Maintaining the *animator* role, IR2 again uses the faithful translation of the term '*jiyuuishi*' in his rendition (line 51). S2 then initiates yet another repair, the term '*jiyuuishi*' having caused a comprehension problem. IR2 takes a turn, but after a hesitation, a 0.5 second pause follows, making his interactional stance ambiguous (cf. Komter, 2005). One possible option is to translate what S2 says, which will be another trouble source for PO2, while the other option is to explain that S2 is having a problem with the term 'free will'. At this point, however, PO2's assisting officer (POa) intervenes and provides an explanation of the question, in which the proposition is presented in a lower register. S2 comes to an understanding and denies having been coerced or influenced by the interviewer during the interview (lines 69–70).

It is noteworthy that POa's turn starts without waiting for IR2's rendition of S2's turn in lines 53–54. The use of the phrase 'The explanation' which prefaces his turn (lines 58–61) suggests that the interviewing officers probably had a prepared explanation for occasions when suspects had comprehension problems with the notion of answering from one's 'free will' and its legal meaning. If this misunderstanding is not uncommon, then it was reasonable for the interpreter to focus on translation activity instead of trying to solve a problem that had more of an institutional than a linguistic or interactional nature.

The source of miscommunication in this extract was S2's lack of knowledge of the legal term '*jiyuuishi*' (free will), but his misunderstanding, emerging after PO2's first explanation (or repair), suggests that there was also a 'global trouble source', a concept which refers to 'the different interlocutors' respective views, beliefs and attitudes in relation to subject matter, to the encounter and to one another' (Wadensjö, 1998, p. 202). As suggested by Rock (2007) and Heydon (2005) in their discussion of monolingual police interviews, formal language about the interview itself in the opening and closing phases of the interview tends to cause suspects problems of understanding. S2 was probably not aware of the legal framework in which police interviews of suspects operated, or of the discourse shift from the 'information gathering' to the 'closing' phase (Heydon, 2005, pp. 53–55) of the interview. S2's turns in this extract shows his concern to claim his truthfulness in his statements, thus to clear the allegation on him, but the officers are trying to elicit the suspect's comment to validate their own behaviour in the interview in order to make it admissible evidence.

This 'global trouble source' may not have been so apparent to the police officers however. Because of POa's interruption of IR2's turn in line 58, S2's repair initiator focusing on telling 'what actually happened' in lines 53–54 was not rendered. Thus, due to the nature of the interpreter-mediated interaction in which 'there is no contiguity between the utterances of the primary speakers' (Komter, 2005, p. 208), the miscommunication is repaired at the local level but not at the global level. POa's institutional power and schema also enabled his intervention to resolve the communication problem. This however came at the expense of blocking the rendition of S2's turn containing the assertion that he had told what happened.

5.3.1.2   *Suspects' attempts to repair problematic questions*

One of the problematic aspects of repair sequences that occur in interpreter-mediated interviews is that the interpreting process may lead to a skewed construction of the trouble source, even in normal format turn-taking organisation in which interpreters engage solely in translatory activities. The next two extracts (5.3 and 5.4) show instances in which interpreting errors lead to miscommunication and suspects attempt to remedy this miscommunication by initiating a repair. In the following extract, interpreting error (presented in Extract 5.3-a) and the subsequent use of the erroneously translated word in English by the police officer leads to the suspect's explicitly pointing out the wrong use of the word. In Extract 5.3-b, the police officer (PO1) asks the suspect (S1) about Mark's 'office', for which the term *'heya'* (room) was used in S1's original utterance. The interpreter has translated this word into 'office' prior to the temporary suspension of the interview (Extract 5.3-a, line 18).

Extract 5.3-a (Interview 1)

```
       1  S1:  Ano: ma,(.) Shookai sareta no ga ano: (0.4) oi
       2       desu kara (0.3) ano: (0.5) soko no: (0.6) Mark
  →    3       no, (0.4) jibunno heya ni (0.6) Wong ga itari
       4       (Um well, the person to whom I was introduced
       5       um was his nephew, so Wong was sometimes um
       6       was in that room, Mark's own room,)
               ((several lines of S1's utterance))
      17  IR1: I've (0.4) er seen uh: Wang when: I visit Mark
  →   18       in his office and he was there,
               ((after a few more exchanges, the interview is
               suspended for a short break))
```

Extract 5.3-b (Interview 1)

```
               ((After a few exchanges in relation to
               recommencing the interview))
       1  PO1: All right. (0.2) Just prior to us ceasing
       2       suspending the taped record of interview,
       3       (0.6) um you mentioned that you had been to:
       4       Mark's office. (0.4) Can you- (.) what can
       5       you tell me about Mark's office.
       6  IR1: Ano izenno teepu no rokuon no toki niwa Mark
  →    7       no jimusho no hooni, ofisu no hoo ni ikareta
       8       toiu kotowo ukagaimashita ga,[nan]i ka (.)
               (Um in the previous tape-recording, we heard
               That you had been to Marks' office, to his
               office, is there anything)
  →    9  S1:                              [ E-]
                                           (What,)
  →   10  IR1: Ah [sono ofi]su nikanshite_
               (Uh about that office)
      11  S1:     [Of: isu ]
                  (Office)
```

```
        12 IR1:  [Oboetemasu k]a,
                 (do you remember?)
 →      13 S1:   [Ofisu janai ]ndesu yo heya tte itte ( )desu
 →      14       yo,(0.4) mae heya tteiu fuuni itta ndesu kedo.
        15       (0.2) [Ofisu janakute]
                 (It's not an office, I said ( ) his room you
                 know, I said 'room' before, not his office. )
        16 IR1:         [well- wasn't r]eally office uh just uh:
        17       Mark's room.
        18       (0.4)
        19 S1:   °Hai.°
                 (Yes.)
        20 PO1:  So, (0.2) that is i- actually (.) his office
        21       is also where he lives.
 →      22 IR1:  Ja Mark ga soko ni sundeiru heya desu ka?
                 (So is that the room where Mark lives?)
        23       (1.4)
        24 S1:   Sun- ya sunderu no wa ano: (0.3) jibun no ie
        25       ni sunderu to omoundesu kedo,=
                 (Liv- no where he lives is um I think he lives
                 in his own house).
        26 IR1:  =no, uh=
        27 S1:   =Jibun no ie tte, okaasan no._
                 (His own house, which is his mother's.)
        28 IR1:  I think uh that's not where he lives. (.) uh I
        29       think he lives with his his mother somewhere?
        30       (0.5)
        31 PO1:  Does he know where this room is.
```

In line 7 of Extract 5.3-b, IR1 uses a Japanese word '*jimusho*' (office)
for 'office' but then switches to the loan word '*ofisu*' (office) in her
rendition in Japanese. Before IR1 completes the rendition, S1 interrupts IR1 (lines 9, 11 and 13) and initiates a repair, pointing out that
'it is not an office' and adding that he 'said "room" before'. At line 14,
there is a short pause after a TRP is reached with the interactional
particle '*yo*', but IR1 neither renders this repair initiator nor produces
a repair turn herself. S1 persists in his correction (lines 14–15). After
another short pause, IR1 renders S1's repair initiator (line 16). This
rendition, however, does not include the projection frame 'I said
before' in S1's turn in line 14. It also contains 'wasn't really', which,
combined with the omission of the projection frame, makes the

translated turn appear to PO1 as if S1 himself, not IR1, were correcting himself.

PO1's next question supports this alternative interpretation as he asks whether S1's associate, Mark, has an office which is also his residence. IR1's rendition of this question neither has a subject (the literal translation would be 'The room in which Mark lives?') nor contains the rendition of 'office', masking the damage created by the incorrect translation 'office', yet at the same time keeping the discourse coherent to PO1.

In this extract, the fact that the problem was to do with interpreting is masked by the omission of the projection frame 'I said before'. In other words, the 'primary reality' (Hale & Gibbons, 1999) of the interview is dropped through interpreting. Such loss of primary reality may conceal from the audience that the statement 'is being constructed in a particular way' (Gibbons, 2003, p. 251). This omission serves to deflect the blame and functions as the interpreter's face saving strategy. Although IR1 made a 'correction', it was presented as a rendition and not brought to the attention of PO1 as an interpreting error. The omission may lead to a possible interpretation by PO1 that S1 corrected 'office' into 'room' so he could downplay the business relationship between himself and Mark. The correction may also be regarded as a sign of inconsistent accounts which could be damaging to S1's case. This is one of the situations in which the interpreter may need to suspend the translation activity and address the miscommunication caused by an interpreting error in a *principal* role.

The following extract shows a similar example, where miscommunication has been caused by an interpreting error, but primary reality concerning interpreting errors is lost through interpreting. In the interaction preceding that shown in Extract 5.4, S3 had mentioned being stopped, upon her arrival in Australia, by customs officials with dogs. This had made her think of dogs sniffing out illegal substances. PO3 uses this idea of dogs brought up by S3 and asks a number of questions to highlight the association of dogs with illegal drugs.

Extract 5.4 (Interview 3)

```
→   1  PO3:  What's: =how does that relate to narcotics,
    2  IR3:  Demo sore wa, mayaku tono kankee wa nan deshoo
    3        ka.
              (But how would that relate to narcotics?)
    4        (1.0)
→   5  S3:   Ano: (.) Narita- Naritakuukoo de .hh nanka
```

→   6   *sooyatte:* (.) *inu ga ite,*
              (Um at Narita Airport, .hh like, there are
              dogs like that and)
    7 IR3:   *Un.*
              (Yeah.)
→   8 S3:   *Ano nioi:: kagiateru toka.*
              (and they sniff things out for example).
    9   (0.5)
→ 10 IR3:   At Narita Airport there were some dogs and
   11   they were sort of you know going around
   12   [sniffing].
→ 13 S3:   [*Kiita ko*]*toaru,* (.) *kiita ndesu kedo.*=
              (I have heard about that, I have heard.)
   14 IR3:   =And she's heard about that,
   15   (1.1)
   16 PO1:   How does she kn*o*w that they are looking for
   17   narc*o*tics,
              ((13 lines, in which a problem arises due to
              IR3's pronunciation))
   31 PO3:   Wh*e*n she saw
   32   (0.2)
   33 IR3:   m[m,]
   34   [th]e d*o*gs in Narita airport,=
   35 IR3:   =mm,
   36   (1.0)
   37 PO3:   h*o*w has she (0.3) come to the concl*u*sion (0.2)
   38   that they were searching for narc*o*tics,
→ 39 IR3:   *Ano* (.) *Naritakuukoo de ano inu o mita to*
   40   *iimashita ga,*=
              (Um you said you saw dogs at Narita Airport,)
→ 41 S3:   =*Iya, mita njaari*[*mase*]*n.*
              (No, I did not see them.)
   42 IR3:   [A,]
                                  (Ah)
   43 IR3:   *Un.*
              (Right.)
   44 S3:   *Hanashi ni kiita ndesu.*
              (I heard about it.)
   45 IR3:   Ah (.) no she didn't actually s*ee*, (.) s*ee*
   46   dogs at that airport =she h*ea*rd a story about
   47   it.

```
   48        (1.6)
→  49  PO3:  Well I'm sure she said a second ago she saw
   50        dogs at Narita airport.
   51        (1.5)
→  52  IR3:  Naritakuukoo: de inu o (0.2) ano mimasen
→  53        deshita ka,
             (Didn't you see dogs at Narita Airport?)
   54  S3:   Mimasen deshita.
             (I didn't see them.)
   55  IR3:  No.
```

In response to the question asking about the relationship between dogs and narcotics, S3 responds by mentioning the dogs used at Narita Airport to locate narcotics (lines 5, 6 and 8). The rendition (lines 10–12) presents the response as based on S3's first-hand experience at Narita airport, but this is problematic. It appears that IR3 missed the '*toka*' (for example/among others) at the end of S3's turn (line 8) and rendered verbs that did not in this context indicate past tense in Japanese (line 6 '*ite*' [there are] and line 8 '*kagiateru*' [sniff out]) into past tense in English. Whether S3 recognised the past tense in the rendition in English or not is uncertain, but somehow she immediately adds in line 32 that she has 'heard about it', to suggest that she did not actually see dogs at Narita Airport. This addition is rendered (line 14), but the use of past tense in the earlier rendition (line 10) means that PO3 understood that S3 had seen dogs at Narita.

The police officer keeps on probing S3's reference to dogs in lines 16–17. However, a comprehension problem due to IR3's pronunciation of '*sagasu*' (to search for) arises (not shown in the extract), and PO3 paraphrases the question in lines 31, 34 and 37–38. This question contains the phrase 'when she saw the dogs', which prompts S3 to interrupt IR3's rendition and initiate a repair in line 41. However, instead of providing a repaired question, in lines 49–50 PO3 accuses S3 of giving contradictory accounts (cf. Drew, 1990), using a projection frame 'she said'. The accusatory tone is emphasised by the use of 'well', 'I'm sure' and 'a second ago'. The police officer also challenges S3 that she said 'she saw dogs at Narita Airport', but neither S3 nor IR3 has said that S3 'saw' dogs. This turn is followed by a 1.5 second pause before IR3 renders it. IR3 may have become aware that miscommunication has occurred due to an interpreting error from an earlier rendition. However, the rendition in lines 52–53 contains neither the features emphasising the accusation nor the projection frame. Again, the primary realities – that

PO3 is sure about his memory of S3's utterance and that he thinks S3 *said* that she saw dogs at Narita – are lost through the interpreting. The primary reality that S3's responses have been negatively evaluated is masked. This omission also puts S3 into a vulnerable situation, casting a negative light on her story and credibility. At the same time, it diffuses the threat to S3's face and a possible conflict between the primary speakers (cf. Mason & Stewart, 2001; Wadensjö, 1998).

These two examples of miscommunication and repair sequences occurring due to interpreting problems suggest that interpreters have the capacity, as the mediator with access to two languages, to redress a translation-related trouble source while engaging in translatory activities and giving the impression that the miscommunication occurred due to a primary speaker's lack of alignment. The normal format of turn-taking requires the interpreter to play an *animator* role, but in these two examples the interpreter role shifts to that of an *author*. Wadensjö (1998) also shows a similar example in which an interpreter omits the police interviewer's explicit comment on misunderstanding, stating that by this move the interpreter 'kept away from giving a possible reason to doubt her own competence' (p. 210).

5.3.2   Repairs initiated by police officers in the normal format of turn-taking

In the four examples of normal format repair sequences above, the trouble source was the interviewing officer's turn with which the suspect had a problem. In the next extract, the trouble sources are the suspect's responses, or the renditions of them. The miscommunication takes some time to resolve because of translation problems and the primary speakers' non-standard turn-taking behaviour. In Extract 5.5 below the police officer (PO4) is asking the suspect (S4) about his contact with Pat, who, S4 claims, gave him a bottle containing stimulant drugs to be taken to Australia as a souvenir.

Extract 5.5 (Interview 4)

```
1  PO4:  U:m the per- (.) Pat, whose name is featured
2        on the business card of XXXTour, uh: (1.5)
3        how many times have you met the person previously.
4  IR4:  Ah hai, Pat san ni wa nankai oaishita koto ga
5        arimasu?
       (Ah yes, how many times have you met Pat?)
```

```
    6        (0.3)
    7  S4:   Ya Ikkai dake desu [sono].=
             (Well only once, that time.)
    8  IR4:                   [Only] once.
    9  PO4:  Only once? = And was that at the airport?
→  10  IR4:  Sorega, (.) [kuukoo ]
             (That's- airport)
→  11  S4:               [Eapooto] ni (.) iku: made.=
             (Travelling to the airport.)
→  12  PO4:  =Oka[y],
   13  IR4:     [E]e.
   14  PO4:  W[ho arran-]
→  15  IR4:   [on the wa]y to airport.
   16  PO4:  On the way to the air- whereabouts on the
   17        way to the airport.
→  18  IR4:  .hh ee dokokara eh: ( [        ] made)
             (.hh um from where uh to [ ])
   19  S4:                         [Tai no::](.) Sentoraru
   20        Hoteru no naka.
             (Inside the Central Hotel in Thailand.)
   21  IR4:  Ah, (0.2) from the Central Hotel in: (0.2)
   22        <Thai[la:nd].>
   23  S4:        [Machi]awase ga Sentoraru Hoteru datta
   24        node:=
             (Because we were to meet at the Central
             Hotel.)
   25  IR4:  =Yeah, I met her at the Central Hotel.
→  26  PO4:  °Right° so you met her at the Central Hotel on
   27        the way to the airport = is that correct?
   28  IR4:  De Sentoraru Hoteru kara [eapooto no (hoo) ]
             (And you went from the Central Hotel to
   29  S4:                           [Takushii ni notte],
                                      (By taxi)
   30  IR4:  ni itta.=
             (the airport.)
   31  S4:   =Ee ee, soo desu.=
             (Yes, yes, that's right.)
   32  IR4:  =Yes.
   33  PO4:  And [is]
   34  IR4:      [By] taxi.
```

→ 35 PO4: Uh er by t<u>a</u>xi? (.) Was she travelling in the
   36   t<u>a</u>xi with you?
   37 IR4: .hh de sono Pat san m<u>o</u> sono: takushii no naka
   38   ni [irashita] ndesu ka?=
              (.hh and was that Pat also uh in the taxi?)
   39 S4:   [Hai, hai]
              (Yes, yes.)
   40 IR4: [°*Takushii wa*]°
              (Taxi)
   41 S4: [*isshoni itte*], (0.4) *Ryoogae mo isshoni yat-*
              (We went together, and she also assisted me
   42 IR4: Yeah.=
   43 S4: *yat*[*te moratta ndesu*].
              with changing money.)
   44 IR4:   [and then h<u>e</u> exch]anged the m<u>o</u>ney to
   45   Australian d<u>o</u>llars.
→ 46 PO4: Oka:y, uh h- h<u>ow</u> come: (0.2) you wer-, i- (.)
   47   when you were travelled in the ho-, did you
   48   travel from the hotel to the airport w<u>i</u>th Pat?
   49 IR4: *Sorede*, .hh e: (0.2) *Sentoraru Hoteru kar<u>a</u>*
   50   *kyuukoo made no aid<u>a</u> wa Pat san toissho n<u>i</u>*
   51   *takushii ni no*[*tta nde*]*su ne?*=
              (And then .hh uh from the Central Hotel to the
              airport you were in a taxi with Pat, right?)
   52 S4:   [*Soodesu*].
                  (That's right.)
   53 IR4: =Y<u>es</u>.

The rapid pace of turn-taking and frequent interruptions are apparent
in this extract. The interpreter (IR4) struggles to hold the floor, and her
difficulty in rendering the primary speakers' utterances appears to be one
of the causes of miscommunication (see Wadensjö, 1998 for fragmentation of discourse in relation to miscommunication). For example, in line
10 before she was able to produce a full rendition of PO4's question, S4
provides his response. The rendition would have been '*kuukoo de desu ka?*'
(lit. 'was it at the airport?') but rather than waiting for the TRP (Transition
Relevance Place), S4 responds with '*Eapooto ni iku made*' (lit. until I/we
arrived at the airport, that is, travelling to the airport). S4 blocks IR4's
sentence before the core verb of the sentence 'atta' (met) is produced, and
he himself does not produce the main clause, which makes the exchange

vulnerable to miscommunication. Moreover, when PO4 hears the loan word *'eapooto'* in S4's response, he assumes the answer to be affirmative, and latches onto S4's response, acknowledging the response (line 12). However, since PO4 blocked the interpreter's rendition, his understanding is that it was *at* the airport that S4 *met* Pat, and has not realised that it was during the trip to the airport that S4 was with Pat. (For a similar problem of not waiting for a rendition when meaning is assumed to have been understood without translation, see Dimitrova, 1997.) IR4 is therefore the only interlocutor who becomes aware of the miscommunication at this point, and she interrupts PO4's next question (line 14) to render S4's response in line 11 to clarify where S4 met Pat. This however leads to another layer of miscommunication due to the translation of the particle *'made'* (to) (line 11) into 'on the way to' (line 15). PO4's question in line 16 suggests that his new understanding is that S4 met Pat at one location *on the way to* but not *at* the airport.

The divergent understanding of the location of the meeting between S4 and Pat persists when PO4's question (line 16) is rendered with *'doko kara'* (from where) in line 18. S4's response is 'inside the Central Hotel in Thailand', although *'kara'* (from) may be assumed here as its ellipsis would be grammatically possible. IR4's rendition of this response in lines 21–22 is coherent with her rendition 'from where' (line 18) but not totally so with PO4's original question (line 16–17) as he is referring to a place *at* which the meeting occurred. IR4 may have become aware of this divergent understanding when she slows down her speech in line 22, but when S4 says their rendezvous point was the hotel, IR4 quickly renders the statement that S4 'met her at the Central Hotel', which is a more coherent response than the previous response in line 21–22. Had it not been for S4's self-selected elaboration on his response in line 23, in the normal format of turn-taking it would have been PO4's turn to either clarify the preceding response or ask a new question. The preposition 'from' in line 21 may have prompted PO4 to initiate a repair following IR4's rendition. However, PO4 ignores this earlier rendition in line 21 and attends to the immediately preceding rendition turn (line 25), and initiates a repair to clarify, in lines 26–27, exactly where the meeting took place.

The rendition of this repair initiator, however, contains neither the translation of 'you met her at' (line 26) nor any nominative or objective pronouns in Japanese. The particle *'kara'* (from) appears again in *'Sentoraru Hoteru kara'* (from the Central Hotel). Since IR4 heard at line 11 that S4 was with Pat *traveling to* the airport, this rendition is sill discursively coherent as far as the Japanese sequence goes. However, it seems that IR4 is not aware of the divergent assumptions on where the meeting is assumed to have occurred – in one location in PO4's mind but between the hotel and the airport in the minds of IR4 and S4. Since IR4 and S4 share their assumption, the ellipsis-laden rendition in lines 28 and 30 causes no problem to S4, who responds with an affirmative response (line 31). However, the first part of his response '*Takushii ni notte*' (in the taxi) overlaps IR4's rendition of the question (lines 28–29), and IR4 renders the part of the response that was produced after the overlap (lines 31–32). Before IR4 can then produce the rendition of the overlapped part of S4's response, PO4 starts asking the next question (line 33). At this point, PO4 understands that the meeting took place at the hotel before S4 made his way to the airport. Therefore PO4 is taken by surprise when IR4 interrupts his question and renders 'By taxi' (line 34), and he initiates a repair with the repetition of the trouble source 'By taxi?' followed by a clarification request as to whether Pat was travelling in the taxi with him. Again, the suspect's overlapping talk delays the rendition of an important piece of information ('by taxi'), by which time the interviewing officer has formed a certain understanding based on the rendition that he has heard so far. The miscommunication and PO4's confusion become obvious in his stuttering speech 'h- how come' (line 46) in his next turn.

In the above extract, the interpreter remained in an *animator* role and did not engage in problem solving using 'asides' as a *principal*. However, because the primary speakers initiated their turns too early or deviated from the normative turn-taking format and self-selected their turns without waiting for interpreter rendition, they aggravated the miscommunication caused by problematic translation. While the interviewing officer managed to solve the miscommunication and came to the same understanding of the meeting between S4 and Pat in the end, neither of the primary speakers had any way of knowing the causes of the miscommunication. It should also be noted that S4 was possibly not aware of the miscommunication since the contextualisation cues signalling divergent understanding (for example, line 35 'er by taxi?' and line 46 'how come-') were not rendered. It is also possible that IR4 may not have been aware that the root cause of the divergent understanding was her use and understanding of the term 'on the way'.

The analysis of repair sequences with 'normal format' turn-taking organisation above suggests that, while interpreters can remain in the *animator* role and let the primary speakers deal with miscommunication by themselves, the nature of interpreter-mediated tripartite interaction does not always guarantee an orderly eight-part repair sequence. This can be due to a lack of contiguity in turn-taking or a lack of access to contextualisation cues in the other's language. Overlaps and early turn-taking allow for premature processing of information before a full rendition of the primary speaker turn is completed, and miscommunication may persist for several turns.

This section examined repair sequences mediated by the interpreter in the normal format of turn-taking organisation. This is the 'text-book' and normative framework for resolving miscommunication in interpreter-mediated interaction. However, interpreting errors, overlapping talk, interruptions, premature assumptions and interpreter role-shifts from *animator* to *author* can complexify, and sometimes worsen, miscommunication. The problems in the repair sequences discussed above are more detrimental to the suspects, but in those cases where the police officers were confused, they are prevented from eliciting accurate information concerning the crime and from constructing their preferred version of events.

In the next section, repairs initiated by one of the primary speakers and repaired by the interpreter will be examined. In these cases, repair sequences deviate from the 'normal format' of turn-taking since repairs take place in 'asides', or side sequences, between the primary speaker and the interpreter.

5.4 Repairs initiated by primary speakers: interpreter-repaired

This section examines repairs initiated by one of the primary speakers and responded to directly, if not repaired, by the interpreter. The police interpreter may at times abandon translation activities and engage in dealing with miscommunication themselves, taking the role of a *principal*. As mentioned earlier, this creates a repair sequence as an 'aside', containing content which one of the primary speakers cannot access. First, examples of repairs initiated by suspects and responded to by interpreters will be examined, and then officer-initiated repairs responded to by interpreters are discussed.

5.4.1 Repairs initiated by suspects in asides

5.4.1.1 *Repair initiation used as a discourse strategy of delaying*

Extract 5.6 shows an example of a repair sequence in which the interpreter (IR2) and the suspect (S2) temporarily engage in an 'aside' in Japanese. S2 initiates a repair after PO2's question has been rendered.

Extract 5.6 (Interview 2)

```
 1 PO2: Who- who paid, (0.2) who paid (0.2) for
 2       the ticket.
 3 IR2: Dare ga, okane o haraimashita ka?
         (Who paid the money?)
 4       (0.8)
→ 5 S2:  Dare ga desu ka?=
         (Do you mean who?)
→ 6 IR2: =Hai, kono hikooki no.
         (Yes, for these flights.)
→ 7 S2:  Hikooki no oka[ne desu ka,]
         (Do you mean the airfare?)
→ 8 IR2:              [okane wa dare]
 9       [ga harai mashita ka]?
         (Who paid the money?)
10 S2:   [Sore wa watashi no] otooto.
         (That is my brother.)
11       (0.3)
12 IR2:  Oh, that's my brother.
```

S2's repair initiation in line 5 is a partial repetition of IR2's rendition of PO2's question, which was asked prior to this stretch of interaction. Instead of rendering this repair initiator, IR2 responds, of his own accord, by providing a clarification with *'Hai'* (Yes) and referring to the flights that S2 took. S2 then produces another repair initiator (line 7) with *'hikooki no'* (of the flights) as the trouble source. Yet again the repair initiator is not rendered into English for the interviewing officer, but instead the repair turn comes from IR2 in lines 8–9. This repair turn is an interruption as it starts overlapping S2's turn before its TRP, at the end of line 7. Moreover, IR2's repair turn does not provide an answer to the question in S2's repair initiator. Instead, IR2 asks a question, reiterating his rendition in line 3.

In this stretch of talk, IR2 takes the role of an interrogator by not only engaging in repair sequences with S2 in Japanese but also by not providing the type of repair prompted by S2's second repair initiator. This interactional choice seems to be driven by the commitment to elicit an answer to the police officer's question. In other words, the interpreter's role shifted from that of an *animator* to a *principal*. This role shift by IR2 is inappropriate in terms of the impartiality required in the interpreting code of ethics (see Chapter 2, Section 2.2.3), and as part of the legal process.

However, there is a contextual factor that is likely to have motivated IR2 to engage in this 'aside'. Prior to the above interaction, S2 had been asked who had paid for his and his girlfriend's airline tickets, but he repeatedly responded, 'The airfare has already been paid'. To address the miscommunication, IR2 had explained to the police officer the grammatical structure of Japanese that S2 was using in his responses, namely the ellipsis of the agent of the verb 'pay' and use of 'airfare' as the topic of the sentence. Thus, it is reasonable to say that S2's repair initiators in the above extract (lines 5 and 7) are likely to be delaying devices (Pomerantz, 1984, pp. 70–71) or reluctance markers (Blimes, 1988, p. 173), instead of genuine attempts to resolve miscommunication, since S2 had not previously avoided answering the same question from PO2. IR2's interruption and recycling of an earlier rendition of PO2's question in lines 8–9 suggests that he regarded S2's repair initiators as avoidance or delaying strategies, and that as the mediator, he was frustrated by S2's reluctance to provide a simple answer to a simple question. S2's second repair initiator in line 7 starts with '*Hikooki no okane*' (The airfare). This was exactly the same phrase used earlier (not presented in the transcript) by S2 when he said '*Hikooki no okane wa moo harattearu*' (The airfare has already been paid) in response to the earlier question regarding who paid the airfare. IR2 may have foreseen the recycling of this response by S2 when he heard the same sentence initial phrase in line 7 and therefore interrupted S2 with the 'who' question in line 8.

Thus, the interpreter in this case temporarily took control of questioning as a pursuer of relevant information, and in that sense took over the police interviewer's power. From the suspect's point of view, the interpreter's decision not to stick with the normal format of turn-taking may have shortened the duration of the delay, if the repair initiation moves had indeed been intended as delaying strategies. In fact, this could be a strategy of the 'grammar of non-agency' which suspects or defendants may use as a resistance strategy (Berk-Seligson, 2009, p. 90; see also Ehrlich, 2001). However, because the police officer did not have access to the repair sequence contents and, in the end, a preferred second pair part to the first pair part of the main sequence was produced, the above repair sequence may have shielded the suspect from being perceived as evasive by the officer.

5.4.1.2 *Previous rendition as the trouble source*

The above extract shows a clear example of the interpreter taking up a role as a problem solver and even assisting the interviewing officer as an

interrogator, but 'asides' between the suspect and the interpreter may
also be used for a more subtle off-the-record strategy for dealing with
miscommunication. In Extract 5.7, the interviewing officer (PO3) asks
the suspect (S3) whether she was met by anyone after clearing customs.

Extract 5.7 (Interview 3)

```
→   1  PO3:  Was she met by anybody then,
    2        (0.5)
→   3  IR3:  Sono tokini dareka ni ano mukaeraremashita ka,
             (Were you um met by someone then?)
    4        (1.2)
    5  S3:   Soto de: (.) mukaeraremashita.
             (Outside I was met [by someone].)
    6  IR3:  Um outside we were, yes.
    7  PO3:  .hh who was that person.=
    8  IR3:  =Sono hito wa dare deshita ka?
             (Who was that person?)
    9  S3:   >Wakarimasen.<
             (I don't know.)
   10  IR3:  I don't know,
   11        (1.5)
→  12  PO3:  Why did she meet that person.
→  13  IR3:  Naze sonohito ni aimashita ka,
             (Why did you see that person?)
   14        (0.8)
→  15  S3:   [Wakari]masen.
             (I don't know/I don't understand.)
→  16  IR3:  [Sono hi]-
             (That per-)
   17        (0.3)
→  18  IR3:  Sono hito wa naze ano mukaeni kimashita ka?
             (Why did that person um come to meet you?)
   19        (0.5)
   20  S3:   Annai no hito da tte ittemashita.=
             (They said he was the guide.)
   21  IR3:  =It was- it was a- a tour guide.
```

The verb 'met' in PO3's question in line 1 is rendered into Japanese
with the verb '*mukaeru*' (to meet/welcome someone). S3 did not have a
problem with this question. After saying she does not know who the
person who met them was, S3 is asked why she met that person (line 12).

She does not respond to the question for 0.8 seconds, at which point the interpreter (IR3) starts to render another translation of PO3's question in line 12. This rendition overlaps with S3's response in line 15 '*Wakarimasen*'. Because this phrase means either 'I don't know' or 'I don't understand' depending on the context, it may be an indication of lack of knowledge as to why someone came to meet them at the airport, or of a comprehension difficulty with the rendition or with the point of the original question. Either way, S3's utterance in line 15 is not rendered but followed by a repaired rendition of the question. This indicates that the pause in line 14 and S3's subsequent response were perceived by IR3 as a repair initiator and that IR3 regarded these as indications of a problem in understanding the rendition in Japanese (for a discussion of silence as a repair initiator, see Chapter 6).

IR3's perception of the trouble source may derive from the fact that he has used different Japanese words for the verb 'meet' in PO3's questions. The agent of the verb 'meet' in PO3's first question in line 1 'Was she met...' was 'anybody', but in the second question (line 12) the verb is used in the active voice ('Why did she meet...') with S1 as the subject. Thus, the meaning of the verb 'meet' changes from 'go to a place and wait for someone' to 'come together with someone'. For these two meanings of the verb 'meet', Japanese has two different verbs – '*mukaeru*' and '*au*' – and therefore, in the translation of the second question (line 12), provided 'she' is the subject of the verb 'meet' in the active voice, the verb '*au*' should be used. Thus, the polite past tense of '*au*', '*aimashita*', is used in the rendition in line 13. However, after perceiving a problem, IR3 repairs his rendition in line 18 by changing the subject from 'you' (omitted) to '*sono hito*' (that person) and the verb '*au*' to '*mukae ni kuru*' (to come to meet), which is a compound verb of '*mukaeru*' (meet) and '*kuru*' (come). S3 then responds to the question with a reason for which 'that person' came to meet her.

In the above interaction, the interpreter recognises miscommunication and attempts to solve it by quickly repairing his rendition, without rendering what he has perceived as a repair initiator. Since he was focused on translatory activities through the repair sequence, we could say that he attempted to repair (what he perceived as) miscommunication from an *author* role. However, there is an ambiguity in relation to the addressee of the suspect's response to the police interviewer's question. This is because of the dual meaning of the phrase '*Wakarimasen*' and the fact that there are two preceding turns in different languages to which this turn is directed. The interpreter therefore faces a challenging situation in which two potential interactional contexts exist, to one of which a possible repair initiator can be linked. The problem with this is that the judgment that the interpreter makes about the trouble source has an impact on the interview as an investigative process. If IR3 had rendered S3's response at line 16, PO3 may have regarded it as S3's refusal to answer the question and cooperate (cf. Newbury & Johnson, 2006). PO3 may have become suspicious (Kurzon, 1995) and the trajectory of questioning may have changed. PO3's question in line 12 also implies that S3 is an active participant in the organisation of the tour, while the repaired rendition in line 18 casts S3 as a passive participant. Thus, non-rendition of line 15 (*'Wakarimasen'*) and S3's response in line 20 (although S3's passivity is reduced as the reported speech is turned into direct speech through the translation) makes S3 a cooperative interviewee in the eyes of the interviewer. Without the repair sequence this may not have been the case.

Although by no means exhaustive, the above examples show some of the discursive contexts in which interpreters may withhold the renditions of suspects' repair initiators. The examples include facilitation of investigation when the interviewee is not forthcoming with information, and when the interpreter has some doubts about the rendition preceding the repair initiator.

5.4.2   Repairs initiated by police officers in asides

5.4.2.1   Interpreter as a cultural expert

Asides between the police officer and the interpreter were also found in the contexts where the former relies on the latter as a cultural or linguistic expert. In Extract 5.8, the police office (PO1) and the interpreter (IR1) interact in a side sequence, where PO1 relies on the cultural and linguistic expertise of the interpreter as a competent bicultural/bilingual speaker. PO1 requests a clarification in relation to the place name 'Chiba', where Narita Airport, the airport from which the suspect (S1) departed, is located.

Extract 5.8 (Interview 1)

```
1 PO1:  Which (0.2) city is that airport a part of.
2 IR1:  A kono narita kuukoo wa dono toshi ni
3        arimasu ka?
        (Uh Narita airport which city is this part
        of?)
        (0.3)
4 S1:   E:tto (1.5) °Chiba desu°.
```

```
      5  IR1:  I think it's in uh Chiba prefecture.
               (I think it is in Chiba prefecture.)
      6         (1.2)
      7  S1:   Chiba: ken desu, °kuukoo°,
               (It's in Chiba prefecture, the airport.)
      8         (0.4)
→     9  PO1:  Is that a city?
     10         (0.4)
→    11  IR1:  That's the name of the prefecture.
     12         (0.5)
→    13  PO1:  I'm sorry = Can you explain what- >what you
     14         mean< by the prefecture.
     15         (0.6)
     16         ((PO1 clears his throat))
→    17  IR1:  Uh it's more a type of state uh: Japan, we
     18         have Japan here, (.) and uh we have uh: many
     19         prefectures like uh equivalent to states in
     20         Australia (here).
```

The rendition of S1's answer in line 5 involves additions and refers to 'Chiba prefecture' (this may be due to the fact that the airport does not belong to Chiba city but to Chiba prefecture). It is possible that the 1.2 second silence is caused by PO1's unfamiliarity with the notion of 'prefecture', the official translation of the Japanese term for an administrative division. As if to clarify his earlier answer, S1 at this point self-repairs and adds *'ken'* (prefecture) and *'kuukoo'* (Airport) in line 7. This is not rendered and PO1 initiates a repair to clarify the meaning of 'prefecture' in line 9. IR1 at this point interprets this repair initiator as directed towards herself as a cultural expert and responds to the initiator herself without rendering it in Japanese. Thus the interpreter shifts her role from that of an *animator* to a *principal*. She stays in the *principal* role in her next turn (lines 17–20) explaining the administrative division system in Japan. As part of the investigation process, the content of this 'aside' between PO1 and IR1 is not directly relevant to the case or the issue of culpability. However, the treatment of the two repair initiators is highly relevant to the analysis of interactional dynamics. Neither of the initiators has any element which indicates the addressee. Non-verbal cues such as eye-gaze may have indicated that the addressee was IR1. From IR1's point of view, since it was she who introduced the term 'prefecture' which was absent in the source utterance, it becomes natural for her to respond directly to the repair. However, S1's self-repair containing the term 'ken' (prefecture) also makes a repair turn by S1 relevant. Nevertheless IR1 responds to the initiator herself. The second initiator, in lines 13–14, is also responded to by IR1 even though the referent of 'you' in line 13 in the 'normal format' of turn-taking would be the suspect. This is probably because there is a shared understanding that the interpreter's role is that of a cultural expert in this particular sequence. Similar examples have been reported in studies of courtroom interpreting where interpreters played a role as a cultural expert (for example, Berk-Seligson, 1990; Niska, 1995).

5.4.2.2 *Repair initiation as a discourse strategy?*

As was the case with the suspect's use of repair initiation, the next example contains a possibly similar treatment of repair initiation as a delaying strategy by the interpreter, except that the repair is initiated by the interviewing officer. In Extract 5.9, the interpreter (IR3) directly responds in English (line 7) to the police officer's confirmation request regarding the nationality of a driver involved in the case (line 6). Unlike the 'expert explanation' in the above extract, it is a simple repetition of the trouble source.

Extract 5.9 (Interview 3)

```
      1  PO3:  What nationality was he.
      2  IR3:  Untenshusan wa nanijin deshita ka?
                (What nationality was the driver?)
      3        (0.5)
      4  S3:   Eeto: (0.4) Nihonjin ja nai desu.
                (Uhm He wasn't Japanese.)
      5  IR3:  He wasn't Japanese.
                (1.0)
  →   6  PO3:  He wasn't Japanese,=
  →   7  IR3:  =He wasn't Japanese.
```

It is possible that PO3 asked for confirmation in line 6, after being taken aback by S3's identification of the driver as not Japanese and expecting an affirmative response with a specific nationality. IR4, however, responds to this repair initiator directly. Strictly speaking, the lack of rendition, and direct response, is not appropriate. If the nationality of the driver was to have become a contentious issue in the investigation, then the fact that it had been the interpreter, not the suspect, who had *confirmed* that the driver was not Japanese may have been a problem in terms of legal processes.

However, given that both of the possible trouble-source turns (lines 4 and 5) are straightforward and clearly articulated, and that PO3's repair initiator is also an exact repetition of the trouble source in English, it is possible that the repair initiator may have been a 'delaying device' (Pomerantz, 1984, pp. 70–71) which was used as a sort of filler while the received information is 'digested' and the next question is being formed. IR3's quick turn-taking with latching in offering a repair turn with an exact repetition implies his perception of this function of repair.

Another trigger for this quick repair turn by the interpreter could be the natural conversational orientation to attend to the immediately preceding turn (Levinson, 1983; Sacks et al., 1974). Even if the problem derives from the primary speaker's original utterance and not the interpreter's rendition turn, the interpreter may find it difficult to maintain an *animator* role, especially in the face-to-face consecutive mode of interpreting, as it is easy for the primary speaker to direct their gaze towards the interpreter who has just produced the immediately preceding turn.

The problem is that S3 may have given more details, if the repair initiator had been rendered instead of being directly responded to by the interpreter. The direct repair by IR3 eliminates the possibility of the police officer eliciting more specific information and of the suspect giving more information if she had wished to. Whether or not she had wished to, the repair by the interpreter worked to block the officer from probing further.

5.4.2.3 Previous rendition perceived as the trouble source by the interpreter

In the next example (Extract 5.10) of a repair initiation by the police officer (PO4), the interpreter (IR4) also directly responds to a request for clarification repairs, but in this case she repairs her own rendition, in English (lines 8–9), of the suspect's response (lines 6–7).

Extract 5.10 (Interview 4)

```
1 PO4:  How were you going to travel from the airport
2       to the hotel,
3 IR4:  .hh (.) de kuukou kara:, hoteru made wa
4       donoyouni iku yotei deshita,
        (And how did you plan to travel from the
        airport to the hotel?)
5       (0.4)
6 S4:   M- mada nanimo kangaetenai toki ni kore de
```

```
         7           hh kore [hh dattande heh heh]
                     (Before I thought about anything, because this
                     happened, heh heh)
         8  IR4:                [Ah hah ha: .hhh but] before I think
         9           about tha:t, I was already arrested. (.)
        10           U:[hm I was]
    →   11  PO4:     [What, so]rry?=
    →   12  IR4:     =I- I was already suspended,
        13  PO4:     Right?
    →   14  IR4:     The- before I think about how to get there.
        15  PO4:     Okay.
```

IR4 makes three changes: the sequence of the clauses, the replacement of 'arrested' with 'suspended', and specifying the pronoun 'that' from 'think about that'. PO4 accepts this clarification in line 15. The suspect is probably referring to his arrest when he says '*kore dattande*' ('this happened', line 7), using a gesture of being arrested. Both the trouble source and the nature of the repair initiator by PO4 (line 11) could be interpreted in a number of ways. The trouble source could be S4's response in lines 6–7 which is indirect and not the preferred response, which would have been the transport which S4 had planned to take from the airport. PO4's 'Sorry?' could signal mishearing or hearing doubts but it could be because the unexpected response took him by surprise. It is also possible that the meaning-based translation of the source utterance, turning the subordinate clause ('because this happened') into the main clause ('I was already arrested') may have caused PO4 confusion. The use of non-verbal communication by S4 and the possible attempt by IR4 to self-repair her rendition in line 10 may indicate that IR4 felt unsure, by line 10, about her rendition of S4's answer. This explains her move to repair the rendition in line 12 in response to PO4's repair initiator instead of translating it.

The analysis of the example above, along with Extract 5.5 above where there could have been two possible trouble sources, suggests that the interpreter's perceptions of the source of miscommunication have a significant impact on the interview discourse, because of the nature of turn-taking organisation. The interpreter's turn occurs every other turn and interpreters hold the power to decide what went wrong and how to act on it, at times regardless of the police officer's perceptions of the trouble source.

5.4.2.4   *Ambiguous trouble sources: interpreter's or suspect's words?*

The following extract shows an example in which miscommunication is directly related to one of the key aspects of the police investigation.

Because the extract is long, it will be presented in three parts as Extracts 5.11-a, b and c. The suspect (S3) had told the police interviewer (PO3) that her suitcase had been stolen during the transit but that the contents of the suitcase came back in a new replacement suitcase before their departure from the transit location. S3 says a suitcase was leased and brought to her with her original belongings inside. Because of S3's interchangeable use of the words *'riisu'* (lease) and *'kariru'* (borrow, rent), miscommunication occurs. While, in Japanese, just as in the original English, the loan word *'riisu'* means to use something by paying a fee and *'kariru'* means either borrow or rent, it is possible to say, as she does in lines 4–5, *'riisu de kariru'* ('to lease' or 'to rent through lease'), with *'riisu'* as a noun.

Extract 5.11-a (Interview 3)

```
 1   S3:  (...)sorede:, ano:, sono nakami wa, aru to
 2        omou ndesu kedo, iremono wa (0.3) kari(0.2)
 3        ta toka yutte- Takeda san karita nja nakute,
 4        (0.2) ano:, riisu de, (.) dareka ga kari-
 5        (0.2) karate kita tte.
          (and um, he thought that its contents were
          there, but he said like a container was
          borrowed. Not Mr Takeda, but um someone got
          it on lease, he said.)
 6        (0.3)
→  7  IR3: A, riisu wa nan desuka,
          (Uh what does 'riisu' mean?)
→  8   S3: Riisu wa ano, (0.3) riisu- dareka kara karita.
          (Lease, um lease, borrowed from someone.)
 9  IR3: Hai. (0.4) Uh:
          (Yes.)
10        (0.3)
11   S3: Okane haratte karita no ka, .hh n- nan daka
12        atashi wa shirimasen.
          (I don't know whether they paid to rent it .hh
          or not.)
13  IR3: U:m .hh he said that- that um (.) her original
14        bag was all sort of um (0.2) chopped up? And
15        um (.) was damaged, and this bag here was- had
16        been borrowed but u:m (0.4) where it was
17        borrowed from or sort of who borrowed and sort
18        of how it was borrowed um she doesn't know.
```

```
  → 19  PO3:  What does she mean 'borrowed'?
    20        (0.4)
    21  IR3:  A, karita toiu to,
              (Uh what do you mean by 'karita' [borrowed]?)
    22        (1.5)
    23   S3:  Sore wa, dare kara karita no ka mo, (0.2)
    24        okane haratta no ka mo shiranai n desu.
              (That is, I don't know who they borrowed it
              from or whether they paid for it.)
    25  IR3:  Uh (.) she doesn't know who: (.) who borrowed
    26        it >or sort of how they< paid for it.
    27        (0.4)
  → 28  PO3:  I just wonder on (0.4) Wednesday .hh you spoke
    29        to me >at the record of the interview< and you
    30        stated to me that the suitcase was leased.
    31        (0.5) What do you say to that,
    32        (0.3)
    33  IR3:  °Yes°,
    34        (0.4)
```

The suspect's response regarding what her travel companion Takeda said about the replacement suitcases contains both '*riisu*' (lease) and '*kariru*' (borrow/rent). The interpreter (IR3) initiates a repair by asking the meaning of '*riisu*', creating an 'aside' sequence between S3 and himself. S3's response suggests that S3, incorrectly, uses the two terms interchangeably. After the repair by S3, IR3 goes back to render S3's answer (lines 1–5, the initial part of the response is omitted), but the verb used in this rendition is 'borrow', and S3's comments on payment are not included. This prompts PO3 to initiate a repair regarding the use of the word 'borrow' (line 19). The repair sequence is completed in a 'normal format' of turn-taking, although IR3's rendition in line 26 'how they paid' is not an accurate translation of S3's answer (whether they paid). As we can see in lines 28–31, PO3's main concern is the inconsistent use of the terms '*kariru*' and '*lease*' in relation to the replacement suitcases. Because the illegal drugs were found in the double bottom of the replacement suitcases that the tour group members had been provided in the transit city, whether these suitcases were borrowed or leased would be an important aspect of evidence in the investigation. The reference to 'the record of the interview' and the formal term 'stated' suggest the legal implications of this question. Furthermore, the question in line 31 'What do you say to that' indicates that PO3 is challenging the suspect regarding her inconsistent accounts, using a 'contrasting' strategy (Drew, 1990).

Surprisingly, IR3 provides a token 'Yes' in a soft voice in line 33, instead of rendering PO3's turn. It is possible that IR3 has also been unsure about S3's interchangeable use of *'kariru'* and *'riisu'* and therefore is also unsure about his renditions of these words up to this point in the interview. IR3's 'Yes' token and lack of rendition here is likely to do with PO3's shift in the use of pronouns from the third person *she* to the second person *you*. Although it is not a recommended practice, PO3 used the third person *she* extensively to question the female suspect S3. IR3 at times aligned with this format, and as we can see in line 25, occasionally used *she* instead of *I* in rendering S3's turns. Thus, PO3's switch to the use of the second person pronoun at line 28 may be a shift in the recipient design (Sacks, 1995, p. 230), which points to the interpreter as the addressee. However, the norms of interpreter-mediated police interviews still allow the interpretation that S3 is the addressee as we can see in Extract 5.11-b.

Extract 5.11-b (Interview 3)

```
→  35  PO3:  >I have [a record of the in]terview< with Miss
   36  IR3:           [°(            )°]
   37  PO3:  Take-
   38  IR3:  M[m,]
   39  PO3:   [Mi]ss (0.6) Kanai,=
   40  IR3:  =Yeah,=
   41  PO3:  =on Wednesday morning.
   42  IR3:  Mm,
→  43  PO3:  During that interview I I asked her (0.3)
   44        circumstances relating to this suitcase.
   45  IR3:  Mm.=
→  46  PO3:  =In that record of interview she stated to me
   47  PO3:  .hh that (.) Takeda had stated to her that
   48        the suitcases were leased.
   49  IR3:  Ichioo, suiyoobi ni sono ano, a:no (0.2) kari-
   50        karita,(.) dewanaku ichioo riisu shita to
   51        ii ma[shita] ga.=
             (Actually, on Wednesday, so um u:m borr-
             instead of borrow, you actually said leased,
             however.)
   52  S3:       [ Soo.]
   53        =Riisu, (0.3) dakara, riisu: (.) ka:, (.)
```

```
54        dakara riisu, (.) ri- koo kariru tte koto
55        wa riisu. (0.9) Desho? (0.2) °Chigau no,°=
          (Yes. Lease, so lease bo- so lease, le- like
          to borrow is to lease. Right? Is that wrong?)
56  IR3:  =Ah: (2.5) kari:, karita to iimashita ka,=
          (Ah bor- did you say borrow?)
57  S3:   =Daka- okane o haratte: (.) riisu shita ka:,
58        (0.5) sooiu no wa zenzen, (.) da: riisu.
          (S- whether they paid to lease them and things
          like that, I have no idea. So, lease.)
59        (0.5)
60  IR3:  [It was-]
61  S3:   [Atashi,] riisu, tte iimashitayo,
          (I said lease, you know.)
62        (0.4)
→ 63  IR3:  It was um: m: (2.8) can't hear her >it might
64        have been< my mistake. (0.4) U:m
→ 65  PO3:  .hhh hhhh ((big sigh))
→ 66  IR3:  I wrote d- I wrote down(.) I'd wrote down
67        he'd borrowed but I'm not sure unless I u:m
68        (0.5) she did actually I do remember her
69        saying lease- lease as well just a while ago.
→ 70  PO3:  .hh she said n- you said she said loaned.
71        (0.5)
```

This ambiguity of addressee remains for some time since IR3 does not render or respond other than providing backchannels (although he says something softly in line 36, overlapping PO3's talk) but PO3 elaborates on the record of the interview to highlight the problematic confusion of 'borrow' with 'lease' (line 35 through to line 48). In this elaboration, however, the suspect is referred to by her surname and the third person pronoun *she*. This reversal of the original recipient design, with PO3 using *she* in his question to S3, may have provided a cue to IR3 who then produces a cropped rendition (lines 49–51) of PO3's repair initiation. The challenge 'what do you say to that' (line 31) in the earlier repair initiator is not rendered at all, which suggests again that IR3 may have thought it to have been addressed to himself. The rendition in lines 49–51 neither includes the references to the formal record of the interview from Wednesday nor the reported speech (line 47 'Takeda had stated to her'). Its illocutionary force is weakened by the repeated use of the adverb *'ichioo'* (just/actually), which this interpreter often uses as a slightly unnatural filler. S3's response shows repetitions and false starts, suggesting her uncertainty about the meanings of the two words. At the end of the turn (line 55) she asks IR3 to confirm her interpretation that the two words have the same meaning. This signals a shift into an 'aside' with the interpreter, but instead of responding to S3's request for confirmation, IR3 goes into an 'aside' with a different focus. He asks her if she had said '*karita*' (past tense of *kariru*), probably because he is concerned about his own renditions of the terms during S3's interviews. However, S3 does not answer the question but comes back to the explanation of her use of the terms in line 57. This turn is produced with numerous instances of ellipsis use in Japanese which makes its message vague: '*sooiu no wa zenzen*' (line 58) is literally 'things like that, not at all', and the last part of the turn '*da: riisu*' (so, lease) possibly means 'So, I said lease'. Nevertheless S3 also in a way responds to IR3's question in line 56, stating that she had said '*riisu*' (line 61). However, IR3 gives up on rendering S3's utterances and declares that he is having difficulty and the confusion may have been caused by his mistake. This is however not true, as S3 did say '*riisu*' as she confirms, but she also used the term '*kariru*' which can be used for using another's things either with or without payment.

At this point, the interaction shifts to an aside between IR3 and PO3 about the use of the terms. Here, the discussion concerns the ambiguity of the trouble source, which again emerges as one of the problematic aspects of handling miscommunication in interpreter-mediated police interviews. Because this particular miscommunication could affect the course of investigation and may be an important piece of evidence, it becomes crucial to identify the source of the problem by revisiting the suspect's original words as well as the interpreter's renditions of these words (see lines 66–72). PO3's self-repair in line 70 where he initially says 'she said n-' but repairs it with 'you said she said' is an illuminating example of how complex the nature of resolving this type of miscommunication can be. In the following part (Extract 5.11-c), the suspect breaks off the aside between PO3 and IR3 by saying that the two words have the same meaning.

Extract 5.11-c (Interview 3)

```
72  IR3:  Yeah I actu- I'd wrote written down here, =
73   S3:  =Imi, (.) [iss]ho.
           (The meaning, is the same.)
74  IR3:           [I'd]
75          The- the meaning's (0.6) she says the meaning
76          is the same. (0.7) T- Hold on.
```

```
      77          (1.0)
  →   78   PO3:  Could we clarify this 'cause it's very important,
      79   IR3:  Yep. Chotto, nanka kore daiji desu kara,
      80         Chotto (0.2) kakunin shitaindesuga riisu to
      81         kariru wa,
                  (So like, this is important, so I would like
                  to check if riisu [lease] and kariru [borrow])
      82         (6.6)((IR3 may be checking his dictionary))
  →   83   IR3:  Rii::su wa notte masen ga.
                  ('Riisu' is not in the dictionary.)
      84         (2.1)
  →   85   IR3:  °Riisu° (5.8) Ichioo, .hh riisu to kariru wa,
      86         do- ano dooiu fuuni chigaimasu ka?
                  (Riisu. Actually, .hh 'riisu' and 'kariru',
                  ho- um how are they different?_
      87         (0.3)
      88   S3:   Ano: kariru, kariru no mo:, okane haratee
      89         kariru no to:,
                  (Um kariru, you may pay to borrow, but
      90   IR3:  Mm.=
      91   S3:   =Tomodachi kara tadade kariru no to aru ndesu
      92         yo. .hh riisu mo:,
                  (you may borrow from a friend for nothing, you
                  see. .hh riisu also.)
      93         (0.5)
      94   IR3:  Ah yeah in- in Ja- in Japanese whether you
      95         you u:m, (0.4) um you use the word (0.2) um
      96         the word >which I wrote down here< to sort of
      97         u:m (.) im- either >borrow something for
      98         someone or sort of borrow something< from- (.)
      99         lease >something from someone so you use the
      00         same word<.
      01         (0.8)
      02   PO3:  °Right°.
      03   IR3:  So um=
      04   S3:   =Ya watashi wa kore to kore onaji imi da to
      05         omoimashita.
                  (No I thought this and this had the same
                  meaning.)
  →   06   IR3:  Um but she sort of (0.5) um (.) so yeah the-
      07         the usage of the words is pretty similar.
```

IR3 picks up on S3's self-selected turn (line 72) and shifts his role back towards that of the *animator* in lines 75–76, but not quite, as he uses the reported speech 'she says' (line 75). Then in line 76 he seems to be reaching for the dictionary to check the meaning of the words ('Hold on' and then a 1.0 second silence). PO3's request for clarification in line 78 is made with the pronoun *we*, whose referent is difficult to discern; is it referring to PO3 and IR3, or to all three interlocutors including the suspect? The way in which IR3 checks the dictionary and responds with 'Yep' and then switches to a rendition in Japanese suggests it is actually the latter; all three interlocutors are involved in this process with the interpreter being in the roles of an *animator, author* and *principal*. IR3 translates PO3's request in lines 79–81, then checks the dictionary and talks to S3 in Japanese (line 83, '*Riisu* is not in the dictionary'). Then IR3 'authors' PO3's request for clarification and asks S3 to explain the difference between the two words (lines 85–86). At line 94, IR3 returns to the translatory activity. The rendered explanation, in essence, is that they can be used interchangeably whether or not payment is involved. What should be noted, however, is that the rendition of S3's turn (lines 4–5) does not include the projection frame 'I thought', although there is evidence of IR3's attempt to incorporate it (line 06, 'she sort of'), but somehow this is abandoned through the self-repair. Whether this self-repair was intentional or not, what it achieves is to misrepresent the fact that the word '*riisu*' could only be used for the meaning of the English word lease, involving payment, and therefore the interpreter's loss of face from not knowing the meaning and usage of '*riisu*' is concealed. The suspect's interchangeable use of the two terms was inappropriate.

This example highlights the problem of having two possible trouble sources when the police officer initiated the repair. The nature of the interpreter-mediated interview brings ambiguity and complexity to this type of repair sequence, and in this particular case, the suspect was shielded from giving wrong information on the meaning of the two terms in question. However, interpreters are endowed with interactional power which allows them to mishandle miscommunication according to their perceived trouble source.

5.5   Repairs initiated by interpreters

This section explores repairs initiated by interpreters. When the interpreter initiates a repair, it means that the interpreter's turn is not a rendition of a primary speaker's turn but a turn produced to clarify or comment, as a mediator of communication, on the previous primary speaker's turn. In terms of role, then, the interpreter takes that of a *principal*. This repair initiation move also creates an 'aside' sequence or sequences in which the interpreter and one of the primary speakers engage in addressing miscommunication in one language and the other primary speaker does not have access to what goes on in the 'aside'. First, repairs in which the suspect's turn is the trouble source for the interpreter are discussed, followed by analyses of repairs in which the repair initiation is directed at the police interviewer's turn as the trouble source.

5.5.1 Repairs initiated by interpreters and responded to by suspects

The examples analysed in this section include repair sequences in which the interpreter initiates a repair in an aside with the suspect. Interpreters are sometimes described as mediators who help their clients overcome not only language but also cultural barriers (Berk-Seligson, 1990; Cooke, 1995; Laster & Taylor, 1994; Mikkelson, 1998; Niska, 1995). The extent to which they act as a 'cultural bridge' is a sensitive issue, as accuracy should not be sacrificed. However, as interpreters are usually the only participants who have access to the two languages used in their assignments, they are able to anticipate problems.

5.5.1.1 Repair initiation as a linguistic expert

Extract 5.12 is an example of a repair sequence in which the interpreter avoids a possible misunderstanding by quickly repairing it 'off the record' to remove the risk. The suspect (S2) is asked who his travel companions to Australia were.

Extract 5.12 (Interview 2)

```
1 PO2:  Who have you travelled- (.) who did you travel
2       with, (0.3)(last) Wednesday, (.) who were the
3       other people.
4       (0.4)
5 IR2:  E, sono: juushichinichi no suiyoubi no hi
6       desukeredomo, (.) dare to isshoni ryokou
7       shiteimashita ka?
       (Regarding that Wednesday the 17th, who were
       you travelling with?)
8       (0.3)
9 S2:   Eeeto, watashi: no kyoodai, (0.3) [sannin to:]
       (Uh: my brothers, three of them,)
```

```
      10  IR2:                                        [My brothe-]
      11  S2:   Sore[to]
                (and,)
→     12  IR2:     [my] brothers? (0.2) three of the[m,]
      13  S2:                                       [Ha]i,
                                                    (Yes)
      14        sore[to::]
                (and)
→     15  IR2:     [Jibu]n mo irete desu ne?
                (Including yourself, right?)
      16        Inclu[ding me],
      17  S2:       [Hai sou] watashi mo irete.
                (That's right including myself.)
```

In Japanese, when talking about the number of siblings, it is common to hear, for example, literally 'We are three brothers', which includes the speaker him/herself. Thus, through a direct translation between English and Japanese, there is a risk of understanding the number incorrectly. Being aware of this risk, after rendering a literal translation in lines 5–7, the interpreter (IR2) interrupts S2 in line 10, questioning whether the 'three brothers' includes himself. Without waiting for S2's response to this question, IR2 modifies S2's original reply (line 12) to avoid the risk of the interviewing officer misunderstanding the number of brothers. The subsequent modification of the response to ensure accurate rendition of the original meaning suggests that the interpreter took the role of *author*, moving from being a 'sounding box' towards a 'cultural bridge'. This role shift, however, does not go against the code of ethics which recommends that interpreters 'ask for repetition, rephrasing or explanation' if anything is unclear (NAATI, 2001, p. 14). The repair effectively avoided potential miscommunication that only the interpreter was able to anticipate and ensured accurate rendition of the primary speaker's message.

Extract 5.13 below also shows an example of an aside in which a problem with language is dealt with in Japanese between the suspect and the interpreter. The police interviewer (PO3) asks the suspect (S3) why her passport was stamped on her arrival in Australia.

Extract 5.13 (Interview 3)

```
      1  PO3:  Does she know why it was stamped?
      2        (0.5)
      3  IR3:  Naze tsukemashita ka,
```

```
               (Why have they put this?)
       4       (1.4)
  →    5   S3: Rainichi shita: kiroku da to omoimasu.=
               (I think it's a record of my visit to Japan).
       6  IR3: =E?
               (Eh?)
       7   S3: Rai- (.) Rainichi shita: ki[roku].
               (Com- Record of my visit to Japan.)
       8  IR3:                          [Hai,]
                                        (Yes.)
       9       (0.9.)
      10  IR3: Rainichi.
               (Visit to Japan?)
      11   S3: Hai.
               (Yes.)
      12       (0.6)
  →   13  IR3: Raigoo desu (0.2) [e? ]
               (Visit to Australia, is it?)
      14   S3:                  [Rai]nichi. .hh °huh°
                                (Visit to Japan. .hh huh)
      15       (0.5) ((IR3 may be writing down the word))
      16   S3: Kuru, soo. (1.0) Kita (0.2) hinichi.
               (Come, that's right. The date of arrival.)
      17  IR3: Ichioo Nihon kara kita (0.6) rainichi to iuto,
               (Actually, 'came from Japan', if you say
               rainichi?)
      18       (0.5)
  →   19   S3: Rainichi, dakara:, kekkyoku, (.) kono:
      20       Oosutoraria ni, (.) tsuita hinichi dato
      21       omoimasu.=
               (Coming to Japan, in short, I think that is
               the date of arrival in Australia.)
  →   22  IR3: =They- she thinks it means >it's the date they
      23       arrived in Australia<.
```

S3's response in line 5 contains a problematic use of the word '*rainichi*' (visit to Japan). As evidenced in IR3's turn in line 13 and S3's turn in lines 19–21, S3 assumes that the '*nichi*' component of '*rainichi*' means 'a date' instead of 'Japan' ('date' and 'Japan' are both represented by the same Chinese-derived character in Japanese). Since the '*rai*' component means 'to come', S3 incorrectly uses '*rainichi*' to mean 'the date of arrival'. This leads to IR3's short repair initiation in line 6, but S3 simply repeats her response. IR3 initiates another repair by repeating the trouble source word *'rainichi'* in line 10, and when S3 does not repair her use of the word, IR3 provides the correct word *'raigoo'*, which means 'visit to Australia'. At line 15, IR3 seems to be writing down *'rainichi'*, and S3 explains by providing an incorrect explanation of the Chinese characters for *'rainichi'* in line 16. Being a second language speaker of Japanese, IR3 checks in line 17 whether the word could mean 'coming *from* Japan'. To this, S3 provides an explanation which affirms her misuse of the word; she used it to mean the date she arrived in Australia. IR3 then renders what has been constructed as S3's response to PO3's question in line 1.

In this repair sequence, the interpreter appeared to be the only interlocutor who was aware of the nature of the miscommunication. S3 never seems to have understood why IR3 initiated repairs, and PO3 had no way of knowing the nature of the interaction between IR3 and S3. Yet IR3 dealt with a problem that, had he rendered S3's initial response faithfully without getting into the 'aside', would have led to miscommunication between PO3 and S3. For the local management of language-based problems, which only IR3 can deal with, this may be a reasonable way of handling miscommunication.

The question is, however, whether the police interviewer should have been informed of the nature of this miscommunication and repair in English, and whether it would be better to ensure that the nature of this miscommunication and repair be recorded on the tape in English. In this particular case, unlike the earlier example involving the terms *riisu* (lease) and *kariru* (borrow/rent) which were highly relevant for the investigation, the miscommunication was obviously not so significant and was a straightforward error. It does however give a negative indication of the suspect's literacy level, which may or may not have helped her case had it been made known to the interviewing officer by faithful renditions in the normal format of turn-taking in a repair sequence.

5.5.1.2 *Repair initiation as a facilitator of investigation*

So far, the repair sequences examined have been ones that derive from problems with language and culture, about which the interpreter is the expert. There are however examples of repairs initiated by the interpreters in their attempts to elicit a coherent or preferred response to the police officer's question. In the examples that follow, the trouble sources of interpreter-initiated suspect repairs are related to information-gathering activities rather than translation. In Extract 5.14, the interviewing officer (PO1) asks a simple question about the suspect's (S1) job as a jeweller.

Extract 5.14 (Interview 1)

```
     1 PO1: How long have you been a jeweller,
     2 IR1: A:(.) donokurai houseki:shoo o
     3       itonanderasshaimasu ka,
           (Uh how long have you been a jeweller?)
→    4 S1:  Ie, (0.3) ano: (0.2) houseki wa: sukoshi
     5       nandesu kedo,=
           (No um actually [I deal with] jewellery a)
           little,
     6 IR1: =Hai,=
           (Yes,)
→    7 S1:  =ato tokee da toka,
           (and [I deal with] watches and)
→    8 IR1: Ano, (.) kikan wa dorekurai desu ka,
           (Um how long was the duration?)
     9 S1:  Eetto: juunen kurai.
           (Uhm about 10 years.)
    10 IR1: I: have been a jeweller for the last 10 years.
```

In this example, the 'off the record' repair-initiation strategy goes beyond an ethically acceptable level. In the unmarked role of *animator*, the interpreter should render the suspect's utterances in lines 4–5 and 7 in English. But, judging these utterances as irrelevant to PO1's question, IR1 reformulates her initial rendition (lines 2–3) in line 8, interrupting S1's utterance. This reformulated turn is a next-turn repair initiator, as she deems S1's turns problematic and specifically requests 'the duration'. S1 repairs in line 9, allowing IR1 to render a coherent response to the question posed in line 1. This is a problematic action by the interpreter, who seeks to avoid a threat to coherent interaction and attempts to elicit answers 'acceptable' to the police officers. Consequently, the information that S1 dealt with watches (and possibly other things) is lost here although it actually becomes relevant later in the interview. The information which was not communicated to the interviewing officer could have had implications for the case. In this case, this suspect's business connections with an overseas contact person were probed by PO1 later in the interview. When S1 mentioned a discussion about watches with this contact, the police officer may have made a negative inference as dealings of watches had not been previously mentioned to him. The interpreter takes an interactional role that may be described as bordering *author* and *principal*.

As found in previous studies in legal interpreting, interpreters ask for clarification to facilitate communication and, controversially, to achieve the institutional goal of the discourse which they mediate (Berk-Seligson, 1990, 2009; Hale, 2008; Komter, 2005; Wadensjö, 1998). In Extract 5.15, an interpreter participates in the interview discourse in a *principal* role. The interviewing officer (PO1) asks the suspect (S1) about the nature of the business he discussed with his associate Mark:

Extract 5.15 (Interview 1)

```
     1 PO1: Was any business discussed during that trip
     2      (.) in Japan with Mark.
     3 IR1: Maaku ga Nihon ni taizai shtia toki ni, .hh uh
     4      nanraka no, ano: bijinesu no hanashi wa
     5      demashita ka?
            (When Mark stayed in Japan, .hh uh was there
            some kind of, um business discussion?)
     6      (0.3)
     7 S1:  Da- kono toki mo, ano: (0.2) watte kitatokimo,
  →  8      horidee nandesu kedo, .hh ano: sono: paatsu
     9      kankee datoka, (.) sooiu kankee no hanashi_wa
    10      demashita.
            (S- this time too, um when they came as a
            group, it was for a holiday, but .hh um so:
            things like parts, that kind of things were
            discussed.)
  → 11 IR1: Tokee no paatsu desu ka?=
            (Do you mean watch parts?)
    12 S1:  =Chigaimasu, enjin desu.
            (No, engine.)
    13 IR1: °Enjin. ° (When it) uh: when he: came to Japan
    14      uh: on holiday, uh: in (0.3) May, (.) uh was a
  → 15      discussion regarding the uh: engine parts
    16      (1.0) between Mark and myself.

            ((16 lines later))

    32 PO1: Why, (0.2) why would you be, (.) involved in
    33      business deals, (0.3) concerning (0.2) motor
    34      vehicle parts, if you are a jeweller.
```

S1's response in lines 7–10 refers to 'parts', but the type of 'parts' are not mentioned. Upon hearing this, instead of rendering the response, IR1 initiates a repair in line 11 to clarify whether S1 is referring to watch parts, as he has mentioned earlier in the interview that he deals with watches as part of his work. S1 immediately provides a repair in line 12, identifying 'parts' as engine parts. IR1 then incorporates this repair into her rendition of S1's initial response (lines 7–10). In a monolingual interview the vague reference to 'parts' would either have been left unclarified or caused the interviewing officer to initiate a repair for clarification. Since there was no translatability issue for IR1 to render *'paartsu'* in the above discursive context, it would be reasonable to say that the interpreter's role shifted to that of an interrogator when she initiated the repair. The repair impacts on the trajectory of the interview, with the officer expressing his suspicions about S1's business with his associate Mark in lines 32–34. Had IR1 not initiated a repair, PO1 may have initiated a similar repair to clarify the nature of the parts. However, the significance of the repair sequence above is that the interpreter engaged in discursive activity beyond that of translating to facilitate communication, in this case to facilitate investigation, taking over the power of the interviewing officer.

The analysis in this section suggests that interpreters' repair-initiation moves may provide support for suspects whose responses could potentially lead to miscommunication and negative perceptions of their credibility. On the other hand, if the interpreter initiates a repair because of a problem concerning the institutional relevance of the suspect's talk, there is an issue of interpreter roles. This type of repair initiation may inadvertently affect the trajectory of the suspect's telling of his/her version of events of the 'asides' also means that there are issues with records of interview as evidence. Furthermore, if repair initiation goes as far as the interpreter taking over the role of interrogator, the permissibility of the interview as an evidence-gathering legal process can be threatened.

5.5.2   Repairs initiated by interpreters and responded to by police officers

In this section, interpreter-initiated repair sequences between the interviewing officer and the interpreter are examined. In terms of turntaking organisation, the interpreter's repair initiation turns usually follow those questions from the interviewing officer that are regarded by the interpreter as a trouble source. Repair sequences of this type may occur if the interpreter foresees miscommunication due to linguistic and pragmatic ambiguities in the original question or if the interpreter him/herself does not understand the question. While this type of clarification process is at times necessary for accurate rendition, it may develop into further confusion and failed repairs, if the line of questioning, or the trajectory of the narrative which the police officers have in mind, does not become clearer to the interpreter.

5.5.2.1 Repair initiation to avoid miscommunication

Interpreters in the data set asked police officers for clarification when they found elements in the officers' questions which could potentially cause miscommunication. A common example of this is when the trouble source of the repair is an ambiguous referent of a personal pronoun. In Extract 5.16, the interviewing officer (PO3) is questioning the suspect (S3) who in her tour group asked for help from another passenger in filling out the Australian customs and quarantine forms on their flight.

Extract 5.16 (Interview 3)

```
       1  PO3:  Who asked th<u>a</u>t,
       2        (0.3)
       3  IR3:  Dare ga son- sono koto o kikimashita ka,=
                (Who asked about tha- that?)
       4  S3:   =Takeda Takashi san desu.
                (It was Mr Takashi Takeda.)
       5  IR3:  Takeda <u>a</u>sked him.
       6        (1.0)
   →   7  PO3:  >Asked <u>who</u>,<
       8        (1.0)
   →   9  IR3:  Takeda san wa dare ni sono shitsumon o
      10        kikimashita ka,
                (Who did Mr Takeda ask that question of?)
      11  S3:   Sono: s<u>o</u>bani ita (0.2) [otokono hito desu].
                (The man who was by the- the side of them.)
      12  IR3:                       [he <u>a</u>sked, he ask]ed
      13        the um the man just n<u>e</u>xt to them.
      14        (0.5)
      15  PO3:  That's the older brother, (0.4) Takeda.
      16        (1.0)
   →  17  S3:   Daihyoo de, (.) kiitekureta ndesu.
```

```
                   (He asked as a representative for us.)
  → 18 IR3:  U:m (0.8) Takeda asked as representative for
    19       ev- for all- all of them, (0.2) this guy that
    20       was u:m just sitting behind them, (.) o- over
    21       the aisle and behind them, (.) .hh u:m, (0.2)
    22       about that.
    23       (0.4)
  → 24 PO3:  .hhh did he help fill out all their forms?
    25       (1.0)
  → 26 IR3:  What do you m- who do you mean by he,
    27 PO3:  .hh that (.) Japanese gentleman she's
    28       described.
```

The questions and S3's answers include references to two male persons: to Takeda, one of S3's travel companions, and to a male Japanese passenger who was sitting near the tour group on the flight. According to S3, Takeda asked the Japanese passenger how to fill out the form and was told that ticking 'no' for all questions would be fine (this is not included in the transcript). In line 24, PO3 asks a question whose subject is the third person pronoun *he*. From the grammatical and discursive context, this could refer to either Takeda or the Japanese passenger. IR3 therefore initiates a repair to clarify the referent of the pronoun, and PO3's repair turn (lines 27–28) clarifies the referent to be 'the Japanese gentleman', that is, a Japanese passenger outside S3's tour group. This repair sequence seems to be a less intrusive type of 'aside' compared to other examples of 'aside' in that it does not impact on the core question sequences to the extent that the interview as forensic evidence is affected. It is possible that, in a monolingual interview, the same type of repair sequence may have occurred with the suspect asking for a clarification instead of the interpreter. The interpreter in this example could also have interpreted it and waited for a clarification request from the suspect, but this would have wasted time and efficiency, even if it is correct in principle.

An interesting aspect of the above extract is worth mentioning here in relation to the issue of clarifying referents. The interpreter (IR3) supplies some omitted elements of the primary speakers' turns although it is possible to render the source utterances without doing so. In line 9, the subject of the sentence 'Mr Takeda' is made explicit in the rendition, and in lines 18–22, again the subject 'Takeda' appears in the rendition, and the indirect object in the source utterance omitted in line 17 is included in detail. Those changes mean that IR3 took the role of an *author* to avoid miscommunication in this stretch of interaction.

5.5.2.2 Ambiguous repair-turns causing further miscommunication

The next example shows a more problematic repair sequence. In Extract 5.17 below, the police interviewer (PO2) is asking who paid for S2's flight to Australia (line 1), but this question evolves into further miscommunication through repair sequences:

Extract 5.17 (Interview 2)

```
 1 PO2: Who paid (.) for the ticket.
 2      (0.8)
 3 IR2: Darega, (.) e: kookuuunchin o haraimashita ka?
 4      (.) hikooki [no kippu o ha]raimashita ka?
        (Who uh paid the airfare? paid for the
        airline ticket?)
 5 S2:             [Maa ichioo an]
                   (Well actually u-)
 6      (0.4)
 7 S2: Ano: watashi no bun wa ano jibun de haratte,
 8      (.) watashite: °sore wa harattemasu ne moo°,
        (Um my share, um I paid myself, I gave it,
        I have paid it already.)
 9 IR2: [I pa]i:d (0.5) for (.) my own ticket,
10 S2: [(Ato]
        (And also)
12      (0.6)
→ 13 IR2: >Jibun no bun dake?<
        (Is it only for yours?)
14 S2: E, uchino: ano: soo desune, soreto, (0.5)
15     m kanojo no bun mo watashi, (.) hai. =
        (Ah, our um well, and mm I did that for
        my girlfriend too, yes.)
16 IR2: =And also I pai:d,=
17 S2: =Un, (0.4) Kanai,
        (Yeah. Kanai.)
18 IR2: For [uh] Kanai's tic[ket] (.) as well.
19 S2:     [mm]            [ee.]
20      (1.0)
21 PO2: And Kanai is his girlfriend?=
```

```
    22  S2:  =°Un°.
              (Yeah.)
    23  IR2: Kanai san wa e:to, (0.3) gaarufurendo desu ka?
              (Is Ms Kanai um your girlfriend?)
    24  S2:  Gaarufurendo.=
              (She is my girlfriend.)
    25  IR2: =Yes. (0.2) she is my girlfriend.
    26  PO2: Was (.) what he paid for just the airline
    27       ticket? (0.2) Or: (.) everything.
    28  IR2: .hhhh ano: Takeda san wa (.) tada, ano
    29       kookuuunchin: dake o haratta ndesu ka? (0.2)
    30       Soretomo hoka no zenbu o haratta ndesu ka?=
              (.hhhh um did you pay only the airfare?
              Or did you pay for all other things?)
→   31  IR2: =Are you talking about uh: Kanai's expenses?
    33  PO2: Yes.
    34  IR2: Ano=
              (Um)
→   35  PO2: =Uh, (.) just the accommodation, airline
    36       tickets and,
    37       (0.3)
→   38  POa: Travel,=
    39  PO2: =Travel,
→   40  POa: Tourist places, buses.
    41       (0.6)
    42  IR2: Um (0.4) including Kanai's uh: (0.4) expenses
    43       >you mean.<
    44       (0.5)
→   45  PO2: Y- yeah just what w- what what it cost
    46       him (.) to pay for the ticket to stay (for him
    47       to come).=
    48  IR2: =Regarding this trip.
→   49  PO2: This trip [ yeah,] accommodation tickets,
    50  IR2:           [°Right°].
    51  PO2: vouchers,
→   52  IR2: Konkai no ryokoo ni kanshite,
              (Concerning this trip,)
    53  S2:  Hai.
              (Yes.)
→   54  IR2: Kanai san wa (.) dooiu koto ni (.) okane o
```

```
55        haraimashita ka,
          (What kind of things did Ms Kanai pay for?)
56        (0.5)
57  S2:   N maa okane: wa (0.2) mada haratte nai desu.
58        (0.3) ee.=
          (Mm well [she has] not paid money yet.)
59  IR2:  =I haven't paid yet,
60        (2.2)
61  PO2:  °Oh ↑all ↓right?°
```

The suspect (S2) says that he has already paid his airfare (lines 7–8), but he signals that there is more information with '*Ato*' (And also) in line 10. This overlaps the beginning of the rendition by the interpreter (IR2), who then engages S2 in a repair sequence by asking quickly 'Is it only for yours?' (line 13). S2 then says that he also paid for his girlfriend's airfare (line 15).

At this point, the interviewing officer (PO2) asks whether it was just the airfare that he paid (lines 26–27). This question is probably motivated by the officer's assumption that a number of people in S2's tour group, including S2 and his girlfriend, were mules for importation of narcotics. However, it is not clear whether the question refers to only Takeda's travel costs or Kanai's or the pair's. IR2's rendition (lines 28–30) maintains this ambiguity in the source utterance, but at the end of the rendition he immediately switches to English and initiates a repair (line 31) before S2 can respond. PO2 confirms that the question concerns S2's girlfriend's expenses (line 33), but IR2's attempt to initiate a rendition (line 34) is blocked by PO2's elaboration on the repair turn. This turn specifies some components of travel costs, and is followed by a joint construction of expansion on the repair turn (line 33) by PO2 and her assisting officer POa (lines 38–40). This expansion becomes a source of miscommunication as it changes the nature of the information sought by the original question (lines 26–27) about which the repair was initiated. The short pause in line 41 suggests that IR2 may have been confused, and he initiates another repair in lines 42–43. This initiator is also problematic in that it asks whether the original question concerned S2's travel costs as well as his girlfriend's, although IR2's repair initiator in line 31 is to clarify whether the original question referred to Kanai's expenses only. PO2's repair turn begins with an affirmative response, but the elaboration which follows this 'yeah' modifies the original question to a more general one concerning the overall costs of the trip incurred by S2. Another repair in lines 48–51 also foreground the components of the travel costs, but, surprisingly, IR2 then brings the focus back to S2's girlfriend, Kanai, and her travel costs instead of the components of the trip for which S2 was responsible. S2's answer (line 57) has a problematic ellipsis of the subject of the sentence (the topic is the 'money' but the subject of the verb 'pay' is omitted), which the interpreter assumes to be S2 ('I') as shown in line 59 'I haven't paid yet'. This is despite the rendition of the question having Kanai as the subject in line 54. The unresolved, or aggravated, miscommunication can be inferred from PO2's reaction to this in line 61, which comes after 2.2 seconds of silent pause.

In this extract, the repair sequences develop into an exacerbation of miscommunication as the police interviewer's repair turns bring in new pieces of information and modify the focus of the original question (or trouble source turn). What aggravates the problem is the gap in interpretive frames between the officers and the interpreter, where the focus of the former becomes types of travel costs and the focus of the latter stays with S2's role in covering his girlfriend's travel costs. The interpreter's interpretive frame is interwoven into his inclination to facilitate the investigation process, which seems to affect his approach to repair initiation as well as the rendition of the repaired question. It should also be pointed out that this example of miscommunication is partly caused by a confusing use of ellipsis by all of the interlocutors: the police interviewer (lines 35–36), the interpreter (line 42) and the suspect (line 58). In Japanese, ellipsis occurs far more extensively than in English in spoken interaction, and the verbs and copula do not conjugate according to the person. This makes the interpreting process particularly vulnerable to miscommunication and, in repair sequences in which miscommunication is being handled, it seems to be all the more important to avoid ellipsis as much as possible in order not to aggravate communication problems.

5.5.2.3 *Repair initiation to restore the normal format of mediated interaction*

The next example of repair sequences occurred when the police interviewer (PO3) and the suspect (S3) engaged in the interaction with different contexts as reference points. In this sense, the nature of the miscommunication is similar to the previous example. However, this example is different in that it shows a process in which the interviewing officers (PO3 and POb) and the interpreter (IR3) rectify the miscommunication collaboratively. In Extract 5.18, the first question in the extract (line 1) is asked after S3 explained how her suitcase was stolen during the stopover in Malaysia but a replacement suitcase arrived the next morning with her belongings intact. Thus, the question concerns what she found in her replacement suitcase in Malaysia. However, before S3 gave the account of what happened during the stopover, PO3 had been asking a series of questions in his attempt to reconstruct what happened to S3 at the airport after she landed in Australia.

Extract 5.18 (Interview 3)

```
 1 PO3: What- (0.6) what's inside the suitcase.=
 2 IR3: =A, a suutsukeesu no nakami wa nan desu ka,
        (Uh uh what's the contents of the suitcase?)
 3  S3: Watashi no: (0.3) irui to: (0.4) ato:
 4      shanpuu, rinsu komono desu.
        (My clothes and also shampoo, conditioner and
        accessories.)
 5 IR3: Ano: irui to,
        (Um clothes and,)
        ((several turns between IR3 and S3
        regarding the content of S3's suitcase))
21 IR3: U:m, (0.2) clothes, (0.3) shampoo and rinse,
22      (0.2) dryer, (0.4) u:m underclothes, socks
23      body shampoo toothbrush toothpaste towel
24      tissues shoes.
25      (1.3)
26 PO3: What happened after she picked up the bag,
27 IR3: .hh ano nimotsu o ano totte kara nani ga
→ 28   arimashita ka=nani ga okorimashita ka?
        (.hh um after you picked up the luggage what
        happened, what took place?)
29      (0.9)
→ 30 IR3: Nani ga arimashi[ta ka]?
        (What happened?)
31  S3:                 [totte] kara tte dooiu imi
32      deshoo ka.
        (What do you mean after I picked up?)
33 IR3: A:no:, (0.3) what do you mean by after she
34      took the bag.
35 PO3: .hh (.) would- did she hand another form to
36      Customs.
37      (0.6)
38 IR3: Ichio- (.) nimotsu o totte kara: ano zeekan
```

```
39          ni hoka no shorui o dashimashita ka,
            (Actually, after you picked up the luggage, um
            did you hand in other documents?)
40          (4.6)
41   S3:    °Imi ga wakannai desu°.
            (I don't know what you mean.)
42   IR3:   I'm not I'm not >su- (.) sure what you mean.<=
→ 43   POb:   =I think um (.) that might be unclear because
44          uh she's not sure [as] to whether you meant
45   IR3:                      °[mm]°.
46   POb:   the bag in Australia or overseas.
47   PO3:   In Australia.
→ 48   IR3:   A, Oosutoraria de, suutsukeesu o totta toki
→ 49          ni, (0.4) ah: so do you wanna ask >the
            (Uh when you picked up the suitcase in
            Australia ...)
→ 50          question again after she took the bag up,
→ 51          (.) >after she went to pick up< the bag when
52          [she landed].
53   POb:   [yep, yep,]
54          (0.5)
55   PO3:   Yeah >what happened after she picked the
56          bag up in Aust[ralia],<
57   IR3:                  [ Yep ]=Oosutoraria de sono (.)
58          nimotsu o totta tokini: (.) nan- ano: nani
59          o shimashita ka? (.) Nani ga arimashita ka,
            (Yep, when you picked up the luggage in
            Australia, what did you do? What happened?)
60          (3.0)
61   S3:    Shiraberaremashita.
            (I was searched.)
62   IR3:   I was searched.
```

After the interpreter (IR3) renders S3's response listing the items she found in her suitcase in the stopover country of Malaysia, PO3 asks a question in line 26 which does not include the location in which S3 'picked up the bag'. The preceding exchange is about what happened in Malaysia, but PO3's question, as can be found in line 42 and onwards, concerns what happened when S3 arrived in Australia. The vague nature of the question 'what happened after she picked up the bag' is probably intended to elicit from S3 a narrative including voluntary information about her arrival in Australia leading to her arrest. This vagueness and the sudden shift in the reference to Australia appear to confuse S3, whose point of reference is still Malaysia. S3 then initiates a repair in line 31, and IR3 renders the repair initiation for PO3. However, PO3 does not seem to realise that the trouble source is the lack of reference to the location but instead narrows down the scope of the question by using a polar question and a specific reference to the form and the customs (lines 35–36). This still does not solve the miscommunication, and another repair initiation comes from S3 and is rendered in English (line 42).

Up to this point, there are no 'aside' repair sequences. However, at this point, POb, the assisting police interviewer, intervenes, addressing and explaining to PO3 the nature of the trouble source which caused the confusion over the location of the events referred to in the questions. PO3 accordingly clarifies that he is talking about events in Australia. Because this clarification turn ('In Australia') is given with substantial ellipsis and the repaired question in lines 35–36 is different from that of the original trouble source question (line 26), IR3 ceases his reconstructed rendition at line 49, and asks PO3 in English to provide a repaired question in a full form. Thus, he shifts his role from that of an *animator* to *principal*. Both officers verbally concede this is a reasonable move, and PO3 offers a repair by asking the original question with 'in Australia' at the end. It still takes a short while (and a self-repair of the rendition by IR3 in line 59) for S3 to answer the question, but a coherent response is produced in line 61.

Comparing the two examples above, it seems that a specific identification of the trouble source and a repaired question without ellipsis are required; in other words, not making assumptions about the omitted elements of utterances in the repair improves the chance of rectifying miscommunication through interpreter mediation. The question remains, however, whether, in a case like the one above, the identification of the trouble source should have been done by the interpreter rather than through the intervention of the assisting police interviewer (POb). In both of the above examples, the interviewing officer's question allowed for varied versions of understanding, yet, without the clarification process of the 'aside', it would have been possible for the suspect to be perceived as evasive or the interpreter to be suspected of unskilful translation.

This section examined interpreters initiating repairs to avoid potential miscommunication caused by ambiguities in police interviewers' questions. In some cases, it was possible for the interpreter to remain in the normal format of turn-taking and leave it up to the suspect to initiate a repair if he/she needed clarification. However at times there came a point at which direct intervention became necessary to facilitate communication. In such situations, the interpreter may be providing a 'shield' for the suspect. The examples above also showed problematic omissions and inexplicitness in not only police officers' questions but also their repaired turns, which prevented them from eliciting information efficiently. Because pragmatic assumptions shared and signalled in monolingual interviews, for example though the use of contextualisation cues, cannot always be depended upon in interpreted interviews, it may be necessary for police interviewers to make their language of questioning more explicit.

5.6   Conclusions

This chapter discussed miscommunication by examining repair sequences in interpreter-mediated police interviews. Two categories of repair sequences were identified: those occurring bilingually in the 'normal format' of turn-taking organisation; and those occurring, mostly monolingually, in side sequences or 'asides'.

First, examples of repair sequences within the normal format of turn-taking were examined. Although this is the 'standard' way to address miscommunication, adhering to the ethics of interpreting, in some of the examples the lack of contiguity between the primary speakers made repair processes convoluted. Overlapping talk and fragmented turns in the repair sequence also made it difficult for the interpreter to sustain complete renditions of the turns in repair sequences. 'Global trouble sources' (Wadensjö, 1998, p. 202) may exist in both monolingual and interpreter-mediated police interviews, particularly due to a mismatch between the institutional framework of police interviewing, and suspects' footing based on their versions of events. However, particularly in interpreter-mediated interviews, non-rendition of primary speakers' utterances due to overlapping talk, and lack of contiguity between primary speaker turns may make repair sequences more vulnerable to miscommunication.

Another issue related to interpreter-mediated repairs in the normal format of turn-taking organisation was the loss of 'primary realities' through interpreting (Gibbons, 2003; Hale & Gibbons, 1999). In the examples, even when the normal format of turn-taking organisation was maintained, the loss of primary realities through omissions of projection frames containing 'verbal processes' (Halliday, 1994) made the trouble source of miscommunication ambiguous in terms of whose utterance led to a particular problem. However, maintenance of the 'normal format' could lead to the primary speakers remaining unaware either of how a particular miscommunication has been dealt with or of potentially negative perceptions of their credibility.

In mediated interviews, disturbances of the normal turn-taking format may lead to side sequences or 'asides' – the second category of repair sequences analysed in this chapter. Such asides had several different types of 'trouble source'. One such trouble source was cross-cultural and linguistic gaps. In these cases, police interviewers may directly appeal to interpreters' bilingual and bicultural capacity (cf. Berk-Seligson, 1990; Laster & Taylor, 1994; Niska, 1995; Wadensjö, 1998). The interpreter may also initiate repairs, in a *principal* role, to address what they perceive as cross-cultural or linguistic problems. Addressing these types of trouble sources in asides may be a necessary and effective solution, if not doing so could cause cross-cultural/linguistic misunderstanding. The question is when this type of repair would be considered appropriate in the legal context, particularly given that the suspect's accounts are evaluated throughout the interview and that recorded interviews are part of the evidence used in court if the suspect is prosecuted.

A second type of trouble source addressed by repairs in 'asides' was problems with renditions. At times interpreters responded to the primary speaker's repair initiation by repairing the previous rendition without rendering the primary speaker's repair initiation turn. This seems to have occurred when interpreters had translation doubts or felt challenged by the translation. This type of repair by the interpreter however is based on the interpreter's own perception of the trouble source being their own rendition rather than the source utterance. It therefore entails the risk of removing responsibility from the relevant primary speaker to explain their utterances if they are the actual trouble source of miscommunication.

There were some trouble sources which may not actually have been causing miscommunication, but the primary speaker's discursive needs related to the institutional context of the interview. Primary speakers' repair initiations may sometimes be motivated by a need to buy time: with suspects, for composing answers, and with officers, for composing questions. Some examples of this were discussed in this chapter. Perceptions of repair initiation turns motivated by such discursive needs could have triggered interpreters' deviations from the 'normal format' of turn-taking organisation, offering a repair turn directly by themselves in 'asides'. This may also have been influenced by the normal conversational habit of attending to the immediately preceding turn in everyday interaction (Levinson, 1983; Sacks et al., 1974), making it difficult for the interpreter to maintain an *animator* role, especially in the face-to-face consecutive mode of interpreting. It is easy for the primary speaker to direct their gaze towards the interpreter who has just produced the immediately preceding turn.

Another type of trouble source leading to repairs occurring in 'asides' was suspects' unacceptable or irrelevant responses. Such trouble sources are expected to be dealt with by the interviewing officer, but in their attempt to facilitate the communication, the interpreters shifted their role from that of an *animator* to a *principal* in some examples. These trouble sources appeared to emerge from the 'institutional' framework of the police interview. This type of repair initiation by interpreters to assist the police with their institutional goals goes against the common perception amongst legal authorities that interpreters tend to act in favour of the suspect (Laster & Taylor, 1994).

While trouble sources of repairs are not always clearly identified in monolingual interaction (Sacks, 1995 Part II, p. 413), repair sequences in interpreter-mediated interaction may entail trouble sources which may be perceived differently by different interlocutors or may not be perceived at all by one or two of the interlocutors (cf. Komter, 2005). Nevertheless, on the basis of their bilingual/cultural ability and their designated rendition turn, the interpreter is in a position to decide how to manage miscommunication and potential threat to interactional alignment. Thus, police interviewers must relinquish their power and rely on the interpreter to manage miscommunication to a large extent. However, varying perceptions of trouble sources and miscueing in repair sequences in asides could lead to further miscommunication. If the trouble source is identified explicitly, and if repair initiation and repair turns are produced in full forms (avoiding ellipsis even if it makes the utterances unnatural), some complications of miscommunication through interpreter mediation may be avoided.

The ambiguity of trouble source is also related to interpreter roles. The examples in this chapter showed the interpreter moving back and forth between the *animator, author* and *principal* roles in trying to deal with miscommunication. The *animator* role assumes the trouble source to be that of the primary speaker's turn ('I said X' in the primary speaker's voice), while the *principal* role assumes miscommunication occurring amongst three interlocutors including the interpreter him/herself ('I rendered as X' in the interpreter's voice). The animator role, however, may obscure the trouble source, including interpreting problems. Two examples were given of this, in which projection frames pointing to the primary reality were dropped through interpreting. Furthermore, when the trouble source is the rendition itself, the *author* role allows the interpreter to shift the trouble source from their own utterances to those of the suspect.

Finally, from the evidential perspective, repair sequences laden with overlapping talk, or occurring in 'asides', are problematic in terms of access to the content of the interview discourse as evidence. In this regard, it may make the investigation process more transparent and less problematic if the investigating officer requests a brief explanation about the repair sequence or the interpreter offers a brief explanation (although this would increase the interview time already elongated by interpreter mediation).

The analysis of repairs occurring in 'asides' in this chapter further revealed the potential of interpreter-mediated interviews to exacerbate or prolong miscommunication. The mediation layer appears to have made conversational repair sequences susceptible to changes in the trajectory of discourse, and the divergent perceptions of the interlocutors may lead to multiple interpretations of the trouble source. Another discursive feature which may be vulnerable to varying perceptions is silence, and this will be the focus of the analysis and discussion in the next chapter.

6
Managing Silence

6.1 Introduction

This chapter explores the role which silence plays in interpreter-mediated police interviews. Silence is rarely treated as something that should be translated in the interpreting process, but despite the status of silence as an 'uninterpretable' unit, silent pauses are at times treated as meaningful, not only by interpreters but also by interviewing officers and suspects.

A juxtaposition of the words 'silence' and 'police' is usually associated with the suspect's right to silence. Lack of cooperation through silence has been discussed in terms of power asymmetry and the suspect's resistance to power (Forrester & Ramsden, 2001; Heydon, 2005; Kurzon, 1995, 1997; Moston et al., 1993; Newbury & Johnson, 2006). Police officers may react to suspects' silences in a coercive manner (see for example, Forrester & Ramsden, 2001) or by using subtle questioning strategies (Gibbons, 2003) in order to have the suspect provide the type of answer they are looking for. Thus, in the context of the present research, a question arises about how silence is managed when police interviews are mediated by interpreters. It is the interpreters' turn that selects the suspect as the next speaker (Sacks et al., 1974), and it is also expected that the police officer(s) will take their turn after the suspect's turn is rendered. Given this turn-taking organisation, how do the primary speakers react if the interpreter's rendition turn is delayed or absent? As stated previously, the analysis in this book approaches interpreter-mediated discourse as tripartite interaction, treating all three interlocutors as party to the co-construction of discourse and the social processes. Thus, although discussions of silence in police interviews usually focus on interviewees' silences, this chapter also examines silence occurring in sequential locations where police interviewers or interpreters are expected to take a turn in the 'normal format' of turn-taking (Knapp & Knapp-Potthoff, 1985, p. 457; Wadensjö, 1998). The analysis and discussion explore how the management of silence, who-ever it might be attributed to, can affect the trajectory of discourse and narrative construction processes in mediated police interviews.

6.2 Managing silence in police interviews

Kurzon (1995, 1997), in a discussion of the interpretation of silence in legal contexts in which the witness or the suspect is questioned, arrives at two types of silence: (1) unintentional and (2) intentional. Unintentional silence has psychological causes such as embarrass-ment, shyness or the need to hide ignorance, while intentional silence is 'a deliberate attempt by the addressee not to be cooperative with the addresser' (Kurzon, 1995, p. 55). Intentional silence is likely to be interpreted in a way that is negative for the suspect or the witness, despite the right to silence (Kurzon, 1995). Related to this is a finding by Walker (1985) who showed that evaluation of silent pauses preced-ing an answer given by a witness depended on the social context, that is, on which party interprets the silence. While the police may perceive suspects' silence as a sign of non-cooperation, suspects' silence has also been discussed as a resistance strategy against the institutional power which is reflected and reproduced in the role of questioner given to the interviewing officer (Forrester & Ramsden, 2001; Kurzon, 1995; Newbury & Johnson, 2006).

Silence can also be used intentionally by police officers who are carrying out interviews. Heydon (2005) demonstrated that the police officer may not take the floor even when the suspect appears to have completed their response. In this sense silence can be used as a pressur-ing strategy by the police officer, who avoids taking a turn until some desired information is provided by the interviewee.

In the studies mentioned above (Forrester & Ramsden, 2001; Heydon, 2005), silence in the form of silent pauses is closely examined in the light of the rules of turn-taking originally discussed in the seminal paper by Sacks et al. (1974). The suspect selected as the next speaker by the police officer's question would be expected to follow rule 1(a), in which the selected next speaker is expected to take a turn at the initial transition relevance place (TRP). If the suspect does not answer, this is considered a marked silence caused by a violation of turn-taking rules; it is viewed as the suspect's silence and may be interpreted as indicating their attitude towards the question (Sacks, 1995). If this happens, as demonstrated by Forrester and Ramsden (2001), the interviewing officer may take the floor and ask another question. On the other hand, in a case where the suspect responds to a question, at the next TRP in the suspect's utterance, the interviewer may take a turn and ask another question. There may however be a problem in that the TRP is not as pragmatically or grammatically clear-cut as is the end of a question. Thus, it may be left to the officer's judgment as to how much information is satisfactory as an answer to their question, which could result in long in-turn pauses if the officer expects more but the suspect thinks the answer is complete (Heydon, 2005).

6.3   Analysing silence in interpreter-mediated police interviews

As has been found in previous research in monolingual police interviews mentioned above, silence may have varied functions and interpretations. Questions then arise concerning the function of silence in interpreter-mediated police interviews and how silence is treated by the participants, including the interpreter. In discussing turn-taking in interpreter-mediated interaction, Roy (2000, p. 74) points out that silence 'creates opportunities for talking and taking a turn', which may lead to a finely tuned coordination by the interpreter of their task of mediation. These 'opportunities' created by silence may also become relevant for primary speakers to take a turn.

According to the turn-taking rules postulated by Sacks et al. (1974, p. 704), if the next speaker is selected, for example by a question addressed to a specific interlocutor, the selected speaker is expected to take a turn at the next possible TRP. What is unique in interpreter-mediated interaction is that interpreters are expected to take a turn every time a primary speaker produces a turn. However, this assumed turn allocation does not always materialise (Komter, 2005; Müller, 1989; Roy, 2000; Wadensjö, 1998), and one of the triggers for this deviation may be a silent pause, or a 'gap' as described by Sacks et al. (1994). A source utterance may be rendered in multiple interpreter turns (Wadensjö, 1998), especially when the suspect is providing a narrative with multiple TCUs (Turn Construction Units) (see also Chapter 4, Section 4.3.1). Additionally, since suspects' turns are mostly an answer to a question, they are not intrinsically designed to select the next speaker, although, in the institutional framework, it is expected that the police officer's next question follows the suspect's response. Thus, if a rendition turn does not occur after the suspect has spoken, the relevant turn-taking rule will be applied, namely, if no speaker has been selected, at the next TRP of the current speaker, any speaker may take a turn, including the current speaker (Sacks et al., 1974). Thus the suspect may self-select. This would make what was projected as an 'inter-turn' pause into an 'intra-turn' pause.

On the other hand, if the suspect remains silent after the police interviewer's question has been interpreted, since the next speaker has been selected specifically by the design of the question turn, and due to the institutional framework of the police interview, it can be deduced that the selected speaker has either a comprehension difficulty or refuses to respond and give information. The problem however is that the meaning of the silence is 'interpreted' by two other interlocutors – the interpreter and the interviewer. As we will see, this appears to be a unique, and problematic, aspect of silence in interpreter-mediated interviews.

In a similar way, silence in a sequential location in which the police interviewer's turn is expected can be analysed in terms of how it is managed by the participants. Police officers' turns tend to be any of the following: a 'sequence-closing third' (Schegloff, 2007), that is, a minimal utterance to close, in this case, a question–answer sequence; a first pair part of an expansion sequence; or a question opening a new sequence. When these types of turns do not occur where they are expected, what do the suspect and the interpreter do? Silence in these turn slots may be treated as a possible 'lapse', in which the continuity of interaction is lost (Sacks et al., 1974). Does the silence open up opportunities for the suspect to take a turn? Or is it regarded as a negative evaluation of the suspect's preceding answer?

From the observations above, it can be seen that the sequential location of silence is a good reference point for exploring how participants manage silence and how silence may impact on the trajectory of narrative constructions in mediated police interviews. The following sections thus discuss the management of silence according to its location in the sequence organisation. Following Jefferson (1989), who identified a standard maximum silence as being around 1.0–1.2 seconds, and Walker's (1985) criteria used for courtroom interaction in which pauses above 1.0 but below 1.5 seconds were coded as in-turn pauses and those above 1.5 seconds were coded as switching pauses, pauses above 1.0 seconds in the data were coded according to their location: after the rendition of the police officer's question, within the suspect's response turn, before the interpreter's rendition, and after the interpreter's rendition of the suspect response. Walker (1985, p. 62) accepts that 'what is a pause in some circumstances is not in others', but for the purpose of the analysis, 'a standard of measurement' has to be established.

The discussion covers, first, silent pauses that occurred immediately after the interpreter's rendition of the police officer's question, that is, where the suspect's turn is expected (Section 6.4). Then, the discussion turns to an analysis of how silent pauses were managed when they occurred after the suspect had given their response, or part of it (Section 6.5). Finally, Section 6.6 will consider silences occurring directly after the primary speakers' turns, in locations where the interpreter's rendition is expected.

6.4   Silent pauses after the rendition of police officer's questions

This section examines silent pauses following interpreters' renditions of police officers' questions. The silence in this position of the 'normal format' of turn-taking organisation occurs where the suspect is expected to answer the question, so it can be described as the suspect's silence, but the different ways in which this silence is treated means it does not always 'belong' to the suspect.

6.4.1   Silence as an NTRI for repair of rendition

Interpreters in the data occasionally treat suspect silence after the rendition of a question as a next-turn repair initiator (NTRI). When a problematic utterance has been produced, an NTRI may follow so that the problem that threatens the coherent flow of the conversation can be repaired (Schegloff, 1992; Schegloff et al., 1977). An NTRI may take the form of a request for clarification, a repetition or a repair (Schegloff, 1992; Schegloff et al., 1977; Wong, 2000), but Wong (2000) and Schegloff (2000) point out that an NTRI may be preceded by, or the trouble source may be followed by, a silent gap. Schegloff (2000) in particular argues that such a gap may be due to a preference for self-repair. In other words, a silent gap after a trouble source turn would encourage the trouble source speaker to repair the problem and may possibly lead to the avoidance of other-initiated repair. However, if a self-repair occurs after a gap, without a verbalised NTRI, and if the trouble source is a completed question as a first pair part of an adjacency pair, then it would be possible to consider this silent gap itself as an NTRI. In Extract 6.1 the police officer (PO3) asks the suspect (S3) about a customs and quarantine declaration form.

Extract 6.1 (Interview 3)

```
1 PO3: What did she do with that form,
2       (0.3)
3 IR3: Sono kaado o, a:no sono kaado, nani o
4       shimashita ka, (0.3) sono kaado de.
        (That card, u:m that card, what did you do with
        that card?)
→ 5     (1.5)
→ 6 IR3: Sono kaado de dooiufuuni tsukaimashita = nani
7       o, nani o shimashita [ka?
        (With that card, in what way did you use,
        what, what did you do?)
8 S3:                         [Kinyuushimashita.
                              (I filled it in.)
9 IR3: I ju- yea I just filled it in.
```

The interpreter (IR3) seems to have trouble rendering the question, as indicated by the self-repairs that occur three times (lines 3–4). As has been shown in preceding chapters, the use of the third person 'she' by the police officer is inappropriate but it occurs across the interviews in the data set. The problem with the translation of the question is probably due to the use of 'with' (line 1), which means 'concerning' in this context. The object marker *o* at the beginning is appropriate, but in the first repair IR3 drops it, and uses an interrogative pronoun *nani* 'what' instead of contextually more appropriate *doo* 'what/how'. Then in the last repair in line 4, a case particle *de*, which renders 'with' in the sense of 'by means of', is used instead of *o*. Instead of a response, this is followed by a pause of 1.5 seconds. IR3 then repairs, changing *nani* 'what' to *doo* 'what/how', and the verb *shimashita* 'did' to *tsukaimashita* 'used'. However, in line 7, IR3 reverts to the earlier version '*nani o shimashita ka*', at which point a response from S3 is given with a slight overlap. The multiple repairs before and after the pause in line 5 indicate that IR3 has doubts about his translation and interprets the silent pause as a sign of a problem, and therefore treats it as an NTRI. The interpreter's credibility is at risk if the suspect does not respond to the question, since the police officer may think that the suspect's silence is due to problems with the translation (Wadensjö, 1998).

In Extract 6.2, the police officer (PO4) is asking, after repairing his question twice (line 1), how the suspect (S4) got to know the travel agent who organised his travel to Australia and his short term work there. The police officer's intent is to identify the circumstances in which S4 was given a bottle of rice wine he had been asked to take to Australia as a souvenir, in which a narcotic substance was detected. S4 had told PO4 that the travel agent approached him, and that it was a person from the travel agency who took him to the airport in Thailand, from where he travelled to Australia.

Extract 6.2 (Interview 4)

```
    1  PO4:  Uh how (0.5) when- (0.6) how did the: travel
    2        agent get in contact with you.
    3  IR4:  Mm. .hh demo, e: dooyatte sono
    4        ryokoogaisha no hito ga irasshatta wake
    5        (.)nandesu ka?
             (Mm but uh in what course of event did that
             person from the travel agent come to you?)
→   6        (1.4)
→   7  IR4:  °Dooiu riyuu de°.
             (For what reason?)
    8  S4:   A, e:tto soreto ano nihonjin no tomodachi no
    9        shookai de arubaito ga (0.3) aru kara,
   10        oosutoraria e iku arubaito ga aru kara,
   11        sore de,
             (Oh, uh and through a Japanese friend's
             introduction, because there is a is a part-
             time job to go to Australia, for that reason.)
```

The interpreter (IR4) uses an interrogative *dooyatte* 'in what way/how' in line 3, which is one of the equivalents of 'how' in Japanese, but its combination with the problematic rendition of 'get in contact' into *irasshatta* ('came') makes the question in Japanese sound as if it is about the mode of transportation. It should be noted that this interpreter's renditions *irasshatta* is the past honorific form of *kuru* 'come'. Abundant use of honorifics when translating PO4's questions was observed in this interpreter, but it is not necessary to use an honorific form. That aside, a better option for the rendition of the question would be '*Donoyoona keei de*' ('In what circumstances'). Unsurprisingly, S4 does not reply immediately and a silent pause follows. The interpreter then self-repairs the rendition of 'how', changing it from '*dooyatte*' to '*dooiu riyuu de*' (for what reason). The repaired rendition in line 7 receives a response from S4, although the response outlines the reason for S4's travel rather than the circumstances in which he got to know, or was approached by, the travel agent.

The 1.4 second pause in line 6 may not be significantly long enough to reach an inference that the suspect is confused by the interpreted question. Interpreters do not necessarily initiate repair even when silences longer than five seconds occur after translating questions, some examples of which will be shown. Yet the silent pause in line 6, at a location where the suspect answer is expected, appeared to be treated as an NTRI by the interpreter, probably because of a lack of confidence in the first rendition. It is also likely that the suspect was confused by the first rendition of the question, as he says 'A' ([a], similar to 'oh') at the beginning of his response in line 8, indicating comprehension.

From the point of view of the investigating officers, between the original question and the English rendition of the suspect's response, there is not much they can do, as it is impossible for them to know what is being communicated or what the nature of problem is, if there is one. If the interpreter believes the translation may be the cause of a lack of response and responds accordingly, the interpreter takes away some of the investigating officer's power to deal with the suspect's silence, due to the standard organisation of turns in consecutive interpreting, where an interpreter turn follows each time the primary speaker speaks.

However, a suspect's lengthy silence after the rendition of a question does not always lead to interpreter repairs. Instead of repairing their rendition, interpreters were also found to leave the suspect with long silences. Such silences may put the suspects on the spot (see also Section 6.6.2). In some cases, depending on the nature of the question or the line of questioning, this may pressure suspects into a confession (Gibbons, 2003; Heydon, 2005; Newbury & Johnson, 2006; Shuy, 1998). It has been reported that police officers use such silences in English-only interviews (Forrester & Ramsden, 2001; Heydon, 2005). Interpreters, whether consciously or unconsciously, also seem to adopt this. In Extract 6.3 below, the police officer (PO3) asks a question (lines 1–4) about the discovery of heroin under the false bottom of a suitcase. A question 'Why do you think the heroin would be hidden in the case like that?' had already been asked earlier, to which the suspect (S3) had replied 'I don't know' without hesitation. It seems that PO3, by paraphrasing 'why' with 'what ... for', may be attempting to elicit a specific response or to pressure S3 into confession. Possibly being aware of PO3's motivation for asking this question, S3 hesitates for 2.7 seconds. Her response prefaced by 'I don't know but' suggests that she is trying to give the impression she is guessing and has no involvement in the crime.

Extract 6.3 (Interview 3)

```
 1 PO3:  Why do you think the hero- (.) what do- ah
 2        sorry, what do you think the heroin would be
 3        placed in that, (0.4) placed o:r hidden inside
 4        the case like that for,
 5 IR3:   Nan no tame ni, ano heroin ga suutsukeesu no
 6        nakani, kooiu, aaiu fuu ni kakushite aru
 7        deshoo ka.
          (For what purpose would heroin be hidden
          inside a suitcase like this, like that?)
→ 8      (2.7)
 9 S3:    Wakarimasen kedo:, (0.4) mitsubai: °desho°,
          (I don't know, but isn't it drug trafficking?)
```

During the silence in line 8, the interpreter does not speak. The translation is accurate, apart from not translating 'placed' in PO3's question, which was self-repaired with 'hidden'. It appears that IR3 does not see the 2.7 second pause as an NTRI, particularly since he has already translated an almost identical question, which elicited the suspect's response immediately. However, in light of PO3's repetition of the question after receiving the response 'I don't know', IR3 may be adopting a strategy of silence to pressure the suspect into confession. In this way, IR3 may be, intentionally or unintentionally, going along with PO3's interview agenda. The decision to drop 'placed' in his rendition may also have served PO3's interest here as the word 'hidden' highlights the criminal intent, thus maintaining the pressure on the suspect.

6.4.2 Silence as an NTRI for the interpreter to repair the question

There are some cases in the data set in which the interpreter repairs the police officer's original question, not its rendition, when a short silence ensues following the rendition of the police officer's question. Thus, the silence occurring where the suspect's response is expected is treated as an NTRI, with the police officer's question as the trouble source.

In Extract 6.4, the police interviewer (PO4) asks the suspect (S4) about Pat, who S4 claims gave him the bottle of rice wine in which an illegal substance was found:

Extract 6.4 (Interview 4)

```
 1 PO4:  Okay, is that the only (0.5)um (1.3)piece of
 2        information that Pat (0.4) has given to you?
 3 IR4:   Ye[ah],
```

```
   4 PO4:   [in] regards to her?
   5 IR4:   Yeh, Pat san ni tsuite no joohoo tteiu no wa
   6        kore dake: desu ka,
            (Yeh, is this the only information about Pat?)
→  7        (0.8)
→  8 IR4:   Kono: sono meeshi dake desu ka,=
            (This- is it only that business card?)
   9 S4:    =Hai.
            (Yes.)
  10 IR4:   Ye:s, that's [right].
  11 PO4:                [Okay ].
```

The rendition of the question is followed by a pause (line 7), which occurs where S4 is expected to answer the question. While the rendition is problematic because of its changed nature of 'information', both versions of the question are simple polar questions. Whether S4's silence is due to some external reason or confusion over the question, the interpreter's repair in line 8 clarifies the referent of 'that' (line 1) in the original question. (The deictic 'that' is translated as *'kore'*, or 'this' in Japanese [line 6], probably due to the proximity of Pat's business card to S4.) The repair in line 8 addresses what IR4 seems to perceive as the problem with the referent of the deictic 'that'. This means that the interpreter assumed that the silence in line 8 was caused by a problem with PO4's question in lines 1–2.

Similarly, in Extract 6.5 below, when the suspect (S3) does not respond after the question is rendered, the interpreter (IR3) produces a repair turn, clarifying the item mentioned in the question. The police officer (PO3) asks S3 if she opened her luggage 'at any stage' (line 1). This question was preceded by an exchange concerning a handbag and a suitcase which S3 had brought from Japan.

Extract 6.5 (Interview 4)

```
   1 PO3:   Did you open this luggage at any stage?
   2        (0.5)
   3 IR3:   Itsuka sono su- ano: (0.4) nimotsu akemashita
   4        ka,
            (Did you open the su- um luggage sometime?)
→  5        (3.0)
→  6 IR3:   Nimotsu toiu to sore ano [zen- zen]bu irete,
            (Luggage means that um including all of it,)
   7 S3:                             [Ookii hoo]
```

```
                                         (The big one)
 8  IR3:  (.) [baggu],
              (bags.)
 9  S3:       [ookii] hoo mo. (0.3) Kochira wa
10            akemashita kedo,=
              (The big one too. I opened this one, but
11  IR3:  =Un,=
              (Yeah)
12  S3:   =Ookii hoo no wa akemasen.
              (I didn't open the big one.)
13            (0.3)
14  IR3:  I opened the handbag but >I didn't open the
15            large suitcase.<
```

When the rendition of the question in lines 3–4 fails to elicit a response for three seconds (line 5), IR3 elaborates on the referent of *'nimotsu'* (luggage), saying that it refers to all of the luggage. While the translation of *'at any stage'* into *'itsuka'* (sometime in the future) is unnatural, the past tense of *'akeru'* (open) makes it sufficiently clear that the question is about whether S3 opened the luggage at some point. The problem then becomes the referent of 'luggage'. The exchange which took place prior to line 1 refers to the handbag and the suitcase which S3 had when she left Japan. This suggests that 'this luggage' in the question (line 1) refers to two pieces – a handbag and a suitcase. IR3's repair turn in line 6 suggests that he regarded S3's silence as being caused by the lack of clarity in the original question as to what exactly 'this luggage' referred to. In fact, IR3's rendition (line 3) seems to show him starting to say 'suitcase' but retracting from it to use 'luggage' instead. It seems that S3 also initially understands the question to be about the large piece of luggage (line 7), that is, the suitcase, but then after hearing *'zenbu irete'* (including all) in IR3's clarification, S3 joins to co-construct the clarification sequence in line 7, overlapping IR3's repair turn and finally responding by referring to the two pieces of luggage (lines 9, 10 and 12).

The above two examples suggest an alternative trouble source for the suspect's silence in the turn slot, namely the police officer's question itself. In the previous section, the interpreters treated silence as caused by a problematic rendition, but in this section they directly repaired the police interviewers' original questions. The varying perceptions by interpreters of silence occurring at the same location in the turn-taking system led to different types of repairs.

6.4.3 Silence as an NTRI for the police interviewer to repair the question

Police officers were also found to take a turn to repair their previous turn, although not as often as interpreters, in contexts in which the suspect remained silent after the question had been rendered. This seemed to happen when the police officer became aware that their original question was causing the suspect's silence.

In the following extract, the police officer (PO1) tries to find out how often the suspect (S1) had contact with Wang, a relative of Mark, who helped S1's tour group with their trip to Australia via Malaysia.

Extract 6.6 (Interview 1)

```
 1 PO1: When you've uh: visited (0.3) Mark (.) in
 2       Malaysia, (.) how often has Wang been with
 3       you.
 4       (0.9)
 5 IR1: Ja Mark o ano Mareeshia: de hoomon shita toki
 6       ni wa, .hh ano Wang wa, donokurai no hindo de
 7       Mark to isshoni imashita ka.
         (So, when you visited Mark um in Malaysia,
         .hh um how often was Wang with Mark?)
 8       (2.2)
 9 S1:  Itsu desu ka?
         (When?)
10       (0.3)
11 IR1: Ah you referring to (.) which visit?
12 S1:  Ima madeno (.)[(   )] toki desu [ka?]
         (Until now, when ( ) do you mean?)
13 PO1:               [Any.]           [All],
14       all of the visits.=
15 IR1: =Ja ano imamade itta subete (.) no, na- ano
16       hoomon no naka de, Mark ni (0.2) °Mareeshia de
17       atta toki niwa.°
         (So, um in all of the visits up till now, when
         you saw Mark in Malaysia.)
→ 18     (1.0)
→ 19 PO1: All- sorry, (.) all the visits to Malaysia.=
20 IR1: =De Mareeshia de, e: Wang ni atta toki (.)
21       subete o fukumete, (.) donokurai no hindo de
22       Wang wa Mare- ano Mark to isshoni imashita ka?
```

> (So in Malaysia, uh when you saw Wang, in all
> of your visits, how often was Wang with Mala-
> um Mark?)

Because S1 had visited Mark in Malaysia a few times, something which had already been mentioned in the interview, S1 seems to be unsure as to which visit PO1's question refers to. Thus after remaining silent for over two seconds, S1 initiates a repair in line 9. The interpreter (IR1) renders this NTRI (line 11), and S1 also elaborates on his NTRI in line 12. PO1 responds to the NTRI in line 11 and clarifies his question in line 13, initially saying 'Any'. However, this overlaps with S1's elaboration of his NTRI and moreover, 'any visit' would not give PO1 the kind of information which he required for the investigation. Thus, PO1 self-repairs his repair turn and initiates another clarification at the end of line 13 by changing 'any' to 'all of the visits'. This is immediately rendered by IR1 (lines 15–17), but a 1.0 second pause follows. This pause prompts PO1 to take a turn for another repair, this time adding the clarification of the location being Malaysia. It seems that he is initially trying to repeat what he said in the earlier repair turn (lines 13–14), but then says 'sorry' and specifically mentions the location. The silence in line 18 appears to be perceived by PO1 as caused by his earlier inadequate repair due to overlapping as well as to lack of reference to the location of the 'visits'.

It should be noted that IR1's rendition (lines 15–17) of PO1's first repair ends with a topic marker '*wa*' with a falling intonation. This combination suggests there is more to follow. To signal in Japanese that a response is required, a rising intonation is expected with '*wa*' at this point. It is possible that S1 remained silent expecting more from the interpreter. IR1 herself may have also perceived the silence in line 18 to be caused by this miscommunication, as she adds, in lines 21–22, the core part of the original question ('how often was Wang with Mark?') to the rendition of PO1's second repair. Thus, PO1 and IR1 may have perceived different trouble sources for the suspect's silence in this instance, but PO1's taking a turn in line 19 consequently becomes an 'official' acknowledgement that his turn was the trouble source. However, IR1's subsequent 'unofficial' addition indicates that she may have believed that her rendition of PO1's second repair led to the miscommunication. It is also possible that S1 may have been taking time to formulate his response in the 1.0 second silence. Repairs may occur without a clear identification of the trouble source (Sacks, 1995, Part II, p. 413; see also Komter, 2005), but the ambiguous nature of silence and the mediation process could be making it harder to identify the trouble source.

The following extract shows a similar example in which the police interviewer takes a turn to repair his question after a period of silence following the rendition of the question. The police officer (PO3) is asking the suspect (S3) about the circumstances under which her suitcase was handled as her tour group made their way to the airport in Kuala Lumpur. S3 had told PO3 that her suitcase had been stolen but replaced while in Kuala Lumpur for transit.

Extract 6.7 (Interview 3)

```
 1  PO3:  What sort of car,=
 2  IR3:  =Nan no kuruma deshita ka, (.) Donna kuruma
 3        deshita ka,
           (What car was it, what sort of car was it?)
 4   S3:  Mukae ni kita kuruma to onaji kuruma desu.
           (It was the same car that came to pick us up.)
 5  IR3:  It was the same car as what came- car that
 6        >came to pick us up.<
 7  PO3:  Where was your case then.
 8  IR3:  Sono toki suutsukeesu wa doko deshita ka,
           (Where was the suitcase at the time?)
→ 9        (1.0)
→10  PO3:  Or the maroon suitcase sorry, (well)=
11  IR3:  =A, sono, ru- ano (.) wainreddo no suutsukeesu
12        wa doko deshita ka.
           (Oh, that ru- um where was the wine red
           suitcase?)
13        (0.7)
14   S3:  Ano suutsukeesu wa, (1.0) dokka ni
15        azukemashita.
           (That suitcase, I had left it with someone.)
16  IR3:  Uh: it had been (0.3) looked after somewhere.
```

The topic of the questions moves from the transport used to the handling of S3's suitcase. PO3 asks (line 7) where S3's suitcase was when she and her fellow travellers were driven to the airport. When S3 was searched and arrested on her arrival in Australia, she had with her a handbag and a maroon suitcase, but she told PO3 in the interview that the suitcase was a replacement suitcase after her black suitcase that she brought from Japan had been stolen while in transit in Malaysia. Thus, when 'suitcase' was mentioned it could have been either the black suitcase or the maroon one. However it is not specified in PO3's question ('your case'), and when a silence of one second follows the rendition of this question (line 9), PO3 repairs his question in line 10 by saying 'the maroon suitcase'. The apology 'sorry' in this repair turn suggests his awareness that the question in line 7 was not specific enough.

In Extracts 6.6 and 6.7 above, the police interviewers took a turn to repair their questions after 1.0 second of silence. This has been identified by Jefferson (1989) as the standard maximum length of silent pauses in conversation. However, the police officer's turn is the least expected in this position in the 'normal format' of turn-taking organisation in interpreter-mediated interviews, and there are cases in the data in which neither the interpreters nor the police officers take a turn when suspects remain silent much longer than 1.0 second after the rendition of questions into Japanese (see Extract 6.12 for an example). This suggests that the police officers in these extracts were certain that their original questions were the trouble source to which the suspects' silences were directed and they felt the need to redress the problem. The apologies 'sorry' in the officers' repair-turns in the above two extracts also seem to indicate this stance, although it is also possible that the apologies are directed at either or both the suspect and the interpreter as each officer is aware of taking a turn where he is not expected to.

It should also be noted here that PO3's interpretation of the silence in line 9 in the above extract may not be shared with other interlocutors. While the interpreter's rendition of the original question in line 8 is accurate and easy to understand, the fact that S3's second response (line 14) came after a pause and includes a full second's pause before the predicate is produced may imply that S3 may have needed a full second pause in line 9 to retrieve her memory or formulate her response regardless of her interpretation of PO3's original question. As was the case with the previous example, the interlocutors may have different understandings of silence, in particular due to their varying vested interests in the interview as a speech event. The ambiguous nature of silence as a non-verbal meaning unit also seems to allow for any of the interlocutors to jump in, unlike the verbal NTRIs produced by the suspect.

These varied approaches of the three parties to silence in mediated interviews is also illustrated by Extract 6.8 below. Here, towards the end of the interview, the police officer (PO3) informs the suspect (S3) of the

allegations against her as part of the procedure to request fingerprint-
ing. There are legal terms of the alleged crimes in PO3's utterances in
lines 1–3, and the interpreter (IR3) has considerable trouble in translating these terms.

Extract 6.8 (Interview 3)

```
 1 PO3: Could you also tell her she's suspected of
 2       (0.3) suspected on offence of import and
 3       possess of prohibited import?

         ((Interpreter asks clarification questions and
         checks his dictionary – a couple of minutes))

18 IR3: Do you wanna repeat the question thank you?
19 PO3: .hhh u:m that she's suspected of an offence of
20      import and possess of prohibited import?
21 IR3: Ichioo: (.) a:: (1.5) Possession, possession
22      and importing?
        (Actually, uh:)
23 PO3: Possess, and- (0.5) import and possess of
24      prohibited import, namely that (0.3) heroin?
25 IR3: Ichioo, heroin no (.) ano, motteru, mata
26      mochikomu toiu a: (1.2) kotode, (.) utaga-
27      utaga- (0.2) gawaretemasu ga.
        (Actually, for um carrying, and also bringing
        in heroin, you are suspec- suspec- pected,
        But …)
→ 28    (2.4)
29 PO3: °All right,°
30      (1.9)
→ 31 PO3: Does she understand?
32 IR3: Wakarimashita ka,
        (Do you understand?)
33      (1.2)
→ 34 S3:  Nande utagawareru ndesu ka, = honto no koto
35       shabettemasu yo.
         (Why am I suspected? I am telling you the
         truth.)
36 IR3: Why is she suspected of that >cos she's been
37      speaking< the truth.
38 S3:  Watashi wa, tada tsuitekita dake de:, ikubasho
```

```
39        mo:, nanimo hoteru no namae mo zenbu
40        shiranakatta ndesu.
          (I simply tagged along, and did not know where
          we were going or the name of the hotel or
          anything.)
41 IR3:   I was just sort of taken along I didn't know
42        anything I didn't know the name of our hotels,
43        (0.2) anything.
```

After a number of repair exchanges, IR3 renders PO3's utterances informing S3 of the allegations against her (lines 25–27). The rendition maintains most of the propositional content of the original utterances (including the addition of *heroin* through the repair), but the register is significantly lower in the rendition than in the source utterances. The legal terms 'import' (*yunyuu* in Japanese) and 'possess' (*shoji* in Japanese) are turned into everyday verbs *'motteru'* (to be carrying) and *'mochikomu'* (to bring in), and 'prohibited import' is omitted and replaced by 'heroin'. Thus it should be easy for S3 to understand this communication of allegation, but she does not say anything for over two seconds (line 28). PO3's question following this ('Does she understand?') suggests his interpretation of the silence as S3's comprehension problem. This is understandable given that PO3 is not aware of the change in register through interpreting and that IR3 struggled to translate the legal terms earlier.

However, this interpretation by PO3 may not reflect the cause of the silence from S3's perspective. One possible cause of the silence is that S3 may have been thrown by the official reconfirmation of the allegation, having assumed that the information she provided in the interview would lead to clearing the suspicion. This can be supported by her statements in lines 34–35 and lines 38–40. Another possible cause is that S3 did not think she was expected to take a turn at the point at which IR3 completed his rendition in line 27. The rendition of the communication of the allegation starts with *'Ichioo'* ('actually', which IR3 uses as a discourse marker, often in a non-standard way), which makes the statement (inappropriately) tentative. Then, the rendition ends with *'utaga-warete masu ga'* (you are suspected, but ...). The second clause is usually expected after the conjunction *ga* (but), but this second clause 'is often omitted when it is understandable from the context' or 'when the speaker doesn't want to continue for some reason' (Makino & Tsutsui, 1991, p. 122). IR3 may have used this structure with omission to render the function of the source utterance, which in fact could be ambiguous if it is regarded as the first pair part of an adjacency pair (Sacks et al., 1974). PO3's utterance in lines 1–3 is a *request* for IR3 to *tell* S3 that she is suspected of certain criminal offences. Thus IR3's rendition turn is to have a function of 'telling', or 'informing'. Overwhelmingly the police interview consists of chains of question–answer adjacency pairs, with opening and closing phases of the police interview (Heydon, 2005) containing different types of turns. A long information gathering phase consisting of question–answer sequences took place before this 'informing' turn concerning here and now, or the primary realities (Hale & Gibbons, 1999) of the interview as a legal procedure. This shift in the turn type, reflected in the interpreter's rendition, may have led to S3's silence. Given her stance against the allegation, she could not have simply given an affirmative token response such as '*hai*' (yes) as the SSP (Second Pair Part). It is therefore only when the question 'Do you understand?' is rendered that S3 gives a dispreferred response 'Why is she [am I] suspected ...' refuting the allegation.

This section has examined silences after the renditions of police officers' questions. Since the turn-taking format of interpreter-mediated interviews designates the interpreter as the next possible speaker after the suspect's turn, and the interpreter has also been the last speaker, silence after the interpreter's rendition of a police officer's question tends to prompt the interpreter to take a turn to address a possible problem in communication. The interpreter's perceptions about the nature of silence seem to depend on a number of contextual factors such as the level of accuracy of the preceding rendition or the clarity of the source utterance question. The ambiguous nature of silence also allows for the interpreter's discretion to decide what exactly the trouble source is, although trouble sources are not always clearly identified in repairs (Sacks, 1995, Part II, p. 413). The analysis has also demonstrated that police officers may jump in to clarify their previous question after becoming aware of a problem in it. To a certain extent, silence, as a non-verbal form of communication, allows for this move by the police officer. Verbally produced repair initiation by the suspect in Japanese would make it more difficult for the police officer to step in to address miscommunication and make the police officer more dependent on the interpreter when dealing with miscommunication.

6.5 Silent pauses after the rendition of suspect's responses

Silence is also found in the position following the interpreter's rendition of the suspect's response turn. This is where the police officer's turn is expected, usually a question or an evaluation of the suspect's response followed by another question. Thus, again we could see the silence in this discursive position as the police officer's silence but what unfolds in the position after the silence gives it different roles.

6.5.1   Silence as an opportunity to elaborate on responses

While suspects in non-interpreted interviews are able to give their responses in a long turn containing multiple turn construction units (TCUs), that is unless the police officer interrupts them, the suspects in interpreter-mediated interviews at times have to relinquish their turn to allow the interpreter to render their responses in separate turns before the interpreter's memory is overloaded. This means that the interpreter's rendition of the suspect's response may be followed by the suspect's turn again, to allow for the suspect to continue with the remaining parts of the response.

This practice however may also be adapted to the situation in which the suspect has actually completed his/her turn but decides to elaborate or add to the previous turn after the interpreter's rendition, especially if the police officer does not initiate a turn after a gap. Extract 6.9 shows an example. The police officer (PO4) is trying to find out about the company owned by a friend of the suspect (S4) which has funded S4's trips in and out of Thailand for visa purposes.

Extract 6.9 (Interview 4)

```
 1 PO4: What does- what type of business (.) does that
 2       company do.
 3 IR4: Ah, .hh de koko no kaisha nandesu keredomo,
 4       dooitta (.) e:: shokushu no dooitta koto o
 5       yatteru ndesu ka,
       (Oh, .hh and this company, what kind of
       business, what sort of things do they do?)
 6       (0.3)
 7  S4: Shuu- kuruma no shuuri to,=
       (Rep- Car repair and)
 8 IR4: =Mm:.
 9  S4: Kara: ch- kuruma no chuukosha no hanbai to,
10       (0.4) kara: hokengyoomu desu ne, (.) son-
11       songaihoken.
       (And sec- second hand car sales, and
       insurance business, insurance against damage.)
12 IR4: Hai. .hh the: car repair? (0.4) and then
```

```
       13        second-hand car sales? (0.5) and then (.) car
       14        insurance.
  → 15           (4.5)
  → 16   S4:     De mada (.) hanashitemo ii, (0.9) kono kaisha
       17        jitai ga nisenman kashiteru ndesu.=Kashita
       18        ndesu.
                 (And can I keep talking? This company itself
                 they owe me 20 million yen. I lent them that.)
       19  IR4:  Ah: (.) so the [uh]
       20   S4:               [Be]tsu ni mata, sore to betsu
       21        desu yo. (0.8) Motto mae ni.
                 (On top of the other one. Separately from
                 that, long before.)
       22  IR4:  Ah:, and then I, um (0.5) I let them borrow, I
       23        let them the company borrow my money, (0.4)
       24        about um twenty thousand Australian dollars.
```

After the suspect's response to the question, IR4 renders it in lines 12–14. This rendition is followed by a 4.5 second silence (line 15), during which PO4 takes notes of the types of business which S4 mentioned. S4 had said that he was not employed and that his numerous trips to a neighbouring country were paid for by a friend's company. This would give reasons for the police to regard his lifestyle with suspicion. S4 then self-selects his turn in line 15, asking for a permission to speak, before elaborating on the reason why his trips have been paid by this company. IR4 begins to render S4's self-selected turn in line 19, but S4 interrupts her (line 20) and adds further information to reinforce the justification for having his trips paid for by this company. If it had not been for PO4's note-taking, S4 may not have been able to produce his turn in lines 16–18 and 20–12 to support the narrative desired by him.

In monolingual interviews, police interviewers would also take notes during interviews, creating a period of silence which may give suspects an opportunity to elaborate on their side of the story. What is distinctive about interpreter-mediated interviews is that, as the above example shows, the suspect negotiates a turn with the interpreter. While the request for permission to speak ('can I keep talking?') should be interpreted for the interviewing officer, the interpreter here neither renders it nor says anything in response, which S4 takes as permission to speak. Once the suspect takes a turn, it automatically ratifies the interpreter to be the next speaker, since the suspect's turn should be interpreted.

Extract 6.10 below also shows the suspect elaborating on the earlier response that may have put her in a negative light. The suspect (S3) had claimed that she had been invited by another suspect, who she claimed to be a friend, to join a tour group to go to Australia. The police officer (PO3) asks a question about S3's boyfriend, which implies the officer's suspicions about her motivation in joining the tour group and her character.

Extract 6.10 (Interview 3)

```
  1 PO3: What did her boyfriend think when she was
  2       coming to Australia with Takeshi.
  3       (0.4)
  4 IR3: Ano: Kanai san no kareshi wa, a: (.) Takeshi
  5      san to isshoni oosutoraria ni kuru koto ga
  6      wakatta tokini nani o
        (Um what did your boyfriend- .hh uh when
        he found out about your trip with Takeshi?)
  7 S3:  A, (.) [shittemasu ]
        (Oh, he knows about it.)
  8 IR3:        [omoimashita] ka,
               (What did he think?)
  9 IR3: Nani o omoimashita ka?
        (What did he think?)
 10      (0.7)
 11 S3:  Ano ki o tsukete itteoide, °tte°.
        (Um he said, Take care/Have a nice trip'.)
 12 IR3: He said look after yourself.
→ 13      (3.4)
→ 14 S3:  Ano, (.) iidesu ka?
        (Um, may I?)
 15 IR3: Un.=
        (Yeah.)
→ 16 S3:  =Atashi no koto o shinyoo shiteru n desu.
        (He trusts me.)
 17 IR3: Um um (0.4) her boyfriend believes in her.
 18      (0.4) Trusts her.
```

The interpreter's rendition turn is interrupted by S3's comment ('he knows about it') before reaching a TRP, possibly because S3 expected a question to be about whether she told her boyfriend about her trip with Takeshi instead of what her boyfriend thought about the trip. However, because S3's premature response (line 7) is mostly overlapped with the end of IR3's rendition, it is not rendered, and instead IR3's next turn in line 9 is the remaining rendition of PO3's question. Upon hearing the whole rendition of PO3's question, S3 gives a response which articulates her trusting relationship with her boyfriend (line 11). This utterance is followed by a 3.4 second silence, although in the 'normal format' of turn-taking organisation PO3 is expected to take a turn here. Instead, S3 then self-selects her turn and elaborates on her relationship with her boyfriend. Again, before elaborating, the suspect asks for permission (line 14 'may I?'). Unlike the previous extract, the interpreter gives permission verbally (line 15), immediately after which S3 takes a turn to append to her previous response. Thus, in this example the suspect and the interpreter take control of turn-taking while the police officer remains silent, co-constructing an opportunity on the suspect's part to promote her narrative. However, it should be noted, as Heydon (2005) found, that the suspect's self-selected turn and narrative expansion in the data set, as shown in the above two examples, occurs within the topic which the police interviewer introduced in the interview.

Extract 6.11 also shows S3 self-selecting her turn after a period of silence in the same turn position, but in this example IR3 renders S3's request for permission to speak instead of responding to it himself. The police officer (PO3) asks S3 why her tour group came to Australia via Malaysia.

Extract 6.11 (Interview 3)

```
  1  PO3:  Why did they come to Australia via Malaysia.
  2  IR3:  Naze Mareejia keeki ni oosutoraria ni
  3        kimashita ka?
              (Why did you come to Australia through a
              Malaysian opportunity [sic]?)
  4  S3:   Hai?
              (Sorry?)
  5  IR3:  Naze, .hh Maraiija kei- (.) uh: keeyu ni,
  6        Oosutoraria ni kimashita ka?=
              (Why, .hh vi- did you come to Australia via
              Malaysia?)
→ 7  S3:   =Wakarimasen.
              (I don't know.)
  8  IR3:  I don't know.
→ 9        (2.2)
→ 10 S3:   °IIdesu ka°,
              (May I?)
```

```
      11  IR3:  >[Can she ask] a question?<
      12   S3:   [Watashi wa,]
                 (I)
      13  PO3:  Yep.
      14        (0.3)
      15  IR3:  Doozo.=
                 (Please.)
→     16   S3:  =Atashi wa, ano: (.) tsurete:korareta n de,
                 (I um have been brought here, so)
      17  IR3:  E?
                 (What?)
      18   S3:  Tsure- tsuretekorareta n de,=
                 (Brou- brought here, so)
      19  IR3:  =Hai.
                 (Yes.)
→     20   S3:  Ano (.) kuwashii koto wa zenzen wakannaku tte,
                 (Um I don't know about any details at all and)
      21  IR3:  H[ai].
                 (Yes.)
      22   S3:  [De], (.) saishoni: n sono hikooki de
      23        Mareeshia ni ippaku: toka kiite:,
                 (And I heard that we'd first fly to Malaysia
                 and stay there overnight,)
      24  IR3:  Hai.
                 (Yes.)
      25   S3:  Sorekara: ato: (0.3) nanka Oosutoraria yonpaku
      26        tte: kiita ndesu.
                 (And then I heard we'd be staying four nights
                 in Australia.)
      27        (0.7)
      28  IR3:  So because I was going to be taken on a
      29        holiday, I didn't know anything in- in great
      30        detail, .hh all I found out was you know w- w-
      31        we'll be staying one night in Malaysia and
      32        four nights in Australia.
```

The suspect (S3) responds in line 8 by saying she doesn't know why
her tour group came to Australia via Malaysia. This is followed by a
period of silence, and before PO3 gives any feedback or asks the next
question, S3 takes a turn, asking for permission to speak. The interpreter
(IR3) renders this turn into English (line 10), although assuming this is

a turn asking for permission to ask a question. When PO3 grants the request, S3 explains why she does not know the reason her tour group came to Australia via Malaysia. PO3's silence after the rendition of S3's response could have been attributed to formulating the next question, but also to a negative reaction to S3's response 'I don't know' – which is a dispreferred response. However, S3 manages to take advantage of this silence to shift any negativity by elaborating on the dispreferred response and bringing to the foreground the narrative that she was 'taken on a holiday', 'without knowing anything'. This narrative was in fact repeatedly provided by S3 whenever she found an opportunity in the interview. It is however also possible to view the silence in line 9 as an intentional non-verbal message of dissatisfaction on the part of the police interviewer, which aimed to pressure the suspect into providing justification for her response. Such examples are discussed further in the next section.

6.5.2 Silence as a negative evaluation to prompt further responses

Some silences occurring after the rendition of the suspect's response appear to indicate that the police interviewer does not find the response to be sufficient. However, as Heydon (2005) has shown, police officers prefer, and are trained to use, a participation framework in which the suspect volunteers new information rather than agreeing to the propositions provided in police officer's questions. Because of this preference, police officers may wait for an elaboration by the suspect, recasting the silent pause as an intra-turn pause (although in interpreter-mediated interviews there is a rendition turn between the suspect's turn and the silent pause). The following extracts show some examples of this.

In Extract 6.12, the suspect (S2) is questioned about the weight of the heroin found in his luggage, while being shown a photo in which the heroin is divided into several bags. S2 has been denying his prior knowledge of the heroin in the suitcase and claims that the suitcase had been replaced after a theft in a stopover city.

Extract 6.12 (Interview 2)

```
1  PO2:  How much (0.4) do you think that would we̲igh.
2  IR2:  Kore wa: omosa wa ze̲nbu de (.) donokurai da to
3        omoimasu ka?
       (How much do you think this weighs in total?)
4        (1.0)
→ 5  S2:   Wakarimasen.
       (I don't know.)
```

```
         6  IR2:  I don't know.
         7        (1.2)
    →    8  PO2:  How much do you think would be here,
         9        (0.4)
        10  IR2:  Donokurai aru to (.) omoimasu ka,
                  (How much do you think there is?)
        11        (6.4)
        12  S2:   °(Eeto::)(ichi ni san [shi)] °
                  (Urm) (One, two, three, four)
        13        (Uh::)) (one two three four)
        14  IR2:                      [let] me see, (0.2) one
        15        two three four,
        16        (6.0)
        17  S2:   (zenbu de) juu juuhachi ka,
                  (In total)(there are eighteen.)
        18        (0.5)
        19  IR2:  Eighteen all together? (0.4) eighteen packs
        20        [a:ll togeth]er.
        21  S2:   [(   )dakara],
                  (  ) (so,)
        22  IR2:  Well so:
        23        (1.7)
        24  S2:   ° (Doo daroo) °
                  (Let's see)
        25        (0.8)
        26  IR2:  I wonder:,
        27        (1.4)
        28  S2:   Gohyaku guramu gurai desu ka, (.) (kore).
                  (Is it about five hundred grams, this?)
        29  IR2:  Five hundred gra:ms,
        30  S2:   ( )nai desu.
                  ([I am/I do] not) ( ).
    →   31  IR2:  I don't know.
    →   32        (3.5)
    →   33  S2:   Shashin dake ja chotto wakan nai desu ne,=
                  (I can't really tell you only by a photo.)
        34  IR2:  =I can't tell (0.5) just only by looking at
        35        the picture.
    →   36        (1.9)
        37  PO2:  [what do]-
```

→ 38   S2:   [*Gohyak-*] *gohyaku guramu,*
              (Fiv- five hundred grams,)
   39   IR2: Five hundred grams, I suppose?
   40   PO2: What does he think,
   41   that- that (0.3) black area i̲s̲.

S2's answer to the question from the police officer (PO2) regarding the weight of the heroin in the photo is 'I don't know' (line 5). This is followed by a 1.2 second silence, after which PO2 repeats the question in her attempt to elicit a preferred response. The long silence of 6.4 seconds after the rendition of this repeated question (line 11) suggests PO2's intention to elicit an estimate for the weight of the heroin voluntarily from S2. This stance is aligned with the interpreter (IR2) who also remains silent. S2 then counts the number of bags (lines 12 and 17 and probably during the silence in line 16). After a couple of hesitant utterances in lines 24 and 26, S2 gives a figure of five hundred grams in line 28 in a question form, immediately adding that he does not know.

However, this second response, which required a number of turns and silent pauses to be completed, is followed by 3.5 seconds of silence (line 32). While this response is not as insufficient as the initial 'I don't know' response, the long pause in line 32 suggests that the amount given by S2 underestimated the actual weight (it is most likely that it was more than two kilos), and therefore PO2 was not satisfied with such an underestimated figure. The addition of uncertainty in line 31 may also have contributed to this silence which implies a negative evaluation by PO2. It should be noted here that S2's response in line 28 is a question (although it may have been in a question format to add a sense of uncertainty), and that, at the TRP after the question marker '*ka*', there is a micro-pause. This suggests that S2 may have expected IR2 to render the turn so far as a question, but the lack of immediate rendition prompted S2 to clearly state that he was not sure about the figure which he had given.

As S2 does not hear another question or any evaluation from the interviewer for 3.5 seconds, S2 then elaborates further on his response in line 33, giving the reason why he does not know how much the heroin weighs (that he cannot tell by just looking at the photo), but this at the same time gives him an opportunity to imply his innocence through the preassumption that he had not seen the bags of heroin directly or touched them. However, S2 goes back to giving the estimation of the weight in line 38 when a 1.9 second pause occurs in line 36 after the rendition of S2's justification turn. By this time PO2 gives up on pursuing a preferred response to the question about the weight of heroin and moves on with a question regarding a 'black area' of his suitcase on a photo. The initial attempt to ask this question is overlapped by S2's turn, which is rendered (line 39), but this rendered response is ignored by PO2's next question which is produced immediately after the rendition.

The analysis above is in line with what Heydon (2005) found in her study of monolingual police interviews in Australia in that police interviewers may use silence to elicit the information which they prefer for their case voluntarily from the suspect. As far as the silence after the rendition of the suspect's seemingly completed response is concerned, the interpreter in the above extract remained silent until either of the primary speakers took a turn.

In the next example (Extract 6.13), however, the interpreter (IR2) appears to perceive a silent pause, after the suspect (S2) responds, as a sign of communication breakdown and intervenes as a mediator, and in a *principal* role, to redress the problem. Prior to line 1, the police interviewer (PO2) has been asking S2 what travel expenses, for himself and his friend Ms Kanai, he had paid to come to Australia as part of a privately organised tour group. (This extract is a continuation of Extract 5.17 in Chapter 5.) S2 has previously said that he paid his own airfare and that of his 'girlfriend', Ms Kanai, but as shown in Chapter 5, Section 5.5.2, a chain of repairs regarding who was responsible for what aspects of the travel expenses have made the interview confusing.

Extract 6.13 (Interview 2)

```
   1 IR2:  Konkai no ryokoo ni kanshite,=
          (Regarding this trip,)
   2 S2:   =Hai.
          (Yes.)
   3 IR2:  Kanai san wa dooiu (.) koto ni (.) okane o
   4       haraimashita ka,
          (What kind of things did Ms Kanai pay for?)
   5       (0.5)
   6 S2:   N maa, okane: wa: mada haratte nai desu. (0.4)
   7       Hai.=
          (Mm so she/I haven't paid money yet.)
→  8 IR2:  =I haven't paid yet,
   9       (0.4)
```

```
    10   S2:  Hai,
               (Yes.)
→   11        (1.3)
    12   PO2: °Ah ↑all ↓ri[ght]?°
→   13   S2:              [Ka,] (.) Kanai san wa, °haratte
    14        nai desu ne°,=
               (Ka- Ms Kanai hasn't paid.)
→   15   IR2: =Jaa ano konkai no ryokoo ni kanshite,=
               (Then um regarding this trip,)
    16   S2:  =Hai,
               (Yes.)
    17   IR2: Teiuka,
               (Or rather,)
    18   S2:  Ha[i],
               (Yes.)
    19   IR2: [K]onkai .hh Takada san ga ano: kono
    20        ryokoo shimashita ne?
               (This time, .hh you um came on this trip,
               right?)
    21        (0.3)
    22   S2:  Ee.=
               (Yes.)
    23   IR2: =De maa jibun no mo soo desu shi,
               (And so as well as for yourself,)
    24   S2:  Hai.
               (Yes.)
    25   IR2: Hito no mono mo soo desu shi,
               (also other people as well,)
    26   S2:  Hai.
               (Yes.)
    27   IR2: Sore ni kanshite,
               (Regarding that,)
    28   S2:  Hai.
               (Yes,)
    29   IR2: Ano dooiu, ano:: okane o haratta ka, (0.2)
    30        arui wa hanaru yotee ga atta ka.
               (Um what um costs did you cover, or were you
               planning to cover?)
    31        (1.2)
    32   S2:  Chotto moo chotto imi ga wakan nai .hh (e, nan
```

```
33        te)
          (Well I really don't know what you mean .hh
          (uh what))
34 IR2:   Ano, ((clears throat)) All right, sorry, could
35        you repeat that again?
```

The interpreter (IR2) renders a question in lines 1 and 3, using Kanai as the subject and the topic of the sentence. This seems to be an error since PO2 has asked 'what it cost him' in the question (cf. Chapter 5, 5.5.2, Extract 5.17). It is however possible that IR2 is trying, from a different angle, to clarify the confusion as to whether S2 has covered all of Kanai's travel expenses or only the airfare, and whether some of S2 and Kanai's expenses were covered by the organiser of the tour group. The confusion, however, is aggravated when S2 responds in line 6 with an ellipsis of the agent of the verb *'haratte nai'* (haven't paid). Since the omitted agent would normally be retrieved from the preceding sentence in which the agent is mentioned, discourse grammar naturally points to the agent of the verb 'pay' in S2's response to be Kanai. However, IR2 surprisingly brings the first person 'I' into the rendition of this sentence as the agent of 'pay', which makes S2's response contradictory to his earlier statement that he paid for his airfare and Kanai's.

The reactions to this rendition of S2's response by all three parties suggest that there is a communication breakdown. Although S2's utterance in line 10 is a backchannel, it is produced after a short pause, but IR2 does not render it. PO2 does not respond to this immediately and there is a pause of 1.3 seconds, which is likely to be caused by the surprising contradiction found in S2's response in relation to his earlier statements. PO2's soft-voiced utterance with changes in the pitch following the pause indicates her surprise, but before it is rendered or further moves are made by PO2 herself, S2 comes in, overlapping PO2's utterance. The silence (and probably the reaction of PO2) was also a sign of problematic communication for S2, as S2's turn in lines 13–14 actually repairs IR2's rendition in line 8, to say that it was not S2 himself but Kanai who had 'not paid yet'. However, instead of rendering this repair turn, IR2 latches onto S2's turn in line 15 and elaborates on the question to elicit a response which would redress the earlier miscommunication.

The extract above is an unusual example in which, after a long stretch of 'troubled' interaction, a silent pause after a contradictory response from the suspect appears to cue all parties to react to an apparent communication breakdown. On the part of the police interviewer, a sign of surprise and possibly suspicion towards the suspect may have led to this silence. This may in turn have motivated the suspect to repair the possible misunderstanding caused by his response to avoid appearing unreliable. As for the interpreter, it is possible that the silence prompted him to shift into a *principal* role to rectify the communication problem and to assist the police to achieve their institutional goal of gathering information through the interview (cf. Komter, 2005; Wadensjö, 1998). It should be noted that the interpreter did not render the two primary speaker turns following the silence, but asked a question of his own accord. It is also possible that the interpreter was motivated to react to the silence by the need to avoid the perception by the police officer that the interpreting had been the cause of the communication problem.

In the two examples above, lengthy silences and lack of immediate reaction following the rendition of the suspect's talk appeared to put the suspect under pressure to elaborate his response. Thus silence can on the one hand open up an opportunity for the suspect to expand on their side of the story, but on the other hand it may imply a negative evaluation or communication breakdown, which may pressure the suspect (and at times possibly the interpreter) into defending their positions.

6.6   Silent pauses in or after the primary speaker's turns

In interpreter-mediated police interviews, interpreter turns are expected after one of the primary speakers has taken a turn, that is, in the 'normal format' of turn-taking organisation. This section discusses silent pauses occurring after a primary speaker's turn, at a location in which the interpreter's rendition turn is expected in the 'normal format'. It is not unusual for a short pause to occur between the primary speaker's turn and the interpreter's rendition turn, in consecutive interpreting situations. It may be caused by the interpreter's note-taking, planning of the rendition, or perception that the primary speaker has more to say when he/she actually has given up their turn to allow for the rendition. These types of silences are not considered in the analysis which focuses, rather, on two types of silences occurring in this particular location: silences which open up opportunities for the suspect to self-select a turn, and those which pressure the suspect into providing more information for the police. Interestingly, those types of silences are also identified amongst the ones occurring in the location in which the police officer is expected to take a turn, as discussed in the section above.

6.6.1 Silence as an opportunity to elaborate on responses

When the interpreter does not initiate their rendition immediately, as
was the case with the silence after the rendition of suspects' responses,
discussed above, the suspect may also take advantage of a silent pause.
In other words, suspects may add a justification to their response or give
information that may support their version of events. In Extract 6.14,
the police officer (PO3) challenges the suspect (S3) by asking her how
she could have seen one of the tour guides take a bag from the person
at the front of the queue and did
not see who it was at the front.

Extract 6.14 (Interview 3)

```
   1 sIR3:  I was walking a- >r:ight at the very rear<.
   2        (0.9)
   3 PO3:   Well how did she see the person take, (.) the
   4        bag from the lead person.
   5 IR3:   Sorede, (0.3) moshi ano, ano sore kao o
   6        minakattara,(.) naze sore tsuaagaido
   7        ga ichiban mae ni iru hito no suutsukeesu o
   8        totta tokoro o mimashita ka?=
          (And so, if um um as you say if you didn't see
          the face, why did you see the tour guide take
          the suitcase of that person at the very
          front?)
   9 S3:    =Watashi no MAE no hito desu.
          (It was the person in front of me.)
→ 10        (1.2)
→ 11 S3:    Watashi no mae o aruiteru hito ga suutsukeesu
  12        o, suutsukeesu janakute, bakku o, koo azukaru
  13        tokoro o mitandesu.
          (I saw when the person in front of me took the
          suitcase, not the suitcase, the bag.)
```

After the suspect's initial response in line 9, there is a brief silence.
It is possible that IR3 may be confused due to ellipsis; because of the
lack of any reference to the verb 'take', in line 9, it is difficult to interpret whether the tour guide in front of her *took* the bag, or the person
in front of her had his/her suitcase *taken* away. IR1 may also be taken
aback by the strong tone of the response, as indicated by the strong
emphasis on '*MAE*' ('front'). This is actually a repair of '*ichiban mae*'

('at the very front') in the question, which made S3's utterance almost like a direct 'other repair'. Indeed, S3 had said '*mae no hito*' ('the person in front', which could also mean 'in front of me' in Japanese) earlier, which IR3 has interpreted as 'the person in front of the line'. It is possible that S3's utterance in line 9 may be either a repair or a response meaning 'Because it was the person *in front of me* who had the bag taken away', but in either case this utterance may be unexpected for IR3, which may have resulted in the pause.

As IR3 does not take the turn at line 10, after a short pause S3 starts to give more elaborate repair, which this time has the verb '*azukaru*' ('take away to look after'). It should be noted that the verb is problematic as it suggests that S3 is talking about the tour guide and not one of travellers in her tour group. However, soon after this she says a fellow traveller in front of her had his luggage taken away, using the verb '*azukeru*' ('entrust personal belongings'). Thus, in fact it is possible that S3 may be referring to this fellow traveller in lines 12–13. The silent pause gives S3 an opportunity to emphasise her repair, and at the same time explain that it was because the person was in front of her and not at the front of the queue that she could see the bag being taken away. It would be possible for IR3 to directly render the utterance in line 9 immediately, translating it as 'It was the person in front of me', at the end of which PO3 may or may not ask S3 for further clarification. The questioning could have taken a different trajectory if the interpreter had taken a turn before the suspect at line 10.

In Extract 6.15, the suspect is being questioned about an inheritance from his parents, since he has been living in Thailand but is currently unemployed. The excerpt starts with PO4 asking how much he has received as an inheritance from his mother.

Extract 6.15 (Interview 4)

```
     1 PO4: Yeah. (0.7) Moth[er's?
     2 S4:                  [hahaoya (.) de,
                             (And my mother's,)
     3 IR4: M,okaasan no wa,=
             (Yeah what about the mother's?)
     4 S4:  = yonsen man'en.
             (40 million yen.)
  →  5      (5.2)
  →  6 S4:  Ya dakara sakki hanashita nisen man'en wa
     7      .hhha tai de moo tsukacchattandesu.=
```

```
                (No, so the 20 million yen I talked about
                earlier, I already used that up in Thailand.)
      8 IR4:    =°Ah °.
      9         (1.8)
  → 10 S4:      A, hanashite nai ka na, hh °kocchi wa°.
                (Oh, maybe I haven't talked about this.)
  → 11          (2.4)
                ((IR turns the pages of a writing pad))
     12 IR4:    °Ichi, ni: s:an,°
                (One, two, three,)
     13         (0.3)
  → 14 S4:      (sore demo) boku wa zenbu tsukawanakute, =Isan
     15         desu kara (0.3) kyoodai de mo waketemasu, (.)
     16         hanbun zutsu.
                (But that, I don't [sic] use all of that.
                Because it was inheritance, we took half and
                half each, between siblings.)
     17 IR4:    Ah okay so what they, (.) she left is that um
     18         40 million yen, and this divided to, (.) in
     19         between my- my brothers and sisters
```

Following the interpreter's rendition (line 3), S4 says '*yonsen man'en*'
('40 million yen'). This simple response is followed by 5.2 seconds of
silent pause, in which IR4 seems to struggle with conversion of the
figure, probably due to the different ways in which large numbers are
encoded in Japanese and in English. Taking advantage of this pause,
S4 then takes a turn in which he appears to justify his earlier statement:
that he has used up most of his savings as he has already spent 20 million yen in Thailand. The beginning of his utterance in line 6 with
'*Ya dakara*' ('No, so') suggests that this is a justification, to which IR4
responds softly with 'Ah' in line 8. The response token 'Ah' which suggests that it was news to IR4, prompts S4 to say 'Maybe I haven't told
this' (line 10). However, IR4 can be seen in the video recording to be
writing on a note pad, while S4 speaks, and after that she vocalises her
attempt to translate the number. This prompts S4 to offer extra information in lines 14–16 (that he inherited half of that 40 million yen), which
may serve as an explanation for why he has no savings.

As we can see in lines 17–19, IR4 renders S4's second elaboration in
relation to the 40 million yen inheritance, but S4's utterances in lines
6–7 and 10 about S4's using up the his inheritance, and not having
told the interviewer about it yet, are not rendered. The non-rendition

favours S4 because if the initial response in line 4 had been rendered immediately before S4 took a turn at line 6, it would probably have been followed by a question from PO4 regarding the 40 million yen inheritance. This would have led to S4 saying that he inherited half of it but used it up in Thailand. Instead, the silence gives the suspect an opportunity to provide extra information of his own accord, which may project him as a reliable and forthcoming interviewee.

Thus, it could be said that the above stretch of interaction has two silent pauses in which IR4 may have changed the course of interview if she had taken a turn before the suspect self-selected as the next speaker. Depending on the handling of these silent pauses, information elicited from and the impression made of the suspect could have been different. The suspect in this extract had opportunities that he may not have had in a monolingual context because the interactional constraints in interpreter-mediated interviews mean that the police officers as a rule are not expected to take a turn before the interpreter renders the suspect's response.

In the extract above, the silence occurring after the suspect's turn was broken by the suspect himself. The following extract shows an instance of the suspect self-selecting a turn when the interpreter remains silent after the police officer's question. It should be noted that in this data set, the interpreters mostly initiate a rendition without a long period of silence and where there is silence, the primary speakers simply wait for the rendition turn. In one case, however, the interpreter in Interview 2 did not initiate a rendition for 4.0 seconds, at which point the police interviewer asked 'Do you understand?' indicating that the silence of the interpreter was regarded as a sign of a comprehension problem (and it was). The following example of the suspect coming in during the interpreter silence is therefore unusual. Prior to line 1 in Extract 6.16, the police officer (PO3) has been asking the suspect (S3) how she managed to fill out the customs and quarantine form if she did not understand much English. S3 has said that her tour group asked for help from another passenger in filling out the card. In line 1, PO3 asks who in S3's tour group asked for help.

Extract 6.16 (Interview 3)

```
1 PO3:  Who asked that,
2       (0.3)
3 IR3:  Dare ga sono, sono koto o kikimashita ka?=
        (Who asked that- about that?)
4  S3:  =Takada Takeshi san desu.
        (Takeshi Takada did.)
```

```
 5 IR3: Takada asked him.
 6      (0.9)
 7 PO3: Asked who?
 8      (0.6)
 9 IR3: Takada san wa dare ni sono shitsumon o kiki
10      mashita ka?
        (Who did Mr Takada ask that question of?)
11 S3:  Sono: sobani: ita, (0.2) [(hito ni) desu].
        (That person who was nearby.)
12 IR3:                         [ he asked, he ]
13      asked the um the man just next to them.
14      (1.0)
→ 15 PO3: That's the older brother, (0.3) Takada?
→ 16      (1.0)
→ 17 S3:  Daihyoo de, kiite kureta n desu.
          (He asked as our representative.)
18 IR3: U:m (0.6) Takada (.) asked as representative
19      for ev- for all of them, (.) this guy that was
20      um, just sitting behind them, (0.2) o- over
21      the aisle and behind them, (.) um, about that.
22 PO3: .hhh Did he help fill out all their forms?
23      (1.0)
24 IR3: What do you m- who do you mean by he,
25 PO3: .hh that(.) Japanese gentleman she's
26      described.
```

After S3 states that Takeshi Takada from her group asked for help, PO3 asks who Takada approached (line 7). The response refers to the person who assisted them as 'the man just next to them' (line 13). The next question 'That's the older brother, Takada?' is problematic, since it could be an attempt to clarify either the man who *offered* help or *which of the Takada brothers* asked for help. IR3 remains silent for a second (line 14), most likely due to this confusion caused by his own omission of Takada Takeshi's given name in the interpreting in line 5.

This silence in line 16, however, gives an opportunity for S3 to self-select a turn to give further information which highlights S3's passive stance as a member of the tour group totally dependent on others on her first trip overseas. Another impact of this self-selection of turn by S3 is that, as can be seen in the following turn of IR3 (lines 18–21), PO3's question in line 15 was never rendered and the identity of

Takada was never clarified before PO3 moved on to the next question (which is actually also problematic) in line 22. Thus, the silence triggered a shift in the trajectory of the interview questioning, although the topic stayed in the same domain and S3's self-selected turn did not have a significant impact on the overall narrative or the case itself. What is interesting from the perspective of turn-taking is that the suspect's turn-taking behaviour in line 17 completely ignores PO3's question turn in line 15, and is presented as if it is a continuation of her previous turn. The lack of access to the meaning of the interviewer questions (in cases where the suspect's proficiency level is low) could allow this type of turn-taking move to nullify the police officer's question, something which would be unlikely in monolingual interviews.

6.6.2 Negative evaluation of responses through silences

In this section, the way in which silent pauses within a suspect response may be affected by interpreter mediation will be demonstrated. While interpreters may find it difficult to cut in before the suspect or the police officer speaks too long in one turn, they may also have power to influence turn construction through silences. For example, if the interpreter perceives the suspect's response to the police officer's question as unacceptable or unsatisfactory, then they may not start rendering the translation until the suspect produces a more acceptable utterance as a response. In Extract 6.17, the suspect (S2) is being shown a photograph of bags of white powder in the suitcase which he brought with him, and is asked by PO2 what he thinks the substance is. This seems to be a strategy to encourage the suspect to give new information (in this case, the type of narcotic) in his own words, which would make the record of interview as evidence more reliable (cf. Heydon, 2005). It may also be the case that the police officer is indirectly trying to pressure the suspect into confession.

Extract 6.17 (Interview 2)

```
1 PO2:  What- what sort of narcotic, (0.3) do you
2       think it is.
3 IR2:  Donna shurui no mayaku da to omoimasu ka?
        (What type of narcotic do you think it is?)
4 S2:   Iya, sore wa watashi wa wakarimasen.
        (No, that I don't know.)
5 IR2:  I don't know (.) myself.
6       (2.2)
```

```
        7  PO2:  What does he think=what do you think it is.
        8         (0.9)
        9  IR2:  Desukara, nan da to omoimasu ka?
                 (So, what do you think it is?)
       10         (1.8)
→      11  S2:   E:: (1.0) kore wa hh nan- nan daro.
                 (Uh what- what would this be?)
→      12         (3.2)
       13  S2:   Watashi wa mita- mita kanji de wa
       14         wakarimasen. (.) tada: a: heroin da, tte
       15         iwaranode, (.) kore ga heroin ka na: tte
       16         bikkurishite mitemasu.
                 (I don't know by just se- seeing it. I was
                  told it was heroin, um yeah, I'm looking at it
                  in shock thinking, is this really heroin?)
       17         (0.4)
       18  IR2:  I can't tell by seeing it, (.) but because I
       19         was told it was heroin. (0.3) So I guess: (.)
       20         it is heroin?
```

S2 says 'I don't know' in line 4, but the police officer (PO2) repeats the question in line 7, at which the interpreter (IR2) appears to hesitate, possibly due to the repetition of questions. Nevertheless, adding *'Desukara'* ('So') because of the repetition, IR2 renders the question (line 9). In line 11, S2 hesitates with *'E::'* followed by a pause, and verbalises his thinking process, the end of which is a TRP. However, there is a pause of 3.2 seconds in line 12, during which IR2 does not start interpreting. Only after S2 takes the floor again and mentions heroin (lines 14–15) does IR2 start rendering S2's utterance into English. However, the initial utterance (line 11) indicating uncertainty is dropped in the translation. The rendition in lines 18–20 also has another problematic omission of *'bikkurishite mitemasu'* ('I'm looking at it in shock') in line 16. If IR2 had rendered the utterance in line 11, PO2 would have taken the next turn, and the trajectory of the interview may have shifted, whether or not this oppressive questioning continued. It is possible that by this time, the police may change the question rather than repeating it once more. IR2, however, waits without rendering the first TCU of the suspect response until an acceptable response (from PO2's perspective) is elicited. Thus, in this extract the interpreter held a certain level of power to influence turn-taking and questioning strategies through decisions made in relation to the suspect's silences.

In Extract 6.18, the suspect (S2) is under pressure as he is asked to explain why he filled in the landing card without understanding the questions on it.

Extract 6.18 (Interview 2)

```
 1 PO2:  Why did he fill a form in without
 2        understanding the questions.
 3 IR2:  Shitsumon ga wakaranai noni, dooshite (0.3)
 4        e kono shoshiki ni kinyuushitandesu ka?
        (Why did you fill a form even though you did
        not understand the questions?)
 5        (1.5)
 6 S2:   Hhh (0.8) wakaranai, tabun da- ichioo: (0.4)
 7        ano: sono hito ga, tabun daijobujanai ka, tte,
 8        kankee nai >koto janai (toiukotojanai)< desu
 9        ka, tte sooiu setsumee ga arimasitande, (0.3)
10        ano: no- no: de daijoobu da to omoimasu, (.)
11        tte iu, te iu hanashi ga arimashitande, (.)
12        °no: tte.°
        (I don't know, probably o- actually um that
        person explained to us that it is probably
        okay, that these things probably don't concern
        us, there was that sort of explanation so, um
        'no', ' no' is okay, I heard that, that he/she
        thought so, so I put 'No'.)
→ 13       (1.8)
→ 14 S2:  Ano, sore ja damedesu ka,
        (Um is that no good?)
15 IR2:  Because uh he said it was not important, he
16        said, no would be applied. No would apply, so
17        (0.7), that's why I filled it in.
```

S2 responds with hesitations. The response from line 6 has two TRPs (at line 9 before the pause and at the end of line 11). At any of these points IR2 could render the response without making it incoherent. Another TRP is at the end of line 12, after *'no: tte'* ('I put "No"'), but IR2 does not start a rendition and this creates 1.8 seconds of silence. At this point S2 asks 'Is that no good?' (line 14). Whether the definite pronoun *'sore'* ('that') in this question refers to the acceptability of response or the act of filling in the form without understanding the questions, the silent pause in line 13 seems to prompt S2 to continue speaking. However, IR2 does not render this (line 10) into English. It is possible that the question at the end of S2's turn is perceived to be either irrelevant or directed towards IR2 in the sense of 'Is this a good enough response for you to start translating?', that is, as a request for a rendition.

This observation suggests that IR2 did not find the suspect's response in lines 6–12 acceptable and waited until S2 pleads for his response to be accepted. Given the accusatory nature of PO2's question, it could be said that IR2 is also rendering this attitude through his non-rendition. In other words, IR2 could be re-enacting the power of the interrogator. It could also be said that IR2 is enacting a non-coercive way of inviting elaboration (Shuy, 1998). It should be noted, however, that the silent pause in line 13 after the suspect's utterance could be caused by the interpreter's note-taking activity. If it is, the interpreter may be prompting a longer response from the suspect without any intention of doing so, and this could also be the reason why the last part of the suspect's turn is omitted.

It also appears that intra-turn silences such as those above do not occur so frequently when the interpreter provides frequent backchannels instead of waiting or note-taking in silence. In Interview 4, for example, the kinds of silent intra-turn pauses exemplified in Interview 2 above are rare, and IR4's frequent backchannels appear to be one of the major explanations. Other possible explanations include the suspect's willingness to participate. The suspect in Interview 4 volunteered a considerable amount of information through self-selection of turns and often overlapped the interpreter at the end of questions.

In the two examples above, when silent pauses occur where the interpreter's rendition of the suspect's utterances could be made, the suspect seems to be being pressured into giving responses preferred by the police. However these examples are both from the same interview (Interview 2), which entailed a coercive questioning style from the police interviewer and reluctant responses with hesitations on the part of the suspect. In other interviews in the data, the suspects tended to be less hesitant in their responses and the police officer's questioning style was not as coercive. The role of silence and the way in which it is perceived or dealt with may therefore be a product co-constructed by all the interlocutors involved in the interviews.

6.7   Conclusions

This chapter discussed the role of silence in interpreter-mediated police interviews according to its location in the organisation of turn-taking. In the cases in which silence occurs after a rendition of the police officer's question, it was demonstrated that both the interpreter and the police officer may at times treat the silence as an NTRI and produce a repair turn. For interpreters, two different trouble sources become possible: the police officer's original question and their own rendition of the question. The identification of the trouble source rests with the interpreter, but repairing the original question directly (in other words, in a *principal* role) while the police officer does not have access to the language in which it is done, entails a risk of the interpreter acting as part of the investigation team. In this location police rarely broke the silence by taking a turn. The accompanying apologies however suggested that it was also possible that self-selecting their turn in this location was deviant turn-taking behaviour. Nevertheless, since silence as an NTRI is highly dependent on the discursive context, and importantly, since drawing meaning from silence can be done without translation, the police officer is able to offer a repair of his or her question without waiting for a rendition. Thus, it could be said that silence in interpreter-mediated interaction brings down the language barrier and allows for more flexible turn-taking organisation.

This chapter also examined silence occurring where the interviewing officer is expected to take a turn. When this silence did not end with the police officer's turn, in some instances it became an opportunity for suspects to continue their turn to elaborate on their side of the story. However in some discursive contexts, especially when the suspect had given a dispreferred response, lack of reaction from the police interviewer may have been used to put pressure on the suspect to give a preferred type of response. It should be noted that the interpreters did not seem to read the silence in this location to be signalling an interactional alignment problem requiring a repair. It is possible that there was an expectation amongst the interpreters that any problem would be raised by the police interviewer in this discursive context, verbally and without much delay. Another possible explanation for this silence not inviting the interpreter's repair is that the interpreters may have been more tolerant of the police officer's silence, showing the officers more deference. In other words, the interpreters may have been more concerned about the suspect taking time to respond than the police officer taking time to provide feedback or ask the next question. An ethnographic approach may be able to scrutinise this possibility, which gives rise to questions about the role of institutional power in interpreter-mediated police interviews.

The last category of silence discussed in this chapter occurred where an interpreter rendition is expected. In the examples, silence in this location gave the suspect an opportunity to self-select their turn and elaborate on their preceding turn. One example showed, when a rendition of the police officer's question did not occur for a short period of time, the suspect voluntarily elaborating on her previous response, surprisingly nullifying the police officer's question. This example suggests, again, that the fact that the primary speakers do not need to, or are unable to, monitor the content of each other's talk may make it possible to abandon turn-taking rules (Sacks et al., 1974) without causing a major interactional disarray. On the other hand, in some cases, silence in this category was a consequence of the interpreter's decision to wait for the suspect to produce an acceptable response, turning what the suspect may have projected as the inter-turn pauses into intra-turn pauses. This type of decision may affect the trajectory of the interview, especially when the suspect is not particularly cooperative in giving relevant and/or sufficient information. Furthermore, this silence caused by the interpreter's 'wait' could become coercive, if the interpreter's decision to decide the amount of the suspect's utterance which 'deserves' a rendition is based on the value of the response in the institutional framework of the interview.

The analysis in this chapter also suggests that participants in mediated police interviews may decode other participants' silences in terms of their own understandings of the ongoing discourse, and react according to the judgements they make as to whether the silences are intentional or unintentional (Kurzon, 1995, 1997). If a silent pause is caused by confusion or lack of comprehension resulting from a problem in translation, it could be considered unintentional and the interpreter may break the silence at that point and repair the rendition. However, if the question has been rendered without a problem and the suspect remains silent, the interpreter may judge this as intentional and leave the suspect in a long silence. There were also some instances in which one or both primary speakers took turns to deal with silence where they were not expected to take a turn in the 'normal format' of turn-taking organisation. Primary speakers do not understand what goes on in the interaction between the other primary speaker and the interpreter and all participants in the police interview, including the interpreter, to a certain extent, have different agendas.

This brings us to the question of the role that silence plays in relation to interaction and power. Silence in this type of mediated discursive context may be advantageous or disadvantageous for the suspect. It may favour suspects in the sense that police officers are under interactional constraints due to the layer of mediation and lack of ability to directly monitor the suspect's turns. Police interviewers' ability to exercise power as questioners may be more limited than in monolingual situations where they would have more control over dealing with silences at various locations in turn-taking organisation. On the other hand, interpreter mediation may work against the suspect if the interpreter adopts the power of the interrogator to put the suspect under pressure through interpreter management of silence and turn-taking. However, interpreters are also vulnerable in that a lack of response from the suspect could be interpreted by the police officer as a problem with their rendition. This in turn reduces the possibility of interviewers' drawing inferences directly from suspects' silences, which suggests that interpreter mediation could favour the suspect's position.

The observations above indicate that silent pauses, be they inter-turn or intra-turn, appear to play an important role in police interviews, in particular when mediated by interpreters. The negotiation of power and resistance between the police officer and the suspect may rely substantially on the decisions that interpreters make in and around silences, even when those silences are as short as 1.5 seconds. It also appears to be the case, however, that the ambiguous nature of silence which can communicate meaning without using language opens up freer turn-taking opportunities to all three parties in mediated police interviews.

7
Mediated Reality Construction: Conclusions

7.1 Introduction

In adversarial legal systems, competing versions of an event are constructed through the legal process, from the police interview to the trial (Bennett & Feldman, 1981). Thus, the police interview is the first stage of the story-construction processes in a criminal case. The interviewing officer and suspect in each of the interviews examined in this book attempted to construct different versions of events, through interactional moves to steer the interview discourse in their respectively preferred directions. The main concern of this book has been the impact of interpreter mediation on the process in which these competing versions of events are constructed. This was explored through the analysis of interaction dynamics in interpreter-mediated interviews, on the premise that interactional features such as turn-taking, questioning and resistance strategies, repairs and silences are not only key elements of talk-in-interaction, but also parts of the 'form' aspect of legal narratives (Snedaker, 1991). The way in which the 'form' of the police interview was managed by the interpreter and the primary speakers affected the narratives as recorded evidence and the power relationship between the police interviewer and the suspect. This concluding chapter will synthesise the findings from the preceding chapters, by first summarising the characteristics of talk-in-interaction in interpreter-mediated police interviews, then discussing the impact of mediation on the construction of versions of events and the negotiation of power in police interviews. The final section considers how these three aspects of discourse interact with one another, addressing issues in mediated police interviews as a legal genre.

7.2 Organisation of talk in interpreter-mediated police interviews

The organisation of talk and its key features are building blocks of interpreted police interviews as discourse. Those features of interpreter-mediated interaction and their impact on power relationships are similar to what Dimitrova (1997) and Roy (2000) demonstrated in their analyses of talk-in-interaction mediated by interpreters in medical and educational settings respectively. By identifying characteristics of interpreter-mediated police interviews from this perspective, we are able to explore the impact of interpreter mediation on the construction of versions of events and on the negotiation of power.

7.2.1 Turn construction

One of the characteristics of interpreter-mediated police interviews as talk-in-interaction is that turn-construction is not only governed by turn-taking rules regarding transition relevance place (Sacks et al., 1974) and pragmatic strategies for holding or relinquishing the floor (Jefferson, 1978; Levinson, 1983; Sacks et al., 1974), but also by the interpreter's orientation to and capacity to manage their own rendition turns. As discussed in relation to suspects' response turn lengths (Chapter 4), the need for manageable turn length for accurate interpreting means that long multiple TCU turns entail accuracy risks. However, this also means that the coherent narratives preferred for evidential purposes in monolingual interviews are not always elicited and rendered accurately in interpreter-mediated interviews. This constraint has implications for the quality and amount of information obtained through the mediated interview, and for the trajectory of discourse (see Section 7.4).

7.2.2 Speaker selection

In terms of speaker selection, interpreter-mediated discourse differs from the ordinary conversation governed by turn-taking rules described by Sacks et al. (1974). The most significant aspect of interpreter-mediated interviews as discourse is its 'normal format' of turn-taking organisation (Knapp & Knapp-Potthoff, 1985, p. 457), in which the interpreter takes a turn following each primary speaker's turn. Komter (2005) and Wadensjö (1998) have shown in their analyses of consecutive police interpreting that deviations from this 'normal format' occur. The present study similarly provided examples of such deviations in interpreter-mediated police interviews. When they occurred, it was often to resolve miscommunication or avoid potential miscommunication. Occasionally, the interpreter and one of the primary speakers engaged in talk between themselves in an 'aside', which temporarily excluded the other primary speaker from participation. However, police officers and suspects also self-selected their turns in locations where their turns were not expected in the 'normal format', if the communication seemed to have broken down.

In addition to repairs in side sequences, other examples were found of turn-taking organisation where primary speakers took a turn without waiting for the rendition of the other primary speaker's previous turn. This happened, for example, when suspects suddenly remembered something, when they elaborated on their earlier responses taking advantage of silent pauses occurring in interaction, or when the interviewing officer had to cut in to clarify referential expressions for the 'benefit of the tape' (cf. Stokoe, 2009).

The interaction phenomena summarised above suggest that there is a tension between the interlocutor's requirement to maintain the orderly 'institutional' form of turn-taking in interpreter-mediated interaction and the orientation to the dynamics of more 'spontaneous' ordinary conversation as described, for example, by Sacks et al. (1974). Carter (2011), drawing on her analysis of police interviews conducted in English in the UK, claims that 'talk more typical of the structure of ordinary conversation does creep into the interaction in the police interview' (p. 147). In interpreted police interviews, in addition to the tension between the spontaneous conversational and institutional aspects of talk-in-interaction, fluctuation occurs between the 'natural' orientation to ordinary conversation and the mode of communication required to make mediated bilingual interaction possible.

7.2.3   Overlapping and interruptions

Overlapping and interruptions occurred, not only between one of the primary speakers and the interpreter but also between the primary speakers, as also documented by Wadensjö (1998), Komter (2005) and Russell (2002) in their analysis of interpreted police interview data. Overlapping and interruptions sometimes led to speakers breaking away from the 'normal format' of turn-taking, which in some cases meant that interpreters were unable to render utterances fully or accurately. The consequence of overlapping and interruptions could be miscommunication if some parts of simultaneously produced utterances are not interpreted or heard, or if the current speaker's turn is cut short due to an interruption and the message is not decoded by the primary speaker or the interpreter as intended.

There were also examples of interpreters prematurely cutting off suspects' turns either to avoid inaccurate renditions or to block primary speakers from self-selecting a turn without waiting for a rendition of the previous primary speaker turn. Interpreters in the data set in the present study did not attempt to manage interaction by using explicit language regarding turn-taking. Such an attempt has been reported by Roy (2000) who discussed an example of a sign language interpreter explicitly offering a turn to one of the primary speakers as a discourse management strategy.

7.2.4 Sequence organisation

The dominant pattern of sequence organisation in police interviews is a chain of question–answer adjacency pairs, in which the questioner is the police interviewer and the answerer is the suspect. This makes it more difficult for the suspect to initiate a topic or a new sequence (Heydon, 2005). The data in the present study reflects the dominant pattern in which the suspect is the answerer. However, deviating from the 'normal format', suspects at times took advantage of silent pauses before police officers' or interpreters' turns, and self-selected their turns. They sometimes ignored other interlocutors' turns and pushed on with the sequence to which they had committed themselves, creating two separate sequences running at the same time. This makes it difficult for the interpreter to manage mediation, as Roy (2000) also demonstrated in her study of sign language interpreting.

The fact that the primary speakers are not able to monitor each other's utterances as in monolingual interaction means that without the interpreter's renditions, the mechanism to achieve alignment in interaction and to cope with overlaps and interruptions does not work. In other words, interpreter-mediated interviews may allow more deviation from the rules regulating monolingual interaction, without immediate sanctions. However, this makes the interpreter's work challenging, and involves difficult decisions as to what utterances or whose turn should be ignored (cf. Roy, 2000; Russell, 2002). It also makes interpreter-mediated police interviews more vulnerable to miscommunication and inadequate recording of evidence than monolingual police interviews (Russell, 2002).

7.3 Interpreter mediation and power in police interviews

One might expect that the format of turn-taking in interpreter-mediated police interviews would remove the institutional power from the police interviewer to a certain extent, since they are dependent on the interpreter to elicit information from the suspect. However, the examples analysed in the present study presented a more complex picture of the way in which power is negotiated in the tripartite interaction. This includes interpreters' participation in the process of power negotiation in police interviews as a third interlocutor.

7.3.1 Turn length

In monolingual interviews, police officers have considerable control over how long suspects speak in their answer turns (cf. Heydon, 2005). However, in interpreter-mediated interviews, since the interpreter's turn is expected immediately after each of the suspect's turn, it reduces the police officer's level of control over a suspect's turns. However, the analysis indicated that the interpreters had varied orientations to rendering suspects' turns. It appears that less experienced interpreters had a tendency to intervene early and interpret in smaller chunks of discourse, while the more experienced interpreter waited for coherent responses to be completed before starting renditions. There were however different types of risks and problems associated with both approaches. Interpreting in shorter turns resulted in prematurely making wrong assumptions about the content and intention of suspects' turns, or cut suspects' accounts short and allowed police interviewers to move on to the next questions, therefore preventing suspects from giving as much information as they intended at the onset of their first turn in response. The longer turn approach on the other hand was sometimes complemented by the interpreter's clarification questions which at times put the interpreter into the interviewer's role. It was also the case that the suspect's utterances were rendered in 'tidier' versions.

These two approaches therefore seem to have both advantages and disadvantages in terms of suspects' attempts to construct their versions of events. For police interviewers, the interpreter's orientation to rendition timing may or may not be advantageous. While eliciting fuller accounts without having to ask closed questions frequently may be preferable, potential alterations (and improvements) to the original discourse of the suspects through interpreting may not be so. Meanwhile, although interpreters' orientations to rendition timing may be influenced by their capacity for memory retention and note-taking, there are consequences in terms of giving either party an advantage or a disadvantage in the investigation process. In the light of the recent introduction of cognitive interviewing in Australia, following introduction in the UK, in which trained officers use discursive strategies to enhance the interviewee's memory and to encourage free narratives, balancing the needs for interpreting accuracy and effective investigative interviewing processes appears to be one of the major challenges for both interpreters and investigators.

7.3.2 Turn-taking, overlapping and interruptions

The interview data showed a dominant pattern of turn-taking organisation in which the police interviewer asked questions and the suspect answered the questions, with the interpreter turn following each question and answer. The police officers rarely interrupted the suspects' talk in the data set, which has been discussed as one of the powerful strategies used by police interviewers (Heydon, 2005; Shuy, 1998). Thus, while the asymmetry of power between the questioner and the answerer in the police institutional setting exists to a certain extent in mediated interviews, at the same time the format of turn-taking makes it difficult for the police officer to interrupt the suspect's turn.

Nevertheless, we have seen some examples in which the primary speakers deviate from the norms of turn-taking and interrupt the other or initiate a new sequence without hearing the rendition of the other's turn. The need to satisfy legal requirements appeared to warrant interruptions by the police officer, but when this happened during the suspect's turn, it made it highly challenging for the interpreter to manage mediation and frequent overlapping and interruptions following such moves by the police officer resulted in a chaotic and inefficient stretch of questioning interaction.

With regard to suspects' participation, as mentioned earlier, some examples were discussed where the interpreter mediation layer seemed to have given opportunities for suspects to give their own accounts voluntarily. In this sense suspects may be at an advantage in interpreter-mediated interviews. However, as already mentioned, such extra opportunities for reinforcing or expanding on their version of events did not lead to interviewing officers' changing the line of questioning. Thus, shifts in balance of power at a local interactional level in the interpreter-mediated interview did not seem to affect the power relationship in the wider institutional context.

The examination of overlapping also suggests that the interpreters did not seem to prioritise either primary speaker when they rendered overlapped source utterances. This is not in line with Roy (2000) and Russell (2002) who found that the more powerful interlocutor is given preference, nor with a common perception that interpreters side with the suspect or defendant as advocates (Cooke, 1995; Laster & Taylor, 1994; Mikkelson, 1998).

7.3.3   Repairs

The analysis of repairs also demonstrated that interpreter mediation did not seem to favour either of the primary speakers in particular. On one hand, interpreter mediation at times served as a shield to protect the suspect from miscommunication potentially damaging to them. On the other hand, interpreters at times, intentionally or unintentionally, stepped out of the *animator* role and assumed the interrogator's role, influencing the trajectory of questioning or the suspect's responses. For example, in Interview 2, the suspect's repetitive repair initiation, which may have been an avoidance strategy, was not managed as such, and the interpreter actively guided the discourse process in a *principal* role.

The effects of interpreter mediation on power relations can also be seen in repair sequences occurring in 'asides'. One of the primary speakers cannot address miscommunication if it is handled by the other primary speaker and the interpreter. Again, this was observed for both suspects and police interviewers, and repairs in side sequences were sometimes necessary to efficiently avoid or address miscommunication. However, given that there were instances where these 'asides' themselves became sources of misalignment in interaction, it would be better if the interpreter explained the content of the 'asides' to the excluded party.

One way in which handling of miscommunication may have disadvantaged the suspect was when interpreting itself was problematic but the renditions in the repair sequences included alterations, consequently not bringing interpreting errors to the surface. These changes, whether they were intentional or unintentional, are detrimental to the suspects' standing as they appear inconsistent to the interviewer. Some instances of interpreters' management of repairs also suggested their concern for being regarded as professional, so interpreters' needs to maintain face (Berk-Seligson, 1990; Shlesinger, 1991; Wadensjö, 1998) may have played a role in changes through interpreting.

7.3.4   Silence

Chapter 6 showed that participants in mediated interviews also negotiated their power through silences. The effect of silence as a pressuring strategy was channeled through the interpreting, and in some cases in the form of the interpreter waiting until a desirable response was produced. On the other hand, silent pauses created in and around renditions were taken advantage of by some suspects to push their versions of events. In this sense, the same discursive phenomenon of silence in interpreter-mediated interaction functioned, depending on the local context of interaction, as either a power-enhancing or pressure-exercising tool for both police interviewers and suspects. Unintentional gaps created when the interpreter is planning renditions may be unavoidable; however, interpreters can control interlocutors' turns including their own, for example by explicitly claiming their turn (cf. Dimitrova, 1997) or by using gesture, body language or eye gaze (cf. Dimistrova, 1997; Roy, 2000). The strategy of explicit claim was not found in the present study and the other strategies were either not found in the video-recorded data or were not retrievable from the audio-only data. It would be important to include such turn-management skills in legal interpreter training programs. Another aspect of silence which is significant in interpreter-mediated interviews is that the interpreter has the power to determine when to break the silence by initiating a rendition, when the suspect's responses are fragmented or seemingly incomplete. Such judgments made by the interpreter affect the trajectory of questioning, which is unavoidable given the central role of the interpreter in the turn-taking process (Dimitrova, 1997, p. 161).

7.3.5 Discursive strategies of pressure and resistance

Chapters 3 and 4 discussed a number of discursive strategies used by police interviewers and suspects, and the impact of interpreter mediation on the role of those strategies in the interview. The analysis indicated that discursive aspects of power-negotiating strategies were not always rendered through interpreting. The extent to which pragmatic equivalence can be maintained through interpreting depends on each interpreter's ability in handling the task of translation itself as well as pragmalinguistic differences between the two languages. Nevertheless, accurate and full renditions of power negotiation strategies were also made challenging by the fragmentation of discourse (Müller, 2001) which was caused by the interlocutors' deviations from the normal format of turn-taking or overlapping talk. The level of discourse management skills would probably depend on the interpreter's experience, but the primary speakers' orientation to turn-taking also affects the interpreter's ability to achieve renditions which retain the pragmatic impact of power negotiation strategies. As Wadensjö (1998, p. 152) puts it, interpreter-mediated interaction is a 'communicative *pas de trois*'.

The negotiation of power and construction of versions of events are interrelated. Discourse strategies of power and resistance contribute to the process of constructing versions of events by both parties. It was suggested that suspects' attempts to resist institutional power and put forward their side of the story were at times not rendered with the equivalent illocutionary force. On the other hand, pragmatic equivalence was not always achieved in rendering powerful strategies of police interviewers in the present study, as was the case with Krouglov's (1999) study of interpreted investigative interviews in the UK. If the interpreter provides mediation with an awareness of this interrelationship between discourse strategies and the underlying version of events, it could enhance the quality of interpreter mediation.

Analysis in this book also has indicated that police interviewers and suspects, in efforts to establish their own versions of events, flouted maxims of Cooperative Principles (Grice, 1975) as part of their discourse strategies. However, there were some cases of maxim-flouting which appeared to have been treated as genuine cases of miscommunication by some of the interpreters. This at times led to non-renditions or inaccurate renditions, or the interpreter's unnecessary shift to a *principal* role, which brought disarray into mediated interviews. Skilled interpreters are likely to interpret discursively with an awareness of competing versions of events as features of the legal genre, picking up on contextualisation cues while maintaining accuracy at the semantic level.

Wadensjö (1998) and Komter (2005) suggest that interpreters' renditions may not always reflect the speech style of the source utterances to avoid loss of face. Mediating between interlocutors who attempt to construct competing versions of events may also entail a risk of interpreters themselves being regarded as incompetent. Analysis of examples in this book has also demonstrated that interpreting confrontational or intentionally misaligned talk is a challenging task for interpreters. Wadensjö (1998) claims that experienced and trained interpreters are 'able to let the primary parties be confronted with and take care of possible conflicts' (p. 133). The findings of this research suggest similarly that training police interpreters to develop this capacity is crucial.

7.4   Interpreter mediation and the construction of versions of events

The layer of interpreter mediation in the analysed interviews at times affected the quality, amount and presentation of information as part of the evidence, particularly the process of constructing versions of events related to the crime in question.

7.4.1   Length of suspects' turns

Evidence obtained through police interviews may be influenced by the fact that each of the primary speakers' turns is by default preceded and followed by the interpreter's turn. While following this format is important in avoiding miscommunication, even if the 'normal format' is maintained, turn length also seemed to affect the amount of information gathered through interpreting. The interpreters showed varied orientation to the timing of rendering suspects' turns. Longer turns with multiple TCUs could avoid the risk of suspects' accounts being cut off after the first rendition, by the interviewing officer's taking a turn and initiating a new topic. However, longer turns may lead to omission of information in renditions. We have also seen, in Chapter 6, examples of interpreters' silence pressuring suspects into producing longer responses than they might wish to, withholding a rendition until a relevant response is produced. On the other hand, short turns intended to ensure the accuracy of rendition can lead to fragmentation of the suspect's accounts and legitimise the interviewing officer taking the turn after the rendition of only some parts of the suspect's turn. This also changes the trajectory of the discourse from that of a non-fragmented account provided by the suspect to that of the suspect's fragmented account followed by the police officer's question on the basis of such a fragmented account. Jefferson (1978) argues that stories are locally occasioned and sequentially implicative. They can also be co-constructed and collaboratively concluded (Jefferson, 1978; Lerner, 1992). The interpreting process inhibits collaborative co-construction if the rendition in short turns fragments the discourse.

7.4.2 Overlapping and interruptions

As in previous studies (Komter, 2005; Russell, 2002; Wadensjö, 1998), overlaps and interruptions occurred in the interviews. When they occurred, it was not always possible for interpreters to completely render the overlapping turns of both primary speakers (cf. Roy, 2000; Russell, 2002; Wadensjö, 1998). Although the extent to which interpreters manage to render or handle simultaneous talk would depend on their experience and skills, overlapping and interruptions by the suspect or the interpreter at times prevented the police interviewer from asking relevant questions at a relevant time to elicit the type of information required for their investigation. There were also examples of overlapping and interruptions by the police interviewer or the interpreter which prevented the suspect from providing an important piece of information, whether to support the suspect's version of events or to add to evidence useful for prosecution. Accurate recording of the interview process was also hindered by overlapping talk, affecting the versions of events constructed in the interview. As Russell (2002) suggests, simultaneous talk is best avoided for the accurate recording of interpreter-mediated police interviews.

An important issue related to overlapping and interruptions is the question of whether priority of rendition is given to one party, favouring one of the competing versions of events. As far as the interviews examined for this research are concerned, rendition of overlapping talk did not favour either party, nor were interruptions of primary speakers one-sided.

7.4.3   Repairs and the trajectory of interview discourse

Another key feature of discourse which affected the quality and amount of information elicited in the interviews was repairs. In police interviews in which competing versions of events are constructed, like the ones examined in this book, the attribution of trouble sources in miscommunication is particularly important because credibility of the story-teller matters to the legal process, and versions of events are constantly evaluated in police interview discourse (Johnson, 2006). Perceptions about the trouble source in miscommunication were not always shared by the interlocutors (cf. Komter, 2005; Wadensjö, 1998). However, this did not necessarily lead to communication breakdown or serious misunderstanding. In some cases, while repairs as interactional processes were achieved and the main sequence of interviewing discourse resumed, repairs as legal processes were problematic because the interlocutors had different perceptions of the nature of the miscommunication and/or of the interlocutor to whom the trouble source should be attributed.

In some of the examples, interpreter mediation in repair sequences consequently affected the trajectory of questioning. In both monolingual and interpreted interviews, repair sequences have a potential to shift the trajectory projected by the preceding main sequence, changing the type of questions and questioning strategies used by the police officer or the accounts given by the suspect. This has implications for the construction of versions of events, by both police interviewers and suspects. However, in interpreter-mediated interviews, lack of contiguity between the primary speakers may make the repair process more vulnerable to further misalignment in interaction.

Finally, in repair sequences in 'asides', whose problematic consequences with regard to the negotiation of power in discourse have been discussed above (Section 7.3), the excluded primary speaker could be disadvantaged in strategically constructing a version of events, because of their lack of ability to monitor repair processes which make up an important part of the local context of interaction.

7.4.4 Topic control

Heydon's (2005) analysis of monolingual police interview discourse shows that one of the factors that made it difficult for the suspect to take control of the topic was that they did not initiate sequences apart from repairs. In the present study, the suspects in some cases managed to foreground their side of the story using the opportunities created by repair processes.

Silences at times seemed to open up possibilities for suspects to foreground and expand on their version of events. While it is not possible to obtain comparative data, it appears that the constraints on turn-taking due to interpreter mediation could give more space for the suspect to put their version of events, since the police officer turns cannot directly follow the suspect's turns in interpreter-mediated interviews but can only intervene after the interpreter rendition.

On the other hand, police officers did not take up the newly introduced elements of suspects' turns very often. The 'evaluative third parts', which in institutional interaction such as courtroom questioning are given by the professional to support or challenge responses to questions (Gibbons, 2003, p. 124; see also Eades, 2000), were often missing, especially in the 1992 interviews (Interviews 1–3), after renditions of suspects' turns. Instead, police interviewers moved on to the next question relevant to their own version of events and kept following their existing line of enquiry. In the 2002 interview (Interview 4), the interviewing officer often used the response tokens such as 'okay' or 'right' (which were not observed frequently in the 1992 interviews), but the narrative expansion on the part of the suspect did not go much further than that, because the officer rarely took on board the topics introduced by the suspect. Thus, beyond the level of repair sequences or a few turns, suspects did not contribute a significant amount of information voluntarily. This resonates with Jaquemet's (1996, p. 132) observation of legal discourse in which details of stories that are 'uninteresting' for the audience are 'skipped'. Research has shown what is important to suspects or witnesses is not always relevant to police investigators, whose institutional roles tend to prioritise legally acceptable narratives (Gibbons, 2003; Hall, 2008; Johnson, 2006; Linell & Jönsson, 1991).

7.4.5 Versions of events and their evaluation

Through the process of police interviews, versions of events concerning the alleged crime are constructed (Heydon, 2005; Johnson, 2006; Linell & Jönsson, 1991), as with the case of courtroom examinations (Bennett & Feldman, 1981; Gibbons, 2003; Maley & Fahey, 1991). Johnson (2006), drawing on Labov and Waletzky (1997), states that those versions of events, or narratives, are constantly 'evaluated' by both the interviewing officer and the interviewees during the interview. If the constructed versions of events concern the 'secondary reality' (Hale & Gibbons, 1999), evaluations are part of the 'primary reality' (Hale & Gibbons, 1999), the reality of the interview as a legal process. As found in courtroom interpreting studies (for example, Hale & Gibbons, 1999), this study found examples where linguistic elements encoding primary realities were not interpreted, as a consequence of which suspects' credibility and the coherence of their accounts may have been negatively affected.

In a similar vein, loss or distortion of contextualisation cues (Gumperz, 1981) through interpreting at times seemed to cause misunderstanding as to the evaluation of the version of events projected by the primary speakers. In some of the examples, as a consequence, suspects ended up giving what may have been perceived by the interviewing officers as incoherent or even evasive responses. Studies of courtroom interpreting have shown that pragmatic equivalence is not always maintained through interpreting (Berk-Seligson, 1990; Hale, 2004) or is difficult to achieve (Lee, 2011). Faithful rendition of contextualisation cues is one of the challenges of maintaining pragmatic equivalence. Legal interpreter training therefore needs to include instruction in the interpreting of primary reality elements and contextualisation cues, so as not to put at risk the coherence of narratives. Otherwise there is a risk not only of suspects incorrectly appearing evasive, but also of police officers failing to elicit the information they seek.

7.5   Mediated discourse, power and evidence

In this book, a number of key aspects of the interpreter-mediated police interview as institutional discourse were analysed. The aim, as stated at the beginning, was to explore the interaction dynamics of interpreter-mediated police interviews as a legal process. The analysis revealed that interpreter mediation brings new dimensions to the interaction dynamics of police interviews. There are aspects of interaction that are unique to the consecutive mode of interpreting such as turn-taking principles, repairs and issues with simultaneous talk. These characteristics of interpreter-mediated discourse impact on the balance of power in interaction. Power negotiation strategies pull interview discourse in varied directions and affect the process by which versions of events are constructed in the interview. As previous studies of interpreter-mediated discourse have demonstrated, the interpreter is at the centre of the turn-taking system (Dimitrova, 1997; Leung & Gibbons, 2008; Roy, 2000; Wadensjö, 1998). Moving between roles of *animator, author* and *principal,* interpreters engage in management of discourse (Berk-Seligson, 1990; Dimitrova, 1997; Laster and Taylor, 1994; Roy, 2000; Wadensjö, 1998). In doing so, their decisions and actions influence interactional power relationships between the police interviewer and the suspect, which consequently affect the trajectory of versions of events constructed in the interview.

Versions of events, or narratives constructed through the police interview, are central components of the police interview as a genre (Johnson, 2006, p. 669). Furthermore, how such versions are supported, challenged and evaluated may affect the intertextual value of police interviews as trial evidence (Haworth, 2006; Heydon, 2006; Johnson, 2006). The present study suggests that interpreter mediation has an impact on the police interview as evidence to a certain extent, depending on the experience and skills of the interpreter. It must also be highlighted, however, that even when the suspect's resistance was rendered faithfully or even reinforced by interpreter mediation, the police interviewer's institutional power to push forward their preferred version of events was evident. The preallocation of turns in police interviews, which endows the police officer's role as the questioner and the evaluator of answers, makes it difficult for the suspect to reinforce their version of events beyond a number of sequences in interaction.

The extent to which the legal interpreter is able to manage mediated interaction to achieve conditions equivalent to those of non-interpreted discourse (Hale, 2004, 2008; Mikkelson, 2000) also depends on the orientation of the primary speakers to the particularities of the police interview through consecutive interpreting. In the present study there was evidence of primary speakers oscillating between the 'orderly' mode of interaction (avoiding simultaneous talk and following the 'normal format' of turn-taking) and the more 'conversational' mode. When the balance tends towards the 'conversational' mode, exhibiting the orientation described by Sacks et al. (1974), it makes the police interpreter's work particularly challenging and consequently the legal process more problematic.

Approaching the discourse of interpreter-mediated police interviews by examining its form, content and power struggles enables understanding of the complexity of the legal process involving lay persons and interpreter mediation. It was beyond the scope of this study to examine how these interviews as evidence impacted on the discourse process in the trial phase. A holistic study examining the intertexual aspects of interpreter-mediated police interviews in relation to their trial discourse would yield valuable findings for both research and practice in legal processes.

7.6   Implications for interpreter-mediated police interviews as institutional discourse

The present study suggests that the mediation process is likely to improve if interpreters approach police interviews as a genre that may contain competing versions of events over which the primary speakers engage in a negotiation of power. Such awareness, which experienced and trained police interpreters would have, facilitates accurate interpreting that maintains both semantic and pragmatic equivalence. Jackson (1991, p. 160) argues for recognising the importance of understanding legal phenomena in terms of 'the story of the giving of evidence', in other words, the secondary reality embedded in the primary reality (Gibbons, 2003; Hale & Gibbons, 1999). It is recommended that police interpreter training include developing awareness of the police interview as a process of story construction. Furthermore, it may allow police interpreters to be more sensitive to contextualisation cues if they have heightened awareness of intertextuality, in other words, the role of the interview as evidential discourse in its related legal processes (cf. Haworth, 2006; Johnson, 2006).

In relation to the interview as a storytelling process, repair sequences addressing miscommunication emerged as one of the challenging aspects of interpreter-mediated interviews (cf. Komter, 2005; Wadensjö, 1998). To minimise the impact of interpreter mediation on the trajectory of police interviews, interpreters should in theory remain in their *animator* role and let the primary speakers resolve miscommunication on their own, which is also in line with the interpreters' code of ethics. Given the importance of impartiality in legal interpreting and the vulnerability of such impartiality in repairs occurring in 'aside' sequences, it is recommended that interpreters be trained in how to handle miscommunication (in particular, managing miscommunication as a *principal* should be the last resort). An important lesson from the present study is that if repairs by means of asides are deemed necessary, the content of the asides should be reported to the excluded speaker, be it the interviewer or the suspect, before the interview resumes its main sequence. The reason for this is twofold: the exclusion of the primary speaker, who is likely not to be informed of the nature of miscommunication and its resolution, may lead to a lack of alignment in interaction in the ensuring sequence; at the same time, the excluded primary speaker will not know whether impartiality was maintained in the repair sequence. If police interviewers ask the interpreter to render the utterances in the 'aside' for the excluded primary speaker, retrospectively, the above issues associated with 'asides' are less likely to have an undesirable impact on the legal process. Interpreters should also be trained to take this step even if they are not prompted by the interviewing officer after engaging in 'asides'.

In the process of constructing varying versions of events, the suspect and the police interviewer engage in power struggles, which often manifest themselves in the form of simultaneous talk or divergence from the 'normal format' of turn-taking. This prevents the interpreter from providing full and accurate renditions and brings risks of miscommunication. Police officers should be trained in management of interpreter-mediated interaction. For example, if the suspect tries to speak before the interpreter has finished his/her renditions, then the police interviewer should intervene and advise the suspect to wait until the interpreter rendition is completed. Interviewers themselves should also be aware of the consequences of their own overlapping talk and try to rectify any problems caused by it, for example by asking the interpreter to render the uninterpreted utterances. While it is not possible to 'train' suspects to follow the normal format and avoid miscommunication (and miscommunication may be caused deliberately to dodge questions), it would be possible for police interviewers to advise suspects and witnesses at the beginning of the interview to avoid simultaneous talk or speaking out of their turn. These measures however would mean that the conversational aspect of police interviews would have to be suppressed for the sake of transparency and coherence in interpreter-mediated interviews.

Experienced and trained interpreters have probably developed discourse management skills which can be applied without violating the code of ethics, but where such trained interpreters are in short supply, it is essential to include turn-taking and discourse management skills in the training of interpreters. Even though in theory it should be left to the primary speakers to 'manage' their interaction, interpreters nevertheless will still need to be equipped with a set of discourse management skills, given that they are the only party who is able to monitor the interview discourse in both languages. Wadensjö (1997) suggests that interpreting quality involves the interpreter's skills in coordinating interaction as well as achieving semantic and pragmatic equivalents. Training of interpreters could include strategies to control primary speaker turns, and the use, where necessary, of explicit remarks to avoid problematic simultaneous talk. Those discourse management strategies, however, should be kept to the minimum because their use would entail risks of loss of impartiality, which is ethically problematic.

Finally, the cognitive interview approach, which has been implemented in a number of jurisdictions in recent years, should be mentioned in relation to the future directions of investigative interviews through interpreting. The present study did not examine interviews which had fully adopted the cognitive interview approach, although the 2002 interview data contained fewer instances of coercive tactics used by the police officer. While the cognitive interview approach has been encouraged since the early 2000s in Australia for its potential to elicit reliable information from the interviewee and as a fairer alternative to the problematic coercive approach to questioning (Buckley, 2009; Holmes & Boni, 2001), its application in interpreter-mediated interviews entails challenges. This is especially because of the need to invite information given in a narrative form, which places an increased memory demand on interpreters (Heydon & Lai, 2012). Further research is required to explore the best possible way to implement the cognitive interview approach while not jeopardising the ethical framework and the quality of professional legal interpreting.

The discourse of interpreter-mediated police interviews is still under-investigated compared to courtroom interaction involving interpreters. The author hopes this book serves as a small contribution to a better understanding of interpreter-mediated legal processes.

References

Angermeyer, P. (2008). Creating monolingualism in the multilingual courtroom. *Sociolinguistic Studies* 2(3), 385–403.

Auburn, T., Drake, S., & Willig, C. (1995). You punched him, didn't you? Versions of violence in accusatory interviews. *Discourse & Society* 6(3), 353–386.

Australian Institute of Interpreters and Translators (AUSIT) (2010). http://www.ausit.org/files/code_of_ethics/ethics.pdf. Accessed 17 September 2010.

Australian Institute of Interpreters and Translators (AUSIT) (2013). http://ausit.org/AUSIT/Documents/Code_Of_Ethics_Full.pdf. Accessed 5 March 2013.

Baldwin, J. (1993). Police interview techniques: establishing truth or proof? *British Journal of Criminology* 33(3), 325–352.

Bennett, W. L. & Feldman, M. S. (1981). *Reconstructing Reality in the Courtroom: Justice and Judgment in American Culture.* New Brunswick: Rutgers University Press.

Berk-Seligson, S. (1990). Bilingual court proceedings: the role of the court interpreter. In: Levi, J. N. & Walker, A. G. (eds), *Language in the Judicial Process.* New York: Plenum Press, pp. 155–201.

Berk-Seligson, S. (2002). The Miranda warnings and linguistic coercion: the role of footing in the interrogation of a limited-English speaking murder suspect. In: Cotterill, J. (ed.), *Language in the Legal Process.* New York: Palgrave Macmillan, pp. 127–143.

Berk-Seligson, S. (2009). *Coerced Confessions: The Discourse of Bilingual Police Interrogations.* Berlin: Mouton de Gruyter.

Blimes, J. (1988). The concept of preference in conversation analysis. *Language in Society* 17(2), 161–181.

Buckley, C. A. (2009). *The theory and practice of the cognitive interview in criminal cases [Abstract only].* Doctoral Dissertation. University of Melbourne.

Carter, E. (2011). *Analysing Police Interviews: Laughter, Confession and the Tape.* London: Continuum.

Church, A. (2009). *Preference Organisation and Peer Disputes: How Young Children Resolve Conflict.* Aldershot: Ashgate.

Conley, J. M. & O'Barr, W. M. (1990). *Rules versus Relationships: The Ethnography of Legal Discourse.* Chicago: University of Chicago Press.

Cooke, M. (1995). Aboriginal evidence in the cross-cultural courtroom. In: Eades, D. (ed.), *Language in Evidence: Issues Confronting Aboriginal and Multicultural Australia.* Sydney, NSW: University of New South Wales Press, pp. 55–96.

Cotterill, J. (2000). Reading the rights: a cautionary tale of comprehension and comprehensibility. *Forensic Linguistics* 7(1), 4–25.

Coulthard, M. & Johnson, A. (2007). *An Introduction to Forensic Linguistics: Language in Evidence.* London and New York: Routledge.

Dimitrova, B. E. (1997). Degree of interpreter responsibility in the interaction process in community interpreting. In: Carr, S. E., Roberts, R. P., Dufour, A., & Steyn, D. (eds), *The Critical Link: Interpreters in the Community.* Amsterdam and Philadelphia: John Benjamins, pp. 147–164.

223

Drew, P. (1990). Strategies in the contest between lawyer and witness in cross-examination. In: Levi, J. N. & Walker, A. G. (eds), *Language in the Judicial Process*. New York: Plenum Press, pp. 39–64.

Eades, D. (1994). A case of communicative clash: Aboriginal English and the legal system. In: Gibbons, J. (ed.), *Language and the Law*. London: Longman, pp. 234–264.

Eades, D. (1996). Verbatim courtroom transcripts and discourse analysis. In: Kniffka, H., Blackwell, S., & M. Coulthard (eds), *Recent Developments in Forensic Linguistics*. Frankfurt: Peter Lang, pp. 241–254.

Eades, D. (2000). I don't think it's an answer to the question: silencing aboriginal witnesses in court. *Language in Society* 29(2), 161–196.

Eades, D. (2004). Understanding aboriginal English in the legal system: A critical sociolinguistics approach. *Applied Linguistics* 25(4), 491–512.

Eades, D. (2008). *Courtroom Talk and Neocolonial Control*. Berlin: Mouton de Gruyter.

Eades, D. (2010). *Sociolinguistics and the Legal Process*. Bristol: Multilingual Matters.

Edwards, D. (2008). Intentionality and *mens rea* in police interrogations: the production of actions as crimes. *Intercultural Pragmatics* 5(2), 177–199.

Ehrlich, S. (2001). *Representing Rape: Language and Sexual Consent*. London: Routledge.

Fairclough, N. (1989). *Language and Power*. London: Longman.

Fairclough, N. (1995). *Critical Discourse Analysis: The Critical Study of Language*. Harlow, Essex: Pearson Education.

Flack, S. (1987). *Rett tolk?: en undersøkelse av tolker, språk, rettssikkerhetsproblemer og orllekonflikter innen politi og domstoler*. Oslo: Universitetsforlaget.

Forrester, M. A. & Ramsden, C. A. H. (2001). Discursive ethnomethodology: analysing power and resistance in talk. *Psychology, Crime & Law* 6, 281–304.

Gibbons, J. (1995). What got lost? The place of electronic recording and interpreters in police interviews. In: Eades, D. (ed.), *Language in Evidence: Linguistic and Legal Perspectives in Multicultural Australia*. Sydney: University of New South Wales Press, pp. 175–186.

Gibbons, J. (2003). *Forensic Linguistics: An Introduction to Language in the Justice System*. Oxford: Blackwell.

Gibbons, J. (2008). Questioning in common law criminal courts. In: Gibbons, J. & Turell, M. T. (eds), *Dimensions of Forensic Linguistics*. Amsterdam and Philadelphia: John Benjamins, pp. 115–130.

Gieselman, R. E., Fisher, R. P., Firstenberg, I., Hutton, L. A., Sullivan, S. J., Avetissian, I. V., & Prosk, A. L. (1984). Enhancement of eyewitness memory: an empirical evaluation of the cognitive interview. *Journal of Police Science and Administration* 12, 74–80.

Goffman, E. (1981). *Forms of Talk*. Philadelphia: University of Pennsylvania Press.

Goodwin, C. (1984). Notes on story structure and the organization of participation. In: Atkinson, M. J. & Heritage, J. D. (eds), *Structures of Social Action: Studies in Conversation Analysis*. Cambridge: Cambridge University Press, pp. 225–247.

Goodwin, M. H. (1990). *He-Said-She-Said: Talk as Social Organization among Black Children*. Bloomington: Indiana University Press.

Grice, P. H. (1975). Logic and conversation. In: Cole, P. & Morgan, J. (eds), *Speech Acts*. New York: Academic Press, pp. 41–58.

Gudjonsson, G. H. (1992). *The Psychology of Interrogations, Confessions and Testimony*. Chichester, UK: John Wiley & Sons.

Gumperz, J. J. (1982). *Discourse Strategies*. New York: Cambridge University Press.

Hale, S. (1997). The treatment of register variation in court interpreting. *The Translator* 3(1), 39–54.

Hale, S. (2002). How faithfully do court interpreters render the styles of non-English speaking witnesses' testimonies? A data-based study of Spanish-English bilingual proceedings. *Discourse Studies* 4(1), 25–47.

Hale, S. (2004). *The Discourse of Court Interpreting*. Amsterdam: John Benjamins.

Hale, S. (2008). Controversies over the role of the court interpreter. In: Valero-Garcés, C. & Martin, A. (eds), *Crossing Borders in Community Interpreting: Definitions and Dilemmas*. Amsterdam and Philadelphia: John Benjamins, pp. 99–121.

Hale, S. & Gibbons, J. (1999). Varying realities: patterned changes in the interpreter's representation of courtroom and external realities. *Applied Linguistics* 20(2), 203–220.

Hall, P. (2008). Policespeak. In: Gibbons, J. & Turell, M.T. (eds), *Dimensions of Forensic Linguistics*. Amsterdam/Philadelphia: John Benjamins, pp. 67–94.

Halliday, M. K. (1978). *Language as Social Semiotic: The Social Interpretation of Language and Meaning*. London: Edward Arnold.

Halliday, M. A. K. (1989). *Spoken and Written Language*. Oxford: Oxford University Press.

Halliday, M. K. (1994). *Introduction to Functional Grammar* (2nd edn). London: Edward Arnold.

Haworth, K. (2006). The dynamics of power and resistance in police interview discourse. *Discourse & Society* 17(6), 739–759.

Haworth, K. (2010). Police interviews as evidence. In: Coulthard, M. & Johnson, A. (eds), *The Routledge Handbook of Forensic Linguistics*. London and New York: Routledge, pp. 169–181.

Heffer, C. (2002). If you were standing in Marks and Spencers: narrative and comprehension in the English summing-up. In: Cotterill, J. (ed.), *Language in the Legal Process*. Basingstoke: Palgrave Macmillan, pp. 228–245.

Heffer, C. (2005). *The Language of Jury Trial*. Basingstoke and New York: Palgrave Macmillan.

Heritage, J. C. & Watson. D. R. (1979). Formulations as conversational objects. In: Psathas, G. (ed.), *Everyday Language*. New York: Irvington Publishers, Inc., pp. 123–162.

Heydon, G. (2005). *The Language of Police Interviewing*. Basingstoke: Palgrave Macmillan.

Heydon, G. (2012). Helping the police with their inquiries: enhancing investigative interview with linguistic research. *The Police Journal* 85(2), 101–122.

Heydon, G. & Lai, M. (2012). Cognitive interview vs cognitive saturation: interpreting free narratives in multi-lingual police interviews. Paper presented at *the Regional Conference of the International Association of Forensic Linguists*, Kuala Lumpur, 5–7 July.

Hill, M. D. (2003). Identifying the source of critical details in confessions. *Forensic Linguistics* 10(1), 23–61.

Holmes, M. & Boni, N. (2001). *The Cognitive Interview as a Tool in Australian Policing*. Pyaneham, SA: Australian Centre for Policing Research.

Holt, E. & Johnson, A. (2010). Socio-pragmatic aspects of legal talk: police interviews and trial discourse. In: Coulthard, M. & Johnson, A. (eds), *The Routledge Handbook of Forensic Linguistics*. London and New York: Routledge, pp. 21–36.

Hutchby, I. & Wooffitt, R. (1988). *Conversation Analysis*. Cambridge: UK: Polity Press.

Inbau, F. E., Reid, J. E., & Buckley, J. P. (1986). *Criminal Interrogation and Confessions* (3rd edn). Baltimore: Williams & Wilkins.

Jackson, B. S. (1991). Narrative models in legal proof. In: Papke, D. R. (ed.), *Narrative and the Legal Discourse: A Reader in Storytelling and the Law.* Liverpool: Deborah Charles Publications, pp. 157–178.

Jaquemet, M. (1996). *Credibility in Court.* Cambridge: Cambridge University Press.

Jefferson, G. (1972). Side sequences. In: Sudnow, D. (ed.), *Studies in Social Interaction.* New York: The Free Press, pp. 294–337.

Jefferson, G. (1978). Sequential aspects of storytelling in conversation. In: Schenkein, J. (ed.), *Studies in the Organization of Conversational Interaction.* New York: Academic Press, pp. 219–248.

Jefferson, G. (1984). Transcription notation. In: Atkinson, J. & Heritage, J. (eds), *Structures of Social Interaction: Studies in Conversation Analysis.* New York: Cambridge University Press, pp. ix–xvi.

Jefferson, G. (1989). Preliminary notes on a possible metric which provides for a 'standard maximum' silence of approximately one second in conversation. In: Roger, D. & Bull, P. (eds), *Conversation: An Interdisciplinary Approach.* Clevedon: Multilingual Matters, pp. 166–196.

Johnson, A. (2002). So…? Pragmatic implications of so-prefaced questions in formal police interviews. In: Cotterill, J. (ed.), *Language in the Legal Process.* Basingstoke: Palgrave Macmillan, pp. 91–110.

Johnson, A. (2006). Police questioning. In: Brown, K. (ed.), *Encyclopedia of Language and Linguistics* (2nd edn). Oxford: Elsevier, pp. 661–671.

Johnson, A. (2008). 'From where we're sat …': Negotiating narrative transformation through interaction in police interviews with suspects. *Text & Talk* 28(3), 327–349.

Knapp, K. & Knapp-Potthoff, A. (1985). Sprachmittlertätigkeit in interkultureller Kommunikation. In: Rehbein, J. (ed.), *Interkulturelle Kommunikation.* Tübingen: Gunter Narr, pp. 450–463.

Komter, M. (2003). The interaction dynamics of eliciting a confession in a Dutch police interrogation. *Research on Language & Social Interaction* 36(4), 433–470.

Komter, M. (2005). Understanding problems in an interpreter-mediated police interrogation. In: Burns, S. (ed.), *Ethnographies of Law and Social Control: Sociology of Crime, Law & Deviance.* Amsterdam: Elsevier, pp. 203–224.

Komter, M. (2006). From talk to text: the interactional construction of a police record. *Research on Language and Social Interaction* 39(3), 201–228.

Krouglov, A. (1999). Police interpreting: politeness and sociocultural context. *The Translator* 5(2), 285–302.

Kurzon, D. (1995). The right of silence: a socio-pragmatic model of interpretation. *Journal of Pragmatics* 23(1), 55–69.

Kurzon, D. (1997). *Discourse of Silence.* Amsterdam: John Benjamins.

Labov, W. & Waletzky, J. (1997). Narrative analysis: oral versions of personal experience. *Journal of Narrative and Life History* 7(1–4), 3–38.

Laster, K. & Taylor, V. L. (1994). *Interpreters and the Legal System.* Sydney: The Federation Press.

Lee, J. (2011). Translatability of speech style in court interpreting. *The International Journal of Speech, Language and the Law* 18(1), 1–33.

Leo, R. A. & Drizin, S. A. (2010). The three errors: pathways to false confession and wrongful conviction. In: Lassiter, D. G. & Meissner, C. A. (eds), *Police Interrogations and False Confessions: Current Research, Practice, and Policy Recommendations.* Washington, DC: American Psychological Association, pp. 9–30.

Lerner, G. H. (1992). Assisted storytelling: deploying shared knowledge as a practical matter. *Qualitative Sociology* 15(3), 247–271.

Leung, E. S. M. & Gibbons, J. (2008). Who is responsible? Participant roles in legal interpreting cases. *Multilingua* 27(3), 177–191.

Levinson, S. C. (1983). *Pragmatics*. Cambridge: Cambridge University Press.

Linell, P. & Jönsson, L. (1991). Suspect stories: on perspective-setting in an asymmetrical situation. In: Marková, I. & Foppa, K. (eds), *Asymmetries in Dialogue*. Hemel Hampstead: Harvester Wheatsheaf, pp. 75–100.

Makino, S. & Tsutsui, M. (1991). *A Dictionary of Basic Japanese Grammar*. Tokyo: The Japan Times.

Maley, Y. (1994). The language of the law. In: Gibbons, J. (ed.), *Language and the Law*. London: Longman, pp. 159–173.

Maley, Y. & Fahey, R. (1991). Presenting the evidence: constructions of reality in court. *International Journal for the Semiotics of Law* 4(1), 3–17.

Martin, J. R. (1984). Language, register and genre. In: Christie, F. (ed.), *Children Writing: Reader*. Geelong, Victoria: Deakin University Press, pp. 21–29.

Mason, I. & Stewart, M. (2001). Interactional pragmatics, face and dialogue interpreter. In: Mason, I. (ed.), *Triadic Exchanges: Studies in Dialogue Interpreting*. Manchester: St. Jerome, pp. 51–70.

Mikkelson, H. (1998). Towards a redefinition of the role of the court interpreter. *Interpreting* 31(1), 21–45.

Mikkelson, H. (2000). *Introduction to Court Interpreting*. Manchester: St Jerome.

Milne, R. & Bull, R. (1999). *Investigative Interviewing: Psychology and Practice*. Chichester: John Wiley & Sons.

Momeni, N. (2011). Police genre: interruption and its classification as a sign of asymmetry in police interview/interrogation. *International Journal of Criminology and Sociological Theory* 4(1), 615–625.

Moston, S., Stephenson, G. M., & Williamson, T. M. (1993). Incidence, antecedents, and consequences of the use of the right to silence during police questioning. *Criminal Behaviour and Mental Health* 3(1), 30–47.

Müller, F. (1989). Translation in bilingual conversation: pragmatic aspects of translatory interaction. *Journal of Pragmatics* 13(5), 713–739.

Müller, F. E. (2001). Inter-and intra- cultural aspects of dialogue interpreting. In: Di Luzio, A., Günthner, S., & Orletti, F. (eds), *Culture in Communication: Analyses of Intercultural Situations*. Amsterdam: John Benjamins, pp. 245–270.

Nagano, T. (2003). *Mayaku no Hakobiya ni Sarete*. Tokyo: Fusoosha.

Nagao, H. (2004). Meruborun jiken ni okeru tsuuyaku no fubi. *Kobe Joshigakuin Ronshuu* 51(2), 77–89.

Nakane, I. (2007). Communicating the suspect's rights: problems in interpreting the caution in police interviews. *Applied Linguistics* 28(1), 87–112.

Nariyama, S. (2009). *How Can We Know Who Did What to Whom in Japanese?* Tokyo: Meiji Shoin.

National Accreditation Authority for Translators and Interpreters Ltd. (2001). *Ethics of Translation and Interpreting: A Guide to Professional Conduct in Australia*. Canberra: National Accreditation Authority for Translators and Interpreters Ltd (NAATI).

National Accreditation Authority for Translators and Interpreters. (2013). http://www.naati.com.au/pdf/misc/Outliness_of_NAATI_Credentials.pdf. Accessed 10 October 2013.

Newbury, P. & Johnson, A. (2006). Suspects' resistance to constraining and coercive questioning strategies in the police interview. *The International Journal of Speech, Language and the Law* 13(2), 213–240.

Niska, H. (1995). Just interpreting: role conflicts and discourse types in court interpreting. In: Morris, M. (ed.), *Translation and the Law*. Amsterdam and Philadelphia: John Benjamins, pp. 293–316.

Ord, B., Shaw, G., & Green, T. (2011). *Investigative Interviewing Explained* (3rd edn). Chatswood, NSW: LexisNexis Butterworths.

Ortega Herráez, J. M. & Foulquié Rubio, A. I. (2008). Interpreting in police settings in Spain: Service providers' and interpreters' perspectives. In: Valero-Garcés, C. & Martin, A. (eds), *Crossing Borders in Community Interpreting: Definitions and dilemmas*. Amsterdam: John Benjamins, pp. 123–146.

O'Barr, W. M. (1982). *Linguistic Evidence: Language Power and Strategy in the Courtroom*. New York: Academic Press.

Pomerantz, A. (1984). Agreeing and disagreeing with assessments: some features of preferred/dispreferred turn shapes. In: Atkinson, M. J. & Heritage, J. D. (eds), *Structures of Social Action: Studies in Conversation Analysis*. New York: Cambridge University Press, pp. 57–101.

Psathas, G. (1995). *Conversation Analysis: The Study of Talk-in-Interaction*. Thousand Oaks: Sage.

Roberts-Smith, L. (2009). Forensic interpreting: trial and error. In Hale, S. B., Ozolins, U. & Ludmila, S. (eds), *The Critical Link 5: Quality in Interpreting: A Shared Responsibility*. Amsterdam: John Benjamins, pp. 13–36.

Rock, F. (2007). *Communicating Rights: The Language of Arrest and Detention*. Basingstoke: Palgrave Macmillan.

Russell, S. (2000). 'Let me put it simply ...' The case for a standard translation of the police caution and its explanation. *Forensic Linguistics* 7(1), 26–48.

Russell, S. (2002). 'Three's a Crowd': shifting dynamics in the interpreted interview. In: Cotterill, J. (ed.), *Language in the Legal Process*. New York: Palgrave Macmillan, pp. 111–126.

Roy, C. B. (2000). *Interpreting as a Discourse Process*. Oxford: Oxford University Press.

Sacks, H. (1972). Lecture 5, Topical vs. pair organization. In: Sacks, H. (ed.) (1995), *Lectures on Conversation* (Vol. II). Oxford: Blackwell, pp. 561–570.

Sacks, H. (1974). An analysis of the course of a joke's telling in conversation. In: Bauman, R. & Sherzer. J. (eds), *Explorations in the Ethnography of Speaking*. Cambridge: Cambridge University Press, pp. 337–353.

Sacks, H. (1995). *Lectures on Conversation*. Edited by Jefferson, G. and with an introduction by Emanuel A. Schegloff . Oxford: Blackwell.

Sacks, H., Schegloff, E. A., & Jefferson, G. (1974). A simplest systematics for the organisation of turn-taking for conversation. *Language* 50(4), 696–735.

Schegloff, E. A. (1992). Repair after next turn: the last structurally provided place for the defence of intersubjectivity in conversation. *American Journal of Sociology* 95(5), 1295–1345.

Schegloff, E. A. (2000). When others initiate repair. *Applied Linguistics* 21(2), 205–243.

Schegloff, E. A. (2007). *Sequence Organization in Interaction: A Primer in Conversation Analysis*. Cambridge: Cambridge University Press.

Schegloff, E. A., Jefferson, G., & Sacks, H. (1977). The preference for self-correction in the organization of repair in conversation. *Language* 53(2), 361–382.

Schleiermacher, F. (1813/1992). On the different methods of translating. In: Schulte, R. & Biguenet, J. (eds), *Theories of Translation*. Chicago and London: University of Chicago Press, pp. 36–54.

Shlesinger, M. (1991). Interpreter latitude vs. due process: simultaneous and consecutive interpreting in multi-lingual trials. In S. Tirkonnen-Condit (ed.), *Empirical Research in Translation and Intercultural Studies*. Tubingen: Gunther Narr Verlag, pp. 147–155.

Shuy, R. W. (1997). Ten unanswered language questions about Miranda. *Forensic Linguistics* 4(2), 175–195.

Shuy, R. (1998). *The Language of Confession, Interrogation and Deception*. Thousand Oaks: Sage.

Snedaker, K. H. (1991). Storytelling in opening statements: framing the argumentation of the trial. In Papke, D. R. (ed.), *Narrative and the Legal Discourse: A Reader in Storytelling and the Law*. Liverpool: Deborah Charles Publications, pp. 132–157.

Solan, L. & Tiersma, P. M. (2005). *Speaking of Crime*. Chicago: University of Chicago Press.

Stacey, H. & Mullan, B. (1997). Cognitive interviewing. *Policing Issues & Practice Journal* 5(4), 36–41.

Stokoe, E. (2009). 'For the benefit of the tape': formulating embodied conduct in designedly uni-modal recorded police-suspect interrogations. *Journal of Pragmatics* 41(10), 1887–1904.

Stokoe, E. & Edwards, D. (2008). 'Did you have permission to smash your neighbour's door?' Silly questions and their answers in police-suspect interrogations. *Discourse Studies* 10(1), 89–111.

Supreme Court of Japan General Secretariat Criminal Case Division. (2003). *Saikousaibansho jimusookyokukeejikyoku: tokushu keeji jiken no kisochishiki: gaikokujin jiken hen*. Tokyo: Hoosookai.

Svennevig, J. (1999). *Getting Acquainted in Conversation: A Study of Initial Interactions*. Amsterdam: John Benjamins.

Silvester, J. (2010). Police learn the art of gentler persuasion. *The Age*, 10 September.

Wadensjö, C. (1997). Recycled information as a questioning strategy: pitfalls in interpreter-mediated talk. In: Carr, S. E., Robers, R., Dufour, A., & Steyn, D. (eds), *The Critical Link: Interpreters in the Community*. Amesterdam: John Benjamins, pp. 35–52.

Wadensjö, C. (1998). *Interpreting as Interaction*. New York: Longman.

Walker, A. (1985). The two faces of silence: the effect of witness hesitancy on lawyers' impressions. In: Tannen, D. & Saville-Troike, M. (eds), *Perspectives on Silence*. Norwood, NJ: Ablex, pp. 55–75.

Watanabe, O. & Yamada, N. (2005). *Higisha Torishirabe Kashika no Tameni: Oosutoraria no rokuon rokuga shisustemu ni manabu*. Tokyo: Gendaijnbunsha.

Watson, D. R. (1990). Some features of the elicitation of confession in murder interrogations. In: Psathas, G. (ed.), *Interaction Competence: Studies in Ethnomethodology and Conversation Analysis*. Washington DC: University Press of America, pp. 263–295.

Wong, J. (2000). Delayed next turn repair initiation in native/non-native speaker English conversation. *Applied Linguistics* 21(2), 244–267.

Yoong, D. (2010). Interactional norms in the Australian police interrogation room. *Discourse & Society* 21(6), 692–713.

Index

Printed and bound by CPI Group (UK) Ltd, Croydon, CR0 4YY